A CONSEQUENTIAL PRESIDENT

ALSO BY MICHAEL D'ANTONIO

The Truth About Trump

Mortal Sins

A Full Cup

Forever Blue

Spend Shift (with John Gerzema)

A Ball, a Dog, and a Monkey

Hershey

The State Boys Rebellion

Mosquito (with Andrew Spielman)

Fun While It Lasted (with Bruce McNall)

Tour '72

Tin Cup Dreams

Atomic Harvest

Heaven on Earth

Fall from Grace

The Legacy of
BARACK OBAMA

A CONSEQUENTIAL PRESIDENT

Michael D'Antonio

Thomas Dunne Books
St. Martin's Press
New York

THOMAS DUNNE BOOKS.
An imprint of St. Martin's Press.

A CONSEQUENTIAL PRESIDENT. Copyright © 2016 by Michael D'Antonio. All rights reserved. Printed in the United States of America. For information, address St. Martin's Press, 175 Fifth Avenue, New York, N.Y. 10010.

www.thomasdunnebooks.com
www.stmartins.com

Designed by Omar Chapa

The Library of Congress Cataloging-in-Publication Data
is available upon request.

ISBN 978-1-250-08139-1 (hardcover)
ISBN 978-1-4668-9327-6 (e-book)

Our books may be purchased in bulk for promotional, educational, or business use. Please contact your local bookseller or the Macmillan Corporate and Premium Sales Department at 1-800-221-7945, extension 5442, or by e-mail at MacmillanSpecialMarkets@macmillan.com.

First Edition: January 2017

10   9   8   7   6   5   4   3   2   1

For Toni

CONTENTS

A CONSEQUENTIAL
PRESIDENT

INTRODUCTION

Black mascot of Wall Street oligarchs and a black puppet
of corporate plutocrats.

—Cornel West, 2011

One hundred days into his second term, Obama has
already lost control of the agenda, if he ever had control
in the first place.   *—Dana Milbank, 2013*

Unfortunately he still has not learned how to govern.

—Maureen Dowd, 2013

With friends like his liberal critics, Barack Obama didn't need any
Republican antagonists. Beginning with the academic/activist Cornel West, who campaigned for Obama to be elected in 2008 and
then became a fierce critic, many top-rank figures on the Left criticized him with particular impatience because he had not met their
expectations. None expressed the disappointment more pointedly
than Maureen Dowd of *The New York Times*, who alternately attacked Obama as too cool and too emotional.

Dowd's criticisms, like those voiced by Dana Milbank and
Cornel West, were sharpened by the kind of disappointment that

would inevitably arise among those who welcomed Obama's election with excitement. In November 2008 Dowd had called him "elegant and disciplined" and wondered, in print, if the nation might one day build an Obama monument in Washington. This enthusiasm was driven by three main factors. The first was the tragedy of George W. Bush's presidency and ruinous war in Iraq. The second was the optimism that so many felt as the nation elected its first black president. The third, and most significant, was the man himself.

Throughout his presidency, Obama would experience both a benefit and a burden based on the circumstances of his election. For a brief period, when the nation and most of the world felt profound relief that the Bush era was over, Obama's mere presence seemed enough to guarantee great success, However, the power generated by his popularity inspired an equal and opposite force among his political opponents, who determined to thwart him with a just-say-no response that was so consistent that they would reject Obama even when he offered to promote their own policies. This intransigence, combined with timidity in his own party, would deny Obama immediate, sweeping victories and require his administration to wage a daily struggle to claim progress by the inch.

Although many who were overcome with the sense of possibility when Obama was elected lost faith, the president and his administration adapted to the hyperpartisan reality in Washington. The administration sought advances wherever they could be achieved, using incremental legislative acts and regulatory shifts and the executive's discretionary powers to make steady progress on the president's agenda. Initiatives in energy, transportation, environmental protection, and foreign policy were tailored to complement each other. The result was not the revolution that some liberals had hoped to see, but the gradual progress the American political system permits.

The record, laid out here, shows a president whose calm and analytical temperament allowed for adaptation and perseverance.

These qualities frustrated many of his backers because they seemed at odds with the energy Obama sometimes displayed as a leader. A truly inspirational figure, he was also a determined politician who was willing to do the hard, unglamorous work of legislating and steering a bureaucracy. This effort would directly improve the lives of American schoolchildren, workers, college students, and tens of millions who had been shut out of the health care system. Obama would restart the economy, set a modern record for job creation, reduce pollution, curb wasteful energy consumption, and make a start in the campaign against climate change. Roads, bridges, and railroads were rebuilt. Health care cost inflation was curbed. Soldiers were brought home from foreign conflicts, and outlaw countries—Iran and Cuba—were brought into the community of nations.

That Obama was both an outsider symbol *and* an effective insider in action made it difficult for some to recognize his many achievements, which were realized piecemeal. Those who expected him to be perfect, struggled to accept that he was, instead, extremely good. This is understandable given his rapid ascent from obscurity to worldwide acclaim.

An inspiring speaker who was both passionate and cerebral, Obama had followed a most unlikely path from the Illinois legislature, to the US Senate, to the Oval Office in just twelve years. In the previous century only two candidates—Warren G. Harding and John F. Kennedy—had gone directly to the White House from the US Senate. In the case of Obama, the country had elected, to the most powerful position in the world, a man who, in 2004, was little known outside Illinois. The big opportunity that transformed this politician with an unusual name into an immediate presidential contender came with a cell phone call that Obama received as he was campaigning for the US Senate. On the other end of the call he heard the voice of Mary Beth Cahill, who was Democratic presidential nominee John Kerry's campaign manager.

Cahill's boss had been impressed by the forty-two-year-old Obama during a recent swing through the Midwest and had picked him to deliver the keynote address at the Democratic Party's 2004 national convention. But as she tried to deliver the news, Cahill had to dial three times, due to bad cell connections.

"Yes, that's great," said Obama when he finally heard the request. "I'd be honored to do it."

The conversation was overheard by David Axelrod, Obama's chief political aide. As Axelrod would recall in his 2015 memoir, *Believer,* his candidate had already benefited from extraordinary good fortune. First, he had bypassed the usual route to political power and joined the political game in Illinois without the benefit of a patron. Then in the US Senate race his opponent, Jack Ryan, was forced to withdraw because his exploits at sex clubs had been revealed. (That Ryan's wife at the time of the incidents was a semi-famous actress and beauty pageant winner spiced up the scandal.) The invitation to deliver the keynote was another stroke of luck for Obama, albeit one that he had earned in his time with Kerry. Turning to Axelrod, Obama said, "I know what I want to say. I want to talk about my own story as part of the larger American story. I want to talk about who we are at our best."

Axelrod had been pushing Obama to add heart to the basic speech he was delivering on the stump. The positive and personal themes Obama imagined for the convention showed that the message had gotten through. Instead of detailed policy prescriptions from the mind of a man who had taught constitutional law at the University of Chicago, the convention delegates would hear about shared hopes, feelings, experiences, and dreams. In the roughly three thousand words Obama wrote and showed to Axelrod, Obama described himself as part of a long national narrative of hope. He claimed the faith, grit, and patriotism that Republicans had long tried to reserve for themselves, and he called for unity in response to divisiveness.

The text would be true to the experience of a man who had been born in 1961 to a white mother from Kansas and a black father from Kenya and carried a name—Barack Hussein Obama—that often required an explanation. Obama could readily recall the challenges he had surmounted as a child in Hawaii and Indonesia and then as a young man trying to find his place in college and law school on the US mainland. Frequently denied the comfort of blending in with the majority, he had noted the assumptions he encountered in others and reflected on his own responses. Highly intellectual, he had made a study of human nature that caused him to regard people in a generously nuanced way. (Speaking of political adversaries, he would one day write that they are "possessed of the same mix of virtues and vices, insecurities and long buried injuries, as the rest of us.") This process, combined with family influences and a calm demeanor, had made him a stubborn but realistic optimist. He was so cool that he couldn't be dragged into the gutter even when a notorious local gadfly tried to disrupt his 2004 campaign by insisting Obama was "a Muslim who has concealed his religion."

By the time he walked onto the national-convention stage on July 27, Obama had added to his speaking style many of the flourishes and decorations—repetition, shifting tone, alliteration—favored by certain black preachers. However, he did not sound these notes in the beginning of his talk, when he confessed that "my presence on this stage is pretty unlikely" and then dwelled on his own story. From this bit of autobiography he moved on to the policies his party favored. He called for better access to health care, reduced use of fossil fuels, tax breaks to encourage new jobs, and improvements in education. He did not mention President Bush, or his policies, and he only used the word *Republican* to acknowledge the GOP in a positive way.

After praising his party's ticket, which included Kerry and vice-presidential nominee John Edwards, Obama turned to his core message, in which he used the word *hope* thirteen times. He said, "Even as we speak, there are those who are preparing to divide us, the spin masters and the negative-ad peddlers who embrace the politics of anything goes. Well, I say to them tonight, there's not a liberal America and a conservative America; there's the United States of America. There's not a black America and white America and Latino America and Asian America; there's the United States of America."

As he delivered that last phrase—"there's the United States of America"—Obama spoke more slowly, and more deliberately, stressing the word, *united*. His call to unity rang with rhetorical energy and brought the cheering men and women in the hall to their feet. They remained standing as he said:

> The pundits, the pundits like to slice and dice our country into red states and blue states: red states for Republicans, blue states for Democrats. But I've got news for them, too. We worship an awesome God in the blue states, and we don't like federal agents poking around our libraries in the red states.
>
> We coach Little League in the blue states, and, yes, we've got some gay friends in the red states. There are patriots who opposed the war in Iraq, and there are patriots who supported the war in Iraq.
>
> We are one people, all of us pledging allegiance to the Stars and Stripes, all of us defending the United States of America. In the end, that's what this election is about. Do we participate in a politics of cynicism, or do we participate in a politics of hope?

With his references to "red" and "blue" Americas, Obama relied on a commonly used expression, drawn from the maps used on TV newscasts, to evoke a hyperpartisan style of politics that had been the norm since the Republican Newt Gingrich of Georgia became

Speaker of the House of Representatives. (Gingrich threw the nation into a constitutional crisis when he tried and failed to drive President Clinton from office through impeachment. His crime was not a Nixonian scheme against supposed enemies, but lying about a sexual encounter with a White House intern.) In the years since Gingrich's rise, the number of Democrats who considered Republicans "a threat to the nation's well-being" had risen from 16 percent to 29 percent. The number of Republicans who felt the same about Democrats had also increased, reaching 21 percent.

Seen live by more than 9 million TV viewers, Obama's seventeen-minute message of hope would be remembered as a welcome call for a return to civility in politics. Seconds after Obama finished, the conservative commentator David Brooks told viewers of the PBS television network that they had just seen a master at work: "Even in delivery, the way he used the different prompters, the way he used his hands, the way he used his body, this was like watching Tiger Woods play his first tournament." The analogy was apt. Just like Woods, Obama had joined a game that had been all but closed to African-Americans with a talent that was superior and a temperament to match.

Obama also won Brooks's praise for the socially conservative points he made—"people don't expect government to solve all their problems"—which would appeal to those beyond the party faithful. "He talked about America," said Brooks, "and his story is the American story." On the same broadcast, the liberal analyst Mark Shields noted that Obama had pointedly called for eradicating "the slander that says that a black youth with a book is acting white." Added Shields, "He's the only person who could have said that, and he said it so well."

Long the most troubling factor in American politics, race had often been a stumbling block for African-American politicians. Los Angeles mayor Tom Bradley's unexpected loss in the 1982 gubernatorial race in California, a result no poll predicted, suggested that the quiet racism of white voters could be debilitating for strong black candidates. In a century's time just two African-Americans—Republican senator Edward Brooke and Democratic senator Carol Moseley Braun—had been elected to a statewide office anywhere in the country. Political scientists traced this reality to persistent bigotry, which produced what they called the Bradley Effect in elections. Similarly, Richard Nixon's acknowledged Southern Strategy had played on racism to draw disaffected Democrats into the GOP fold where, beginning in the 1970s, they helped create a formidable block against African-American candidates for high office.

But while bigotry persisted, American attitudes had changed considerably during Barack Obama's adult life. Between 1982 and 2004 the percentage of Americans who told survey takers that they "approved" of interracial marriage grew from 42 to 73 percent. In that same period the number of whites who said they would move if a black family "moved in next door" had dropped from 10 percent to almost zero. Population trends also pointed to major change. When Obama was born, the United States was more than 88 percent white. In 2004 the figure was 75 percent and headed lower.

The America that tuned in for Barack Obama's speech at the Boston convention was ready to regard a young African-American politician as a credible leader. Just as important, Obama was prepared to address the country from a unique position. Though technically a member of the postwar baby boom generation, he had been born at the tail end of this cohort and would have little in common with children of the forties and fifties who grew up under Truman and Eisenhower and came to lead both political parties.

Indeed, Presidents Clinton and Bush, who were both born in 1946, were fifteen years older than Obama. Born into the greatest period of middle-class prosperity in history, they came from an era when divorce was still scandalous and two-parent households were the norm. (Clinton, whose father died, was raised by his mother and stepfather.) Clinton and Bush had attended college at the height of the antiwar protests of the 1960s and would recall the day when President John F. Kennedy was assassinated in personal terms.

Obama was just two years old when President Kennedy was killed. The defining news events of his young life were the Watergate scandal, which drove Richard Nixon from the White House, and America's defeat in the Vietnam War. The United States had never before lost in war, and the disgraced Nixon had been the first president to resign from office. Coming after the turmoil of the sixties, these traumas pushed public faith in the government, as reflected in opinion polls, to record lows. In addition to coming from a different time, Obama came from a different place and culture. Hawaii's population was predominantly nonwhite. Also, the state was not so troubled by problems common to the mainland, including racism. Consequently, Obama would say, "My identity might begin with the fact of my race, but it didn't, it *couldn't,* end there." From this perspective, he was able to speak plainly about the realities of racism but also call on all Americans to do their part to make things better. Combined with his optimism, this focus on shared responsibility marked Obama as a leader with a generous and expansive view of his country.

On the day after the event that *Chicago* magazine came to call simply "The Speech," Obama was mobbed on the streets of Boston, the city that hosted the 2004 Democratic National Convention. His memoir, *Dreams from My Father,* which had been published in 1995 and sold modestly, leaped onto bestseller lists. In its pages, readers discovered a young man who gave up a career path that promised wealth and security to work as a $13,000-per-year community activist in Chicago's poorest neighborhoods. There he conducted an intense but openhearted study of race, politics, and human nature. He notes in his memoir the importance of self-interest as a motivator and explains how he learned to be more patient, more flexible, and more self-critical. It is clear in these pages, written before he turned thirty-five, that Obama was working toward the perspective that would guide his political path. He noted the fears of many white Americans, the diminished hopes of many in minority communities, and both the successes and failures of the American experiment.

Back in Illinois, candidate Obama opened up such a wide lead in his bid for the open US Senate seat that he was able to give substantial amounts of his time, and campaign cash, to fellow Democrats around the country. On Election Day, when Kerry lost to Bush and the Democrats gave up seats in both houses of Congress, Obama crushed his GOP opponent. His forty-three-point margin of victory was the largest ever recorded by an Illinois candidate for the US Senate.

With his reissued memoir reaching first place on the *New York Times* Best Seller List, Obama accepted an offer of $1.9 million to write three more titles, one of which would be a book for children. Days later, *Newsweek* featured a picture of Obama—big smile, arms folded confidently—on its end-of-year cover with the headline "Seeing Purple: A Rising Star Who Wants to Get Beyond Blue vs. Red." Inside, the magazine noted Obama's "star power" and said he would be on every short list for vice president come 2008. This note presumed that someone else—Hillary Clinton, John Edwards, and Joe Biden were early favorites—would top the Democratic Party ticket. It also ignored the talk of an Obama presidency that had swirled in the Midwest for more than a year.

Two weeks after *Newsweek* hit the stands, Obama took the oath of office to become a senator. He was assigned to committees that dealt with veterans, environment and public works, and foreign relations, which was always an interest for senators with presidential aspirations. With his party out of power Obama wouldn't find many opportunities to shine as a lawmaker, but he continued to attract an inordinate amount of attention. Even he seemed a bit chagrined.

"I've got a celebrity that's undeserved and a little overgrown relative to the actual power I have in this city," Obama told

Michele Norris of National Public Radio in March 2005. Having described the limits of his influence, Obama added that he understood he had an opportunity to "help frame" his party's position in a public conversation "about the kind of America that we want" and he intended to seize it.

Early in his tenure in the Senate, Obama faced the skepticism of those who considered him remarkably lucky and unproven. The editorial page of the conservative *Washington Times* noted "signs that Mr. Obama might not live up to his own hype." However, George W. Bush, of all people, welcomed Obama as a senator who might bridge partisan divides, and Michael Steele, who would soon become chairman of the GOP in 2009, praised Obama's support for "the true values that we talk about in the Republican Party."

What Steele and President Bush noticed in Obama was that he favored strict parenting and individual responsibility and recognized the limits of government's ability to solve problems. Others would say these values were conservative, but Obama would not concede this point. He made them his own, even as he built one of the most liberal voting records in the Senate. He also busied himself with practical matters, including bills to fund highway and energy projects back home in Illinois. He built relationships with more senior members of the Senate and used his outsize celebrity to raise money for his colleagues. With a single e-mail he raised $800,000 for the reelection campaign of Senator Robert Byrd of West Virginia.

Byrd had served in the Senate longer than Obama had been alive. He was famous as a leader of the Democrats in Congress and as a former organizer of the Ku Klux Klan. By the time the two men met, Byrd had repudiated his racist past many, many times, calling it "the albatross around my neck." Obama soon took to calling Byrd "a dear friend," and the elder senator tutored him in the ways of lawmaking. Given Byrd's tenure—he was the Senate's longest-serving member—and his skills, Obama could not have found a better instructor.

Whether Obama was helping a colleague from a bygone era or evaluating the opposition, he showed an equanimity that stood in great contrast to that of many in his profession. For example, Obama openly admired Ronald Reagan's style and many of his accomplishments. He had lived under a President Reagan from the age of nineteen to the age of twenty-seven, and like many of his age group Obama appreciated him: "Ronald Reagan . . . put us on a fundamentally different path because the country was ready for it. I think they felt like, you know, with all the excesses of the 1960s and '70s, and, you know, government had grown and grown, but there wasn't much sense of accountability in terms of how it was operating. I think . . . he tapped into what people were already feeling, which was 'we want clarity, we want optimism, we want a return to that sense of dynamism and entrepreneurship that had been missing.'"

And though he was not at ease with the role of the backslapping pol, Obama sometimes practiced the kind of bonhomie that made the powerful comfortable with him. At the annual Gridiron Club Dinner, where journalists and their guests poke fun at themselves, Obama quipped that he was working on his second memoir, which would be titled "The Senate Months." He even sang a song composed for the occasion and matched with the tune "If I Only Had a Brain" from *The Wizard of Oz*. Among the lines:

> I'm aspiring to greatness,
> but somehow I feel weightless
> A freshman's sad refrain

Although he worked at being one of the boys and continued to call for a less partisan kind of politics, Obama was not all modesty and compromise. His celebrity brought requests for interviews from, among others, the *Tonight* show, *Face the Nation,* Conan O'Brien, and Charlie Rose, and Obama used these appearances to polish his style. In the Senate he held fast to key Democratic Party positions including abortion rights and a call for troop reductions in Iraq. Both these concerns came into play when he voted against John Roberts's appointment to the Supreme Court. Roberts was confirmed, but by voting against him, Obama strengthened his appeal to more partisan Democrats.

Whenever Obama practiced a more typical kind of partisan politics, he provided fodder for critics who doubted his sincerity about bridging divides. For example, when he changed his mind about joining John McCain in an effort to rein in lobbyists, the GOP senator from Arizona sent an angry letter about Obama's "disingenuousness" and accused him of "self-interested partisan posturing." Circulated on Capitol Hill in February 2006, the McCain letter caused a stir among members of the political class, who knew, better than the public at large, that Obama was already positioning himself for a run at the White House.

In mid-2006 leading Democrats including senators Harry Reid and Charles Schumer began urging Obama to consider running for president. In October, David Brooks, who became one of a handful of journalists who spoke regularly with Obama, used his *New York Times* column to urge Obama into the race: "Barack Obama should run for president. He should run first for the good of his party. . . . The next Democratic nominee should either be Barack Obama or should have the stature that would come from defeating Barack Obama." Brooks added that Obama's just-published book, *The Audacity of Hope,* made a strong argument for a departure from "the political style of the baby boom generation," which was "highly moralistic and personal."

The "other candidates" referenced by Brooks would include two more experienced campaigners. Former senator John Edwards had been Kerry's running mate. Senator Hillary Clinton, a former first lady, was the odds-on favorite for the nomination and a formidable fund-raiser. Although Clinton and Edwards each seemed to have a head start, they were also vulnerable. Long the subject of vitriolic attacks from the Right, Clinton was a polarizing figure. Edwards, who had served fewer years in public office than Obama, was light on experience and dogged by rumors of personal problems. Obama told his aides to conduct a poll in Iowa, which would be the first state to vote for a nominee, to determine his viability. However, he insisted that a formal discussion of a presidential run be delayed until after the upcoming midterm election.

Although Obama wanted to slow the bandwagon, its momentum continued. Wherever he appeared in public, huge crowds gathered, and people invariably urged him to run. After the Brooks column, *Time* magazine featured Obama on its cover with the headline "Why Barack Obama Could Be Our Next President." On NBC an interviewer asked, "If your party needs you—and there's already a drumbeat out there—will you run?" Talk show host Oprah Winfrey, who by some estimates was the most influential woman in the country, asked, "Would you announce on this show?"

The on-air encouragement coming from Oprah, who was a friend and fellow Chicagoan, led to speculation that she knew that an Obama candidacy was inevitable. More telling was the treatment Obama received in the conservative media, where his name and childhood years spent in Indonesia were presented as evidence that he might be a Muslim, not a Christian, and that he might not even be an American citizen. (After the attacks of September 11, 2001, *Muslim* was synonymous with *terrorist* in some circles.) In San Francisco, radio host Brian Sussman called Obama a "halfrican." His colleague Michael Savage asked, "Are you going to tell me that Obama, Barack Hussein Obama, is going to take our side should there be some sort of catastrophic attack on America?"

Rumors of Obama's supposed Muslim identity circulated so widely that mainstream media outlets devoted time and energy to proving them false. Some of the innuendo came from supporters of Democratic front-runner Hillary Clinton, who found herself under pressure when Obama announced his candidacy for president in

February 2007. Speaking to a huge crowd gathered at the Old State Capitol in Springfield, Illinois, Obama used the words *hope* and *change* seventeen times, but did not name those he might battle in primaries or the 2008 general election. He never mentioned any political party—not even his own—except to praise a Senate colleague, Republican Richard Lugar, for a bipartisan arms-control initiative.

Though nonpartisan in tone, Obama's announcement was hardly toothless. He made strong arguments for liberal policies including universal health care, an end to the war in Iraq, union rights, alternative energy, and expanded access to education. He made a virtue of his scant political experience and jabbed at Washington insiders, whom most Americans loved to hate. He said, "What's stopped us is the failure of leadership, the smallness of our politics—the ease with which we're distracted by the petty and trivial, our chronic avoidance of tough decisions, our preference for scoring cheap political points instead of rolling up our sleeves and building a working consensus to tackle big problems." Fortunately, Obama added, "Beneath all the differences of race and region, faith and station, we are one people. . . . Together, starting today, let us finish the work that needs to be done and usher in a new birth of freedom on this earth."

Most polls showed that Hillary Clinton led Obama by almost twenty points on the day he announced. However, as voters came to know him, the gap closed. He scored an upset victory in the Iowa caucuses and made strong showings in New Hampshire, South Carolina, and Nevada. He surpassed Clinton in national opinion polls, and when a sex scandal drove Edwards from the field, Obama picked up many of Edwards's supporters. The race to the nomination was hard fought, with Obama prevailing. At the convention, Delaware senator Joe Biden became Obama's running mate, and the party turned to confront the Republican Party nominee, John McCain, and his surprise running mate, Sarah Palin, who had been elected governor of Alaska in 2006.

One of the strangest pairings in political history, the McCain-Palin ticket joined a respected elder statesman of the GOP with a neophyte who seemed unsure of the vice president's duties. Palin would notoriously accuse Obama of "palling around with terrorists." This kind of language echoed the angry comments about Obama—"Treason!" and "Kill him!"—that were reportedly heard at GOP rallies. For his part, McCain took pains to disabuse voters of the notion that his opponent was somehow un-American. He suffered boos and calls of "Liar!" when in a show of political integrity he patiently explained to a rally crowd that Obama was not an Arab and that he is "a person you don't have to be scared of as president of the United States."

As the GOP standard-bearer, McCain was also burdened with the legacy of outgoing Republican president George W. Bush, whose 30 percent approval rating in a Gallup poll was the lowest of any president in history. McCain's association with Bush became a greater liability as the financial crisis that began in the mortgage business in 2007 spread through other sectors of the economy. In September 2008 the US government rescued two giant home-loan insurers, Fannie Mae and Freddie Mac, and the Lehman Brothers investment bank collapsed. As stock markets plummeted, the Bush administration rushed to address the widening crisis. With the worst economic crisis since the Great Depression looming, the presidency became a prize that many reasonable people would refuse to accept.

The financial crisis was so severe that Bush administration Treasury Secretary Hank Paulson frequently briefed the Democratic Party's nominee so that he would be fully informed if he was elected president. Obama absorbed the information with his usual reserve, but his opponent, John McCain, became so alarmed that in late September he publicly suspended his campaign and rushed to Washington, where he demanded to meet with President Bush. Many Republicans were surprised by McCain's decision, and Paulson thought McCain was being rash, given the signal it would send financial markets. He told McCain that if he wound up contributing to a market meltdown, "it is not going to be just on me. I am going to go and say what I think to the American people."

Paulson told the story of McCain's panic in his 2010 book, *On the Brink,* where he also described a White House session attended by both candidates. At that meeting Obama expressed his support for the Bush administration's planned response to the economic mess and added, "The Democrats will deliver the votes" that Bush needed to get his program through Congress. When Obama pointedly asked to hear McCain's thoughts, the senator from Arizona had little to offer beyond what he saw on a note card he held in his hand, wrote Paulson. As other Democrats at the meeting pushed to hear specifics, which weren't forthcoming, the meeting devolved into such chaos that Vice President Cheney began to laugh. President Bush announced, "Well, I've clearly lost control of this meeting. It's over."

McCain's overreaction to the financial crisis and Obama's contrasting cool marked a turning point in the campaign. On the day after the White House meeting, the candidates faced each other in their first debate. McCain seemed tight and somewhat guarded, while Obama showed himself to be more nimble than his more experienced rival. Obama looked vibrant and forceful as he declared the country to be at "a defining moment" and blamed the policies of the Bush White House, which his opponent had supported. McCain offered a crankiness—"I've been not feeling too great about a lot of things lately"—that made him seem tired and disengaged.

Voters chose energy over testiness, and Obama won the largest percentage of the vote recorded by any Democrat since 1964, becoming the nation's first African-American president and the first born outside the contiguous forty-eight states. Estimates of the crowd that gathered to hear him at Chicago's Grant Park on election night ranged as high as 240,000. When the TV networks reported his victory, the crowd in the park erupted in cheers and chants of the campaign slogan, "Yes we can!" Strangers embraced, couples danced, many wept.

When the roaring crowd quieted for him to speak, Obama joined his success with the stream of change that had moved the nation through history. He noted the day's events as merely the beginning of an effort that would require millions to act. He also warned against the persistence of the rancor that made politics so troubling. "In this country, we rise or fall as one nation, as one people. Let's resist the temptation to fall back on the same partisanship and pettiness and immaturity that has poisoned our politics for so long." He concluded, "This is our time, to put our people back to work and open doors of opportunity for our kids; to restore prosperity and promote the cause of peace; to reclaim the American dream and reaffirm that fundamental truth that, out of many, we are one; that while we breathe, we hope. And where we are met with cynicism and doubts and those who tell us that we can't, we will respond with that timeless creed that sums up the spirit of a people: 'Yes, we can.'"

Communicated in JumboTron splendor to a crowd that filled Grant Park and, thanks to television, circled the globe, the election of a black man to the highest office in the land signaled a setback for racism and a high point for inclusion. Writing on the editorial page of The Wall Street Journal, where conservatism reigned, Juan Williams echoed Martin Luther King Jr. as he declared, "In terms of racial politics, the arc of justice took a breathtaking leap." Of course Obama was more than a symbol, and Nobel Prize–winning economist Paul Krugman of The New York Times reminded readers that the winner was a flesh-and-blood leader who had used the campaign to call for programs such as health care reform that prompted his opponents to label him a socialist. Voters chose him anyway, which suggested that the new president had been given a powerful mandate. Krugman encouraged him to be "sufficiently bold" as he sought to end the economic crisis and reform the health care system.

While supporters such as Krugman encouraged Obama, Right-wing politicians, writers, and activists sought to block his agenda and delegitimize his presidency. In Congress, Republican leaders decided they would try to deny Obama any successes by refusing invitations to bipartisanship and, in the Senate, by using the rule that permitted a lockstep minority to block the will of the majority. Away from Washington, fringe figures seized upon long-discredited claims that Obama was somehow foreign-born and thus ineligible to serve as president, to create a so-called birther movement that persisted for many years. (The racism beneath this effort to cast Obama as the "other" was apparent to all but the birthers themselves.) In think tanks and at media outlets, Right-wing polemicists rushed to offer distortion and alarm in much-publicized books that purportedly revealed the true Obama. Many of these were offered by the highly partisan publisher Regnery. One, *The Roots of Obama's Rage* by Dinesh D'Souza, was a tour de force of rabbit-hole logic.

D'Souza, whose work was often subsidized by well-funded conservative organizations, described Obama as a dangerously cynical, "anti-colonial" thinker who had decided that if he could "look black but act white," he might seize power. His ultimate goal, as Regnery described it in promotional materials, was to "reduce America's strength, influence, and standard of living."

According to D'Souza, Obama's "close-cropped hair, a Midwestern-accent, and [conservative] dress" all meant that he was somehow acting white. The bigotry inherent in this line of thinking had been identified by Obama and a string of black leaders stretching back to Frederick Douglass and beyond. Nevertheless, D'Souza insisted that Obama's election had been "the triumph of lactification," by which he meant a strategy black men could use to appear white. D'Souza argued, through a series of issues and incidents, that Obama's long-dead father, whom the president had barely known, had transmitted to him a radical philosophy. According to D'Souza, Obama was consumed by "an often masked, but profound rage that comes from his African father; an anticolonialist rage against Western dominance, and most especially against the wealth and power of the very nation Barack Obama now leads."

Barely noted outside the conservative media echo chamber, *The Roots of Obama's Rage* was most useful as an indicator of the divisive quality of modern politics. Thanks primarily to the Fox News network, which pioneered the nightly delivery of overheated rhetoric into American living rooms, fear and anger had become common currencies in debates over policies and parties. This dynamic, paired with the latent racial anxieties of those who felt threatened by Obama's rise, made for political hysteria in some corners of society. As a result, D'Souza's crackpot book sold well enough to make many bestseller lists. It also became a primary text for like-minded writers who would cite *Roots* as if it had been a rigorous work.

Fortunately many serious writers and scholars also addressed the Obama phenomenon early in his first term. Harvard historian James Kloppenberg examined every word the president had published and every speech he ever gave and then interviewed his former professors and classmates. The result was an analysis, *Reading Obama,* that placed him among a small number of presidents who were also intellectuals, including Thomas Jefferson, Abraham Lincoln, and Woodrow Wilson. Published by Princeton University Press, which is the polar opposite of Regnery, *Reading Obama* concluded that the new president was a pragmatic thinker who encouraged debate and was willing to adapt to changing circumstances.

More fulsome, and more relevant to general readers, was David Remnick's *Bridge: The Life and Rise of Barack Obama,* which revealed the new president to be no less calculating and ambitious than other politicians, but also fiercely intelligent, hardworking, open-minded, and preternaturally calm. In his review of the book, historian Douglas Brinkley called it "brilliantly written" and "flawlessly constructed." Its greatest virtue, added Brinkley, was its revelation of Obama as a man whose "lifetime ambition was to be an American leader, not a Black History Month poster."

Seen in the light of Remnick's book, Obama was a true American: optimistic, patriotic, ambitious, and hardworking. Obama accepted complexity and even contradiction as part of the human condition. Thus a great nation—America, to name one—could commit serious mistakes even as it stood as a beacon to the world. Although opponents noted anti-Americanism in this nuanced approach, Obama was actually offering realism and prudence. Critics were also confounded by Obama's expansive sense of identity. Refusing to accept the trope of a man divided between white and black, he embraced every aspect of his heritage. Growing numbers of people shared Obama's perspective on this, choosing to identify as members of multiple racial groups. Instead of accepting old, negative ideas about racial mixtures, these Americans felt proud and advantaged by their backgrounds.

But even as Obama refused to be defined solely by race, the president discovered that others frequently assessed him in racial terms. People as varied as the actor Morgan Freeman and the conservative media mogul Rupert Murdoch speculated about the quality of his racial identity, and many others seemed unable to accept that his particular traits, such as his passions for both basketball *and* golf, were sincere and compatible.

Events outside his control also often forced the issue of race relations upon Obama. Many but not all of these events involved police officers and black men who, as the country came to understand, were more likely than whites to be killed by law enforcement officers. Time and again Obama was drawn into a national conversation about race and justice as these tragic incidents attracted global press attention. Missing from many of these dialogues was acknowledgment that these problems were not new. What was new was Obama's presence in the Oval Office, which surely encouraged more vigorous and persistent discussions. The overarching debate reached a crescendo when a white gunman killed nine people at a black church in Charleston, South Carolina. The killer was quickly recognized as a racist, and officials across the South moved to remove racist symbols of the Confederacy from public spaces. Whites had defeated such efforts many times in the past, but this time their opposition melted away.

The Charleston massacre prompted criticism of Obama's response to the intractable problems of gun violence and racism. When it came to race, he had, in fact, provided the kind of leadership and example that brought people together. The shift on Confederate symbols was proof of this. On the issue of gun violence Obama ran up against a majority in Congress and hugely powerful special interest groups that have, for decades, thwarted every attempt at real regulation. Those who criticized him on this policy problem sought to hold Obama to the same standard they would apply against any politician, and this matched the president's own perspective. From an early age, as he tested himself against the best competition he could find, he sought to be judged as a man, and not a black man. Any other approach would be condescending, bigoted, and would diminish the consequence of his achievements.

Of course the first African-American's presence in the Oval Office was consequential. As the Obama family took up residence in the White House, they lived, in part, as powerful and effective symbols. However, Obama was a consequential president in so many ways that to focus on his symbolic importance would be, not just a mistake, but an insult to the man and the historical record. Indeed, in his two terms of office Obama reached a long list of goals set during the election campaign and at the start of his presidency. Among them were:

Stabilization of the crisis-stricken financial system
The largest economic stimulus program in history

The turnaround of the failing auto industry

Sweeping reform of the health care system

Regulatory reform of Wall Street and the consumer
   credit business

Reversed the rise in unemployment begun under his
   predecessor

Expanded alternative energy

Achieved substantial reductions in air and water pollution

Advanced the Paris climate-change treaty

Ended Iran's progress toward acquiring nuclear weapons

Advanced rights of women, gays, lesbians, and the
   transgendered

Dramatically reduced US military presence in Iraq and
   Afghanistan

Improved international regard for the United States

Replaced No Child Left Behind education policy with
   Race to the Top

Began to normalize relations with Cuba

Though significant, these achievements constitute just a small sample of the successes realized by the forty-fourth president of the United States. This book will describe these and others in greater detail, taking note of the creative methods Obama used to make progress against great resistance in Congress and despite pernicious campaigns to persuade the public that he was unworthy of his office.

No other modern president has been subject to such a concerted effort to paint him as not-quite-American, and none had been treated with such immediate and constant disrespect. The depth of partisan derangement toward Obama was made clear just nine months into his first term when Obama, addressing a joint session of Congress, heard a Republican member of the House, Joe Wilson of South Carolina, bellow, "You lie!" At the time, no observer could recall a similar incident involving a president of either party.

Despite all of the derision and distortions offered by his critics, Obama resisted being drawn into a gutter fight, even when the topic was his very identity as an American. Here, his cool temperament and practiced reserve served him well, even if some complained that he didn't try hard enough to be a buddy to members of Congress. While his administration was often accused of wrongdoing, his two terms were rarely marked by genuine scandal. Obama and his team endured fewer investigations by special prosecutors and fewer prosecutions than all their predecessors going back at least to Lyndon Johnson. By this measure, and many others, Obama has restored the White House to a legal and moral plane not seen, one could argue, since the days of Dwight Eisenhower.

Remarkably, for all of his successes, many Americans did not know the full Obama record and failed to appreciate all that he had achieved under the unique pressure that arose from his race. Continually monitored by those who looked for him to favor one group over another or for him to reveal some form of prejudice, Obama would be criticized for showing both too much and too little racial sensitivity. This burden makes it all the more remarkable that Obama was underappreciated by many members of his own party. Among them were many, millions perhaps, who had invested in him such high hopes that they would inevitably feel disappointed because he didn't work any actual miracles.

Surely in time most if not all of Obama's fellow citizens will develop a fuller appreciation of the president's policy achievements, moral successes, and historical significance. This book is a step toward that understanding.

1

ENDING THE GREAT RECESSION

It Was the Economy, Stupid

On the day before he became president of the United States, Barack Obama put on faded jeans and went to the Sasha Bruce House, a shelter for runaway youth on Capitol Hill, where he used a roller to apply blue paint to a bedroom wall. Obama also visited with hundreds of volunteers who had gathered at a Washington-area high school to write letters to American military personnel stationed abroad. And he made an impromptu stop at Walter Reed Medical Center to meet more than a dozen wounded veterans of the wars in Iraq and Afghanistan. The day before the forty-fourth president's inauguration was the national Martin Luther King Jr. holiday, and Obama quoted the great civil rights leader as reporters listened: "Everybody can be great," said the president-elect, "because everybody can serve."

In the evening, Barack and Michelle Obama participated in a Washington custom, attending bipartisan events to honor, among others, his campaign opponent Senator John McCain. The senator may be best known for surviving as a prisoner of war in Vietnam, and Obama referred to him as an "American hero." Obama also praised him for understanding the need for "common purpose and common effort" in an age of intense partisanship.

The next day, Obama took the oath of office before a crowd of more than 1.8 million people, which was, by some estimates, the largest ever gathered in Washington. According to a Gallup poll, the number of Americans who felt more hopeful about the future outnumbered those who did not by six to one.

Parts of Obama's inaugural address, including a firm commitment to security, won vigorous applause even from the Republicans seated on the platform that had been built beside the US Capitol. Other items in his speech appealed mainly to the 53 percent of voters who had cast ballots for him. He repeated many of his campaign promises, including health care reforms, an increase in clean energy production, and closing the controversial Guantánamo Bay prison camp. But clearly this president knew he was taking office at a moment of crisis, and he dwelled at length on the three big challenges facing the country: the most severe economic recession since 1929, the terrorism of Islamic extremists, and climate change. He said:

> That we are in the midst of crisis is now well understood. Our nation is at war against a far-reaching network of violence and hatred.
>
> Our economy is badly weakened, a consequence of greed and irresponsibility on the part of some, but also our collective failure to make hard choices and prepare the nation for a new age. Homes have been lost; jobs shed; businesses shuttered. Our health care is too costly; our schools fail too many; and each day brings further evidence that the ways we use energy strengthen our adversaries and threaten our planet.
>
> These are the indicators of crisis, subject to data and statistics. Less measurable but no less profound is a sapping of confidence across our land—a nagging fear that America's decline is inevitable, and that the next generation must lower its sights.

Today I say to you that the challenges we face are
real. They are serious and they are many. They will not
be met easily or in a short span of time. But know this,
America—they will be met.

Of the three big challenges, resolving the economic mess was
the most acute. The pain of the recession was not theoretical, not a
matter of numbers in ledgers. Layoffs, foreclosures, ruined retirement accounts, and shuttered businesses were making it more difficult for millions of people to provide themselves with food and
shelter. (Two signs of economic pain could be seen in the rising use
of antidepressants and declining rates of pregnancy.) The Great Recession was draining the resources available for business to grow
and for the government to perform its basic functions, including
antiterrorism efforts and environmental protection. Worst of all,
some economists had begun to warn that the recession might become something worse. Some, such as Nobel Prize winner Paul
Krugman, feared the arrival of the first depression—a double-digit
decline in gross national product and high unemployment—since
the 1930s. Others worried of a "lost decade" of the sort endured by
Japan in the 1990s. The Japanese had experienced a bubble in asset
prices and subsequent burst in the same way that America's real-
estate and financial-asset bubbles popped in 2007–8. Although commonly called the lost decade, the decline in Japan had actually
continued for almost twenty years.

The specter of Japan's extended crisis and the suffering of individuals and families who'd lost jobs and homes and were losing
hope made the Great Recession the most important problem the
president faced. To borrow a phrase made famous during the 1992
presidential election, the first concern was "the economy, stupid."
Everything else, including national security, the environment, and
even the nation's ability to provide basics such as education and

health care, depended on the vigor of the economy. It would be the highest priority for Obama throughout his presidency.

As he considered the challenge, Obama prayed for a change in Washington's ways, quoting Scripture—"the time has come to set aside childish things"—and calling for an end to "the petty grievances and false promises, the recriminations and worn-out dogmas, that for far too long have strangled our politics." The new president did not have to mention the attempt to remove Bill Clinton from the White House after a sex scandal or the election of 2000, which was decided in Republican George Bush's favor in a party-line vote of the Supreme Court. Every informed American understood that political division had grown in recent decades, and the rift was pronounced in Congress. In 1982, two-thirds in Congress held centrist views as defined by the *National Review.* By the time of Obama's presidency, the centrists would comprise just 4 percent.

Political scientists Thomas E. Mann and Norman J. Ornstein would place the responsibility for the polarization in Congress mainly on Republicans. Neither Ornstein nor Mann were known to indulge in partisan rhetoric. Mann leaned a little Left, Ornstein a little Right. Together they were among the most moderate and widely respected political experts in the country. In their much-praised book *It's Even Worse Than It Looks,* they concluded, "The Republican party has become an insurgent outlier—ideologically extreme; contemptuous of the inherited social and economic policy regime; scornful of compromise; not persuaded by conventional facts, evidence, and science; and dismissive of the legitimacy of its political opposition."

The drift toward the extreme politics noted by Ornstein and Mann had been a factor in Obama's choice of a running mate. The new vice president, Joseph Biden, had served thirty-six years in the US Senate, where he was perhaps the most well-liked person in Washington of any political stripe. Affable and gregarious, Biden had learned to be a senator in the time when centrists from both parties ran the place. He counted many congressional Republicans as friends, and it was hoped, by some Democrats, that he could help move the new administration's agenda forward on Capitol Hill. Biden was an old-school sort who thought the Senate was a truly deliberative body and that compromise was one of the political arts.

This is not to say that Joe Biden was a political Pollyanna. He had experienced the hyperpartisanship of House Speaker Newt Gingrich, who infamously orchestrated a government shutdown and was also the first House Speaker ever disciplined for an ethics violation. The vice president had weathered the Clinton impeachment trial and acquittal, which had been achieved thanks to the votes of the few GOP moderates remaining in the Senate. A decade later, many of the cooler heads who had saved the country from a constitutional crisis, by refusing to support one or both of the articles of impeachment, were gone from the Senate. One who remained, Arlen Specter of Pennsylvania, told Biden to expect trouble from the GOP. Biden surely understood Specter's warning, but he couldn't know the extent of the opposition the new administration faced.

Voters had given Obama a mandate and repudiated congressional Republicans by adding twenty seats to the Democrats' majority in the House and seven to their majority in the Senate. However, Republican leaders in both houses of Congress were already pushing for a united front of opposition to everything Obama might propose. Although the strategy would become obvious as Congress voted on the president's initiatives, its political purpose would be revealed more gradually. In time Obama would learn that the less than loyal opposition united against him so that its leaders could point to his failure when it came to winning bipartisan support. According to their logic, that the president couldn't win Republican support was proof, not of their intransigence, but of *his*. Obama's embrace of many ideas, especially in health care, that originated with Republicans wouldn't matter. What mattered was that GOP leaders could claim that Obama, who had been elected with enormous support, was out of touch with the country he was chosen to lead.

Hostile Republicans could enforce their blockade with a parliamentary procedure called the filibuster. Historically this technique required that senators speak for hours on end, until exhausted colleagues capitulated or a supermajority of sixty voted to break the logjam. In modern times the threat of a filibuster was often enough to force the Senate to assemble a supermajority or move on to other business. Though rarely invoked in prior generations, the rate of filibusters had risen sharply beginning in the 1990s. Both sides used them, although Republicans practiced this form of obstruction more often.

Rules in the House do not permit filibusters and thus do not require a supermajority to end parliamentary delays. There, the GOP minority would have to content itself with symbolic opposition if the Democrats got in line behind the new president. Toward this end Eric Cantor, the vote-counting House Republican whip, told aides that he would organize the minority party to fight Obama in an extremely disciplined way. Obama had won more than 9 million votes than John McCain, but Cantor didn't feel any obligation to honor the mandate. He put it bluntly: "We're going to fight these guys." The top Republican in the Senate also rallied his colleagues to the cause of blocking the new president. Ohio senator George Voinovich would reveal that Minority Leader Mitch McConnell of Kentucky had declared in private, "If he [Obama] was for it, we had to be against it."

The motivation behind this strategy was power. Having analyzed the election results, GOP strategists determined that the other party's control of the House and Senate was not as strong as it may have seemed. Many of the seats recently won by Democrats were in districts with lots of conservative-leaning voters who voted against Obama. These representatives could be vulnerable to challenges in the next elections if they were painted as too loyal to the president. This was explained by Representative Pete Sessions of Texas, who made a presentation at a meeting of his fellow House Republicans where he offered a PowerPoint slide that said, "The Purpose of the Minority Is to Become the Majority."

As Washington writer Robert Draper would recount in his book *Do Not Ask What Good We Do,* a dozen or so congressional Republicans and strategists spent much of inauguration night devising a plan to block the new president's efforts to lead the country. While the Obamas and Bidens danced at various balls celebrating their election, Eric Cantor, Pete Sessions, Newt Gingrich, and others explored ways to deprive Obama of legislative victories, which would position the GOP to prevail in future elections. Draper reported that when the evening ended, Gingrich told the other men, "You'll remember this as the day the seeds of 2012 were sown."

More concerned with 2009 than 2012, the new president could not wait to extinguish the Great Recession, which had begun burning across the American economy in 2007 and had consumed millions of jobs. (Eventually the toll would reach more than 7.4 million.) The value of real estate, including the homes that sheltered the wealth of most American families, was in the middle of a $10 trillion decline. Stocks traded on various exchanges, which underpinned retirement accounts, were headed toward a loss of $7.4 trillion. In 2008, more than 860,000 homeowners received foreclosure notices. In the coming year the number would reach a record of nearly 3 million. The numbers represented men, women, and children forced to abandon their homes, and entire communities where unoccupied houses, with their windows boarded and their landscapes growing wild, outnumbered those where signs of life could still be seen. Tumbleweeds skittered into culs-de-sac. Coyotes loped through backyards.

The financial disaster that loomed over Obama's presidency was so powerful that it seemed like a purpose-built monster. In a way, it was. Beginning in the early 1980s, Democrats and Republicans in Washington had created the conditions for crisis by dismantling the regulatory system that would have prevented it. Conceived after the Great Depression, these rules were imposed by leaders who believed that finance was so essential to the well-being of the nation, and so rife with potential for abuse, that it required special over-sight. But as politicians born well after the Crash of 1929 came to power, and the experience of the Great Depression faded into his-tory, many found fault with the laws that constrained banks and brokerages and insurers. Unshackled, the argument went, financiers would produce new ways to lend money where it was needed. Since these men and women were obligated to keep their firms strong and thriving, they had more than enough incentive to act with pru-dence and responsibility.

The key moment in deregulation came in 1999, after an elec-tion that saw political candidates and parties rake in $58 million in campaign donations from groups and individuals associated with fi-nancial institutions. Urged on by these donors, Congress essentially gutted the Glass-Steagall Act of 1933, which had kept banks, in-surers, and stock brokerages separate for almost seventy years. In that time, the United States had not seen a return of the type of crisis that started in 1929. The repeal effort was led in the Senate by Republican Philip Gramm of Texas, who saw nothing but up-side in a bill that would, he said, make banking easier and cheaper. Among the handful of senators who opposed him, Democrat Paul Wellstone of Minnesota predicted that banks would merge and cre-ate much larger entities that could place great burdens on the taxpay-ers, who, ultimately, insure bank deposits. "Why on earth are we doing this?" he asked.

President Clinton did not share Wellstone's worries. During his presidency, declining unemployment, generally lower inflation, and the longest period of sustained economic growth in US history had

led to the first federal budget surplus since 1970 and prom
pay-down of federal debt. The Clinton years would pa
one recession and be recalled as the Roaring Nineties by
Prize–winning economist Joseph E. Stiglitz. In this decade the stock
market surged almost 150 percent and the value of Americans'
homes increased every year, in every region of the country.

A close look would have turned up signs of trouble. In Reagan's time a New Gilded Age began as those at the highest income
levels reaped a disproportionate share of the economy's growth.
Well-paid jobs in manufacturing were continuing a long decline.
Contrary to the complaints of the deregulators, the financial sector
captured a greater share of the total economy—increasing from about
6 to 8 percent—which made its risk-taking even more dangerous
to bystanders.

No caution appeared in the statement President Clinton made
as he signed the Glass-Steagall repeal. Instead he invoked the holy
trinity of American politics—businesses, consumers, and freedom—
as he announced that the bill changes would spur innovation,
heighten competition, and "alleviate burdens" on financiers. "Re-
moval of barriers to competition," said Clinton, "will enhance the
stability of our financial services system."

Unburdened, the financial industry continued a spree of mergers and concentration that had begun during the Reagan administration. Many smaller banks disappeared, and the business was soon
dominated by a few dozen institutions with regional, national, and
global reach. Investors, including many from abroad, flooded lenders
with cash, with which they funded mortgages for "subprime" borrowers, including many not worthy of the credit they received. Although a few words of warning came from the likes of Federal
Reserve governor Susan Bies, who worried about risky real estate
loans, her minority perspective was countered by the famous Federal
Reserve chairman Alan Greenspan, who spoke repeatedly of the
ways deregulation had made finance safer. In his cryptic speaking

style he credited new financial instruments, including the sales of bundled mortgages to investors, with "the dispersion of risk." This dispersion of risk—to insurance companies, hedge funds, and others—supposedly helped protect everyone.

As a young man, Greenspan had been an acolyte of self-taught philosopher Ayn Rand, who exalted "the virtue of selfishness." Throughout his career he had helped lead a retreat from the theories of John Maynard Keynes, who had reserved a role for government as both a careful business regulator and consumer of last resort. Keynes urged special attention to banking and finance, where mischief-making could have tidal-wave effects on communities and countries. The government could respond to a collapse in confidence that made people pull back from the marketplace by spending money to "prime the pump." Greenspan favored government inaction and faith in private enterprise. He expressed this faith with the kind of certainty and devotion to unfettered markets that his mentor would have admired.

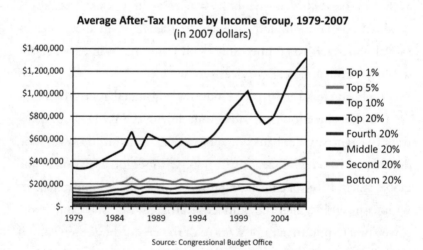

Average After-Tax Income by Income Group, 1979-2007
(in 2007 dollars)

Source: Congressional Budget Office

When he addressed the National Italian American Foundation in 2005, Greenspan said new, risky forms of debt were stabilizing influences, and he announced that America was "rediscovering the benefits of competition and the resilience to economic shocks that it fosters." All this Greenspan hailed even as benefits had concentrated even more at the highest levels. According to the Congressional Budget Office, incomes for the top 1 percent of earners rose 250 percent between 1979 and 2005. In the same period more than two-thirds of Americans had seen their incomes stagnate.

Greenspan had heard warnings about looming dangers in the economy. Weeks before the Fed chairman spoke to the Italian Americans, economist Raghuram Rajan had bravely sounded an alarm at a conference at Jackson Hole, Wyoming, which had been organized to celebrate Greenspan's career. The warning came in a paper—"Has Financial Development Made the World Riskier?"—that Rajan had begun researching with the assumption that Greenspan had been right about deregulation. Rajan concluded that under Greenspan lightly policed financiers had actually taken huge risks that could upend the economy. This had happened because the key players on Wall Street were motivated by short-term gains, which they could make with risky decisions, and their tendency to move together, like a herd, to avoid getting out of step with their peers. Rajan described this as unexpected "perverse behavior" that defied what Greenspan and his allies assumed about a world full of rational people making coolheaded choices.

Dismissed at Jackson Hole, Rajan nevertheless turned out to be right. Deregulation had permitted the rapid growth of unconventional financial institutions such as hedge funds, which operated without the kind of federal deposit insurance that made regular banks secure places for investors. Deregulation also allowed the expansion of risk-taking by banks and of exotic financial instruments such as collateralized debt obligations. Banks could undertake riskier lending without setting aside money or other assets that could be used in the event of big failures. This is how leverage works. The greater the leverage, as allowed under law, the greater the risk, the greater the gamble, for banks, and ultimately for taxpayers, who stood behind the insurance system that guaranteed the banks' solvency.

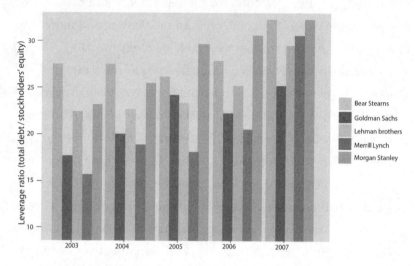

Leverage Ratios for Major Investment Banks

Many of the riskiest new forms of debt were based on mortgage payments made by American homeowners. These payments were, in essence, assets, and in theory they were reliable streams of income because lenders make careful evaluations of applicants, and borrowers will do almost anything to stay current on their mortgages and stay in their homes. However, with real median household income falling from its 1999 peak, lenders had loosened their standards to continue lending to applicants and continually increase the flow of monthly payments. This "subprime" mortgage market helped create artificially high rates of homeownership and a false run-up in home values, which in turn made people feel rich. At the height of the frenzy, lenders allowed people to borrow without proving their income or putting any money down on the property they were buying. In some cases the mortgages exceeded the price of the real estate. As one real estate agent would tell CBS News reporter Steve Kroft, borrowers were "getting paid to buy a house."

Although some insiders were worried about the risk created by excessive leverage, for a time Greenspan's confidence steadied markets. However, by early 2007 Treasury Department officials were quietly developing a plan to rebuild the financial system in the event of its collapse. The need for this plan became obvious in late summer of 2008 with a steep plunge in the stock market and the demise of the investment banks Bear Stearns and Lehman Brothers. As lenders stopped giving new loans and businesses began to suffer the consequences, President Bush and Congress committed $700 billion to bail out bankers. Writing in the *Guardian,* economist Nouriel Roubini, who was among the few who predicted the real estate bust, declared the plan a "rip-off" that shifted risk to taxpayers and profited financiers. It was enacted as the Troubled Asset Relief Program (TARP). Soon federal money would pour into financial institutions to bail out executives and shareholders, and to limit the chaos in the economy.

President Bush got his TARP only with the help of congressional Democrats, who gave him the votes he needed to overcome the opposition of his own party. However, TARP did not stop the decline in the securities markets. After a brief pause the Dow Jones Industrial Average continued to plummet from its height of about 14,000 toward a low, to be reached in the coming April, of just above 7,000. Unemployment continued to rise about half a percent per month. Worst of all, the US economy was actually getting smaller and at an accelerating rate. The huge auto industry had been staggered when consumer credit evaporated. With a severe drop in sales, automakers lost so much revenue that even four hundred thousand layoffs couldn't fix their finances. The chief executive officers of Chrysler, Ford, and General Motors went to Washington seeking help from the TARP fund. Both Chrysler and General Motors were headed for bankruptcy.

Rising unemployment. Markets in free fall. Credit frozen. The economy shrinking. It was too easy to imagine that the recession could become a depression with the kind of suffering not seen since the 1930s.

With the post-TARP economy getting worse, Obama's solution—the American Recovery and Reinvestment Act of 2009—would call for hundreds of billions of dollars in deficit spending, which previous presidents had used to deal with recessions. Direct government spending could create demand for goods and services, and jobs, but in many cases this activity built slowly. Even road projects deemed ready to start required months of contract preparations. Other actions, such as tax cuts, unemployment benefits, food stamps, and financing for private initiatives, could work more quickly by putting money in the hands of people who would spend it. This jolt of spending was called a stimulus because it was intended to cause ripples of buying and selling that would radiate across the economy. Thus stimulated, the economic activity would begin to flow on its own.

Missing from the package, which took shape prior to the inauguration, were impressive projects that would change the landscape and win history's acknowledgment. There would be no Hoover Dam (Franklin Roosevelt), no federal highway system (Eisenhower), and no moon shot (Kennedy). Obama had once pressed his aides to come up with impressive projects that would match the legacies left by his predecessors and satisfy those of his fellow Democrats who dreamed of something comparable to the New Deal programs that provided direct employment to millions of people. However, the Great Recession was not yet a depression, which meant that Obama would meet skepticism over projects that would take years to gear up and complete. For this reason the president set aside anything so big it could be seen from space and stuck with a varied mix of proposals to get money into the economy.

To sell his plan to lawmakers and citizens, Obama would declare his plan "timely, targeted, and temporary," which framed it as a response to a crisis. It was. But federal spending is always an expression of policy—hawks feed the Pentagon, doves do not—so the American Recovery and Reinvestment Act was also an opportunity for the president to move quickly on his agenda. His chief of staff, Rahm Emanuel, announced the president's intentions quite explicitly, and unapologetically, when he appeared at a *Wall Street Journal* forum held days after the election. His eyes shadowed with postcampaign exhaustion, Emanuel sat in a swiveling chair and answered a moderator's questions for an audience of leading corporate executives. In time his remarks would be edited by critics to suggest he was an opportunist. In full his statement was more like a call for calm but also decisive action:

> You never want a serious crisis to go to waste. And what I mean by that is an opportunity to do things that you think you could not do before.
>
> I think America as a whole in 1973 and 1974, and not just my view but obviously the administration's, missed the opportunity to deal with the energy crisis that was before us. For a long time our entire energy policy came down to cheap oil.
>
> This is an opportunity, what used to be long-term problems, be they in the health care area, energy area, education area, fiscal area, tax area, regulatory reform area, things that we have postponed for too long, that were long-term, are now immediate and must be dealt with. This crisis provides the opportunity, for us, as I would say, the opportunity to do things that you could not do before.
>
> The good news, I suppose, if you want to see a silver lining, is the problems are big enough that they lend themselves to ideas from both parties for the solution.

Emanuel said a recent meeting Obama had with Republican senators McCain and Lindsey Graham of South Carolina was not window dressing but a genuine consultation. The need for action grew more urgent with every report on the condition of the economy. Job losses, which caused obvious pain for individuals and families but also rippled through the economy, were especially alarming. The president-elect's top economic advisers, Jared Bernstein and Christina Romer, issued an estimate of the effects the stimulus bill might have on employment. After noting that "all of the estimates presented in this memo are subject to significant margins of error," the economists estimated that as many as 3.6 million jobs could be saved or created and that the rising unemployment rate could be halted before it reached 8 percent.

After Obama's inauguration, the new president's first trip to the Capitol was to meet with House Republicans, and not Democrats, with the Recovery Act the only agenda item. House Democrats had formally proposed the program, which was priced at about $800 billion, which was far bigger even than President Roosevelt's Depression-era New Deal. A *Wall Street Journal* poll found a great majority of Americans, including 68 percent of people in their own party, thought Republicans in Congress should support it.

In choosing to trek up to Capitol Hill the president broke with tradition—usually members of Congress visit the White House for such sessions—and he demonstrated his sincere desire for joint action. Obama would need the support of just two GOP senators to break a possible filibuster; However, he was hoping for the political cover that would come from more substantial bipartisan support on both sides of the Capitol. Without it, the recession-fighting project would belong to the Democrats alone, and given the challenge of turning around the economy, they would take all the blame if it didn't work as well, or as fast, as Americans hoped.

Considering the defeats suffered by Republicans in 2006, when they lost the House, and 2008, when they lost the White House, one might have expected them to offer a measure of conciliation. However, GOP members of Congress were not looking back at the voters' rebukes but forward to coming elections—in 2010 and 2012—and calculating that they would fare better if they could stand united against the president. They would distinguish themselves as staunchly opposed, even in a losing cause, rather than dignify the president's ideas with even the slightest support.

Publicly the leaders of the House and Senate Republicans pledged to have open ears. After his visit with the Republicans in the House, the president stopped to speak with the press in the Ohio Clock Corridor, where senators often answer reporters' questions, and said the meeting had been "very constructive." However privately, in the hours before Obama's arrival, House minority leader John Boehner had told his GOP colleagues, "I hope everyone here will join me in voting no." A day earlier, five corporations had announced that another thirty thousand workers would be fired from their jobs, becoming casualties of the crisis. Soon the president would warn that America could suffer a Japan-style "lost decade" of economic suffering if his plan was not approved.

Although Republican representative Paul Ryan of Wisconsin would praise Obama for "starting us off, at least, beginning to talk to one another," the discussion did not continue. Ryan's House colleagues resisted dialogue, and when the president's plan was approved, not one House Republican would support it. In the Senate, Minority Leader McConnell would rally Republican members against every Obama initiative, beginning with the recovery plan. McConnell wanted voters to consider Obama's plans, and indeed, his entire presidency, to be divisive and controversial. He also wanted to resume the age-old claim that his party was better at managing the economy, overall, and employment and budget deficits in particular.

McConnell believed that American voters associated the GOP with stronger economic leadership. If the Recovery Act failed, a GOP united against it might claim their confidence. In the short term, however, Americans blamed the Great Recession on Obama's predecessor, Republican George W. Bush, and they wanted to give the new president's policies a try. The Gallup poll gave Obama a 78 percent favorable rating, which was substantially higher than the margins enjoyed by Bill Clinton and George Bush when they began their presidencies. This trend was matched by an astounding spike in public concern about the economy. Eighteen months before, just 16 percent of respondents said the economy was America's most serious problem. From there it shot almost straight up, to 80 percent. McConnell also had a problem when it came to the GOP's overall reputation. Since the 1950s Gallup had asked the public to rate the parties on the economy forty-two times. The Democrats beat or tied the GOP in twenty-seven of these surveys. Also, during the Bush presidency, when Republicans held the White House for eight years, the House for six years, and the Senate for four, the trend toward deficit reduction begun by Bill Clinton had been reversed. Both deficit spending and the national debt, which were supposedly anathema to GOP economics, had increased during the Bush years.

In January 2009 the tough times that began under Bush got worse. The unemployment rate, swollen by six hundred thousand January job cuts, rose to 7.4 percent. For the individuals who'd lost jobs and homes these facts were devastating. For others, the news provoked a *Grapes of Wrath* kind of anxiety. Republican senators from the more moderate Northeast states began to express concern about the need for substantive action.

Try as they might, partisan critics could point to no actual boondoggles in the Recovery Act proposal. This defied what many people assume about the way Washington works. Prevailing wisdom held that any piece of legislation written in more than a thousand pages of text *must* contain outrageous elements. Conservative media bristled with the false claim that $30 million would be spent to protect a threatened species of mouse. The planned construction of a Homeland Security facility was criticized as a $248 million furniture-buying program. Requests for projects that the administration had rejected were nevertheless trumpeted by critics as included in the plan, which allowed for press releases about frivolities such as Frisbee parks.

Despite complaints about his heavy-handedness, Obama persisted in his pursuit of bipartisan action. He responded to GOP priorities by not including items they thought frivolous, and by adding the party's favorite type of action: tax cuts. He appointed Republicans to his cabinet and won endorsements for his Recovery Act from a handful of GOP governors. The administration even courted and obtained support from both the national Chamber of Commerce and the National Association of Manufacturers, two groups that were normally opposed to government intervention in the economy. Officials at these organizations understood the danger facing the economy. Commerce and manufacturing were slowing at such a rate that the business interests these groups represented were imperiled. These endorsements would provide cover for any Republicans who might support the president: they could tell their constituents they had done what the sober leaders of American business had recommended.

When the big program was finally put to a vote in the House, on January 29, not one Republican supported it. However, the Democrats enjoyed such a large majority in Congress that Obama prevailed even with eleven members of his own party, each of whom represented a conservative district, joining the opposition. The victory, coming so soon after Obama's inauguration, was enabled by the widespread anxiety created by the economic crisis. In the days after the House vote the press reported layoffs at schools in Missouri, the retailer Target headquarters in Minnesota, radio stations in Ohio, and many other places. Each lost job represented not just a crisis for the individual worker, but uncertainty for dependents and the withdrawal of the worker's income from the local economy.

Before the Senate recorded ayes and nays, the new president used the power and emblems of his office to command attention for his plan. He flew in the presidential plane, Air Force One, with the White House press corps in tow, to visit the economically devastated city of Elkhart, Indiana, where he visited a manufacturing plant and addressed a "town hall" gathering of local residents.

No place in America had suffered more in the Great Recession than Elkhart. The region's major employers make products such as musical instruments and recreational vehicles that are never in demand during hard times. As these industries saw a steep decline, unemployment rose from 4.7 percent to 15.3 percent in a single year. "The situation we face could not be more serious," said Obama in a speech in the small city. "We can't afford to wait. We can't wait to hope for the best. We can't posture and bicker and resort to the same failed ideas that got us here in the first place."

The line about posturing and bickering provoked cheers and applause, and Obama seized the energy offered by the crowd to remind those who listened, "That was what the election was all about. The American people rejected those ideas because they hadn't worked. You didn't send us to Washington because you were hoping for more of the same. You sent us there to change things. The expectation was that we'd act quickly and boldly to carry out change, and that's exactly what I intend to do as president of the United States of America."

Upon his return to Washington, the president reiterated the themes he'd sounded in Elkhart at his first-ever prime-time White House press conference. Obama had been alarmed by the depth of the crisis, which, he discovered after winning the election, was worse than he knew. "We can differ on some of the particulars, but again, the question I think that the American people are asking is, 'Do you just want government to do nothing, or do you want it to do something?' If you want it to do something, then we can have a conversation," he said. "But doing nothing—that's not an option, from my perspective." Obama defended the role of government in the recovery, saying, "With the private sector so weakened by this recession, the federal government is the only entity left with the resources to jolt our economy back to life."

Although House Republicans had established and held their united front against him, Obama didn't need any of them to move his program forward. The Senate, which was the target he intended to reach with his Elkhart visit and his televised press conference, was a different matter. He needed not a simple majority, but sixty out of a hundred votes to prove that he could block a filibuster, which would have been fatal to his plan. With the Massachusetts Democrat Edward Kennedy too ill to vote and independent Joe Lieberman of Connecticut wavering, the president needed GOP help. He got what he needed from Arlen Specter of Pennsylvania and Susan Collins and Olympia Snowe of Maine. Specter would soon jump to the Democratic Party and thus escape repercussions. The move by the senators from Maine, who were well supported back home, signaled that their small state might wield outsize power in the Obama presidency.

President Obama wore a Republican-red tie at the White House ceremony where he signed the Recovery Act. He dubbed the moment "the beginning of the end" of the Great Recession. It wasn't the most radical economic policy ever undertaken. This distinction may actually belong to the policies of Republican president Richard Nixon, who unilaterally dropped the gold standard for the dollar, froze private wages and prices, and imposed a 10 percent duty on imports. The Obama bill was, however, the most expensive and most sweeping economic program ever produced by Washington. More than a third of the effort would be measured in tax breaks for businesses and individuals, which conformed with GOP priorities but also figured to get cash circulating quickly. But the rest, about $500 billion, would be spent to shore up social programs—food stamps, unemployment benefits, lunches for poor schoolchildren—and fund a long list of projects that would pump money into the economy, invest in lasting public works, and fulfill a great many of Obama's campaign promises. Among these projects were:

- About $100 billion to repair or upgrade highways, bridges, airports.
- More than $150 billion for health care, including modernization of medical record-keeping.
- Roughly $18 billion for water and sewerage projects and other environmental protection efforts.
- $27 billion for energy conservation and research and to finance renewable-energy efforts.
- $7.6 billion for basic scientific research.
- Almost $15 billion for housing.
- $21.5 billion to improve electric transmission and grids and disposal of nuclear wastes.
- $100 billion for schools, more than half of which would go to prevent teacher layoffs.
- $10 billion in government technology upgrades.

In addition to the large categories of spending, the bill was loaded, critics would say *larded,* with hundreds of millions of dollars for items that were, in light of the overall program, small. Police departments ($4 billion), farmers ($749 million), and small-scale business operators seeking loans ($730 million) all got a boost from the Recovery Act. Relative crumbs of equal size—$50 million—went to the National Cemetery Administration and the National Endowment for the Arts. The cemetery administration oversees military burial grounds. The NEA offers support to artists, including some who court controversy, which has led to occasional calls for its abolition.

The funding for the NEA was, of course, among the sins highlighted by critics of the Obama program. Writing in *The Atlanta Journal-Constitution,* former GOP congressman Bob Barr singled out this spending as an example of "the true evil of this spending boon-doggle." Other examples included $2 billion for child-care subsi-dies, $2.1 billion to advocate solutions to global warming, and $400 million for antismoking and safe-sex programs. Barr was also out-raged by the $20 billion supplement to the "bloated" food program for the poor.

In fact, after settling at a twenty-year low in the Clinton years, the federal food stamp program had begun to grow during the George W. Bush presidency. This was due not to a sudden outbreak of indolence, but to the most anemic job growth since the Great Depression, which made more people eligible for aid. The program was hardly an encouragement for people to go on the dole. It paid a little more than $1 per person per meal. Roughly half of recipi-ents were children, and another 25 percent were the disabled and the elderly. No able-bodied person without children could receive the help for more than ninety days. Adding to the program was also one way of putting money into the economy quickly. Tax breaks for upper- and middle-class people could be diverted to savings. Spending devoted to bridges and highways would take months if not years to accomplish. But poor people in need of food would use food stamps promptly.

With congressional approval for his economic plan in hand, Obama had not just the stimulus he felt the nation required, but also funding for his policy priorities, and he emphasized this sec-ond part of his victory by traveling to Colorado to put his signa-ture on the bill in a public setting. A bit of stagecraft favored by President Reagan, out-of-Washington bill-signing ceremonies had been rare since the Gipper left office. Obama's chosen site was a sci-ence museum in Denver, where the president was given a tour of an exhibit of solar energy panels. The Recovery Act would make the largest-ever federal investment in alternative-energy science and pro-vide loan support for companies that would make solar panels, as well as other alternative-energy equipment. These forward-looking investments reflected the president's personal interest. Having won election in part thanks to Internet-based activism, he was a president of his time who understood and appreciated science and technology.

Careful to avoid raising expectations, the president told the crowd at the museum, "I don't want to pretend that today marks the end of our economic problems. Nor does it constitute all of what we're going to have to do to turn our economy around. But today does mark the beginning of the end, the beginning of what we need to do to create jobs for Americans scrambling in the wake of layoffs."

On Wall Street, unimpressed traders expressed their opinions about the stimulus plan by pushing stock prices down. By day's end the main index of the US stock market would plunge three hundred points. Before Obama returned to Washington, the House Republican leader John Boehner would declare, "The flawed bill the president will sign today is a missed opportunity, one for which our children and grandchildren will pay a hefty price." Republican governors, who were meeting in Washington, also expressed great pessimism. Some, including Mark Sanford of South Carolina and Bobby Jindal of Louisiana, rejected parts or all of the spending marked for their states. In Sanford's case this would be roughly $700 million, which he would decline for the sake of making a partisan point. While laid-off workers in other states would receive additional unemployment benefits, Sanford's constituents would not. Neither would they receive help holding on to their health insurance, which the stimulus bill provided.

In *The Wall Street Journal,* editorialist Daniel Henninger would compare the program to "a recreational drug" and prescribe, instead, penny-pinching of the sort that would dominate economic policy in Great Britain and the eurozone countries, where the Great Recession had also struck. Thanks to diverging economic and political points of view, Obama and his critics would see a real-world macro-experiment unfold as the United States and Western Europe adopted different responses to the crisis. American officials considered the stunningly low cost of borrowing (Treasury-bill interest rates were approaching zero) a historic opportunity to fund public investments and push government money into the economy with deficit spending. Their counterparts in Europe viewed the crisis as a chance to cut spending and therefore government activity, on the theory that the real problem was national debt and, from their ideological perspective, social programs. The Great Recession also provided the conditions for an experiment *within the United States* as governors in some states also adopted austerity on an ideological basis. Officials in Kansas and Wisconsin would pursue cuts in government spending with particular zeal, especially after each state elected austerity-minded governors in 2010.

Although Republican governors could adopt their own economic policies, the party's leaders in Washington had been swamped by Obama's fast drive to get his program approved and lacked the power to act on their own. They could, however, seek to undermine him on the basis of an idle, destructive rumor, and this they proceeded to do. A few days after the ceremony in Denver, Republican senator Richard Shelby of Alabama met with residents in the small city of Cullman, north of Birmingham, Alabama, where he was asked about Internet-fed suspicions that the president was not a US citizen. For forty years, while conservative critics had gone to great lengths to cast the press as biased in favor of liberals, public confidence in the traditional news media had declined, especially among Republicans. This loss of confidence, combined with the power of the Internet to spread and sustain partisan-flavored rumors, created the context in which someone in Alabama might imagine that Obama could sneak into office as a foreigner. Senator Shelby did nothing to correct this perception, saying, "Well, his father was Kenyan and they said he was born in Hawaii, but I haven't seen any birth certificate. You have to be born in America to be president."

Shelby's statement depended on an unnamed "they" to create doubt and amplify suspicion. The idea that someone who was barred by the Constitution could somehow become president, without any officials noticing, was incredible. Besides, no one in politics could have missed that the question had been raised in the 2008 campaign and resolved with release of Obama's official short-form birth certificate. But even if Shelby was ignorant of this, could he know, for certain, that previous presidents had been born on US soil? Had he seen their birth certificates?

Reports on Shelby's comments did not include any suggestion that these deficiencies in his reply to the question were noted at the time. Instead, readers were left with the image of a Southern senator encouraging doubt that the first black president was, in fact, eligible for the office. Shelby would correct himself in July, but the canard would be advanced by another Republican, Congressman Roy Blunt of Missouri. Blunt would say, "What I don't know is why the president can't produce a birth certificate. I don't know anybody else that can't produce one. And I think that's a legitimate question. No health records, no birth certificate."

When Blunt spoke, hoaxers were circulating a fake document they presented as the president's Kenyan birth certificate, which they said proved he wasn't actually an American. State officials in Hawaii repeatedly affirmed the validity of the short-form certificate made public during the 2008 campaign. These statements did not quell speculation, but they were deemed sufficient by the president, who didn't consider the rumors worthy of his attention. Besides, the administration had far bigger worries. Billions of dollars were being funneled into the economy via tax breaks, increased social-program benefits, and new initiatives, but the data measuring the condition of the economy wasn't improving. In May, frozen credit markets began to thaw as banks lowered the rates they charged each other for borrowing funds. In the next month, foreclosures would decline by 6 percent. However, these glimmers of improvement were not meaningful to Americans, who feared the future. Unemployment remained stubbornly high and even crept upward. In October 2009 it passed 10 percent, which some economists considered an especially discouraging milestone.

A double-digit jobless rate gave critics grounds for attack, and several quickly insisted that the president had promised that his stimulus program would keep unemployment below 8 percent. Although the number had been in Christina Romer's pre-inauguration report, where it was subject to numerous caveats, President Obama had never promised such a result. Nevertheless, he faced an extremely difficult challenge in that economic activity depends, at least a bit, on public confidence, which influences people's decisions on purchases and investments. For the good of the country he needed to both encourage optimism and cultivate patience.

As he sought to rally public support, Obama conducted periodic "town hall meetings," where he answered questions and sought to reassure citizens. Extremely relaxed by nature, he performed exceedingly well in these settings. Occasionally the people he called upon offered him encouragement. In New Orleans a ten-year-old named Terrence Scott asked, "Why do people hate you? They're supposed to love you." Obama gave him a hug and with a chuckle in his voice said, "I did get elected president, so not everybody hates me. . . . But it's true that if you're watching TV, it looks like everybody's getting mad all the time."

Obama told Terrence he thought that his critics were just trying to keep him on his toes and urged Terrence to not "take it too seriously."

Although he sought to reassure Terrence Scott, Obama understood that people who had lost their jobs or their homes were at risk of losing hope, too. The American public was probably not much interested in the factors that made the current recession more intractable than others, even though they were well established. Earlier in the year the International Monetary Fund had issued a report predicting the crisis would be "long, deep with slow recovery." In the IMF's view, recessions that began with catastrophe in the financial system and spread around the world, such as the Great Recession, were especially difficult to resolve. These facts were cited in October 2009 by Nobel Prize–winning economist Paul Krugman as he urged the administration to stay the course.

Krugman had been worried that the United States faced an actual depression, and while he believed that it had been averted, he feared any recovery that might be under way could be undermined. This was a human concern for Krugman, who worried about the "blighted lives" caused by child poverty, which would increase if things didn't get better fast. He was dismissed by economists such as Allan Meltzer of Carnegie Mellon University, who noted some hopeful signs in the economy and counseled simply scrapping the stimulus program, which would halt both the spending and policy initiatives it contained. There would be no energy research and investment, no speeded repairs of bridges and roads, no added support for the poor and unemployed.

As politicians and economists squabbled, the Obama administration pressed ahead with its agenda by advancing its plan to overhaul health care, which the president saw as essential to righting the economy for the long term. Opinion polls indicated that the public was losing confidence in him. Then something good happened. In November 2009 the unemployment rate dipped back below 10 percent. For the next five months it would hover between 9.9 and 9.8 percent, then it dropped to 9.4 percent and commenced a bumpy but nevertheless definite decline.

Month after month, as the stimulus took hold, the number of jobs being lost receded, until, at last, by November 2009, more had been created than lost. The trend took a pause in December and resumed for the next five months. Then another retrenchment in the summer of 2010 spread worry among Americans who had endured years of difficulty. For Republicans running in the congressional elections, the bad news was evidence that Obama was failing. In September the president tried to answer that assessment as he faced a group of citizens at a televised event sponsored by the CNBC television network. Although he got a rock star's welcome from the crowd, he acknowledged that many must have deep concerns about the country's condition. Economists believed the recession had ended, he said, but "obviously for the millions of people who are still out of work, people who have seen their home values decline, people who are struggling to pay the bills day to day, it's still very real for them." He also reminded the audience that "the month I was sworn in we lost 750,000 jobs; the month after that 600,000; the month after that 600,000. This is before any of our plans had a chance to take effect. The financial markets were on the verge of meltdown, and the economy was contracting about six percent—by far, the largest contraction we've seen since the thirties."

One of the toughest questions Obama heard during the session came from a woman who had voted for him and was impatient with the slow pace of the economic recovery. "And quite frankly, I'm exhausted," said the woman. "I'm exhausted of defending you, defending your administration, defending the mantle of change that I voted for."

With poll numbers telling him voters were genuinely worried, Obama didn't sugarcoat his reply: "My goal here is not to try to convince you that everything is where it needs to be. It's not. . . . But what I am saying is, is that we're moving in the right direction. And if we are able to keep our eye on our long-term goal—which is making sure that every family out there, if they're middle-class, that they can pay their bills, have the security of health insurance, retire with dignity and respect, send their kids to college; if they're not yet in the middle class, that there are ladders there to get into the middle class, if people work hard and get an education to apply themselves—that's our goal. That's the America we believe in. And I think that we are on track to be able to do that."

The employment turnaround that Obama expected came in October 2010, but would not appear in economic reports until after the election. The GOP won control of the House and cut the Democratic Party's advantage in the Senate to 51–49. On the day after the election the president told reporters at the White House, "Some election nights are more fun than others," and that his party had suffered a "shellacking." But when a reporter asked if he would concede that the election was a "fundamental rejection of your agenda," he wouldn't go that far. He accepted his share of responsibility, saying, "I've got to do a better job," but he added, "just like everybody else in Washington does."

With reporters pressing him on the meaning of the election result, Obama said he was willing to consider ideas offered by Republicans in Congress and that he imagined he would find some

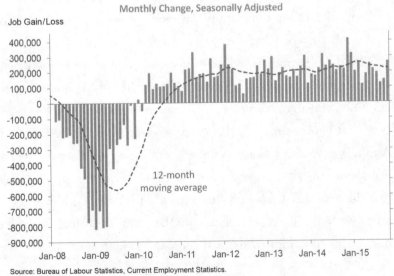

Private Sector Payroll Employment
Monthly Change, Seasonally Adjusted

Source: Bureau of Labour Statistics, Current Employment Statistics.

he was willing to adopt. Asked if he would be "willing to negotiate," Obama replied, "Absolutely."

Although the midterm election brought a difficult outcome for the president, the country would soon recognize the beginning of a long period of positive job growth in the private sector, the longest since the data collection began in 1939.

Jobs represented just one of several positive trends that began after the stimulus program was begun and continued throughout the Obama presidency. Housing starts, which reflect economic attitudes and depend on both growth and job creation, also rose. Contrary to political orthodoxy, which held that liberal-leaning policies are bad for business, the stock market, which had reached a nadir thanks to the financial collapse and the Great Recession, recovered briskly. So, too, did corporate profits.

Even deficit hawks, who were alarmed by the borrowing done to fund stimulus spending, had to be heartened by Obama's performance.

The deficit picture improved in part because revenues increased

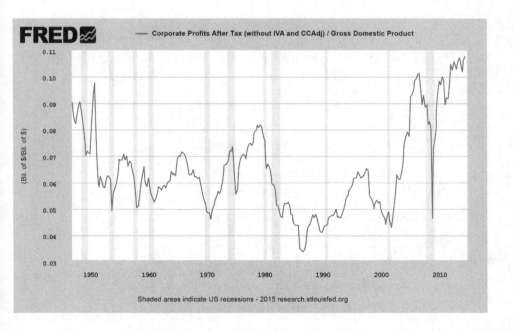

in a healing economy. At the same time, federal spending as a share of the overall economy spiked briefly but then declined.

Critics complained about the slow pace of recovery under the

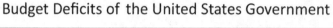

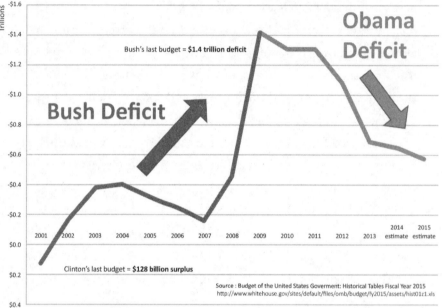

Budget Deficits of the United States Government

Bush's last budget = $1.4 trillion deficit

Bush Deficit

Obama Deficit

Clinton's last budget = $128 billion surplus

Source : Budget of the United States Goverment: Historical Tables Fiscal Year 2015
http://www.whitehouse.gov/sites/default/files/omb/budget/fy2015/assets/hist01z1.xls

Obama stimulus approach, but the American experience was much better than what was seen in the United Kingdom and eurozone countries where the austerity approach—cutting spending to reduce deficits—was tried. Austerity brought rises in unemployment at a time when the jobs picture was improving in the United States and tamped down growth compared with the United States.

Although the country-to-country comparisons demonstrate Obama's success, proof is also available closer to home. In Wisconsin, Governor Scott Walker's use of steep tax cuts, which were intended to spur recovery, actually coincided with worsening unemployment, compared with the rest of the country. And in Kansas, where spending was slashed and taxes on the wealthy were reduced, austerity had a similar effect. It also prompted some strange budgeting gymnastics. Hundreds of millions of dollars were diverted from the Kansas Department of Transportation, which maintains the fourth largest network of state highways in the nation, to pay for other government functions. Some of this money was obtained, not via taxes but by issuing long term bonds, which are

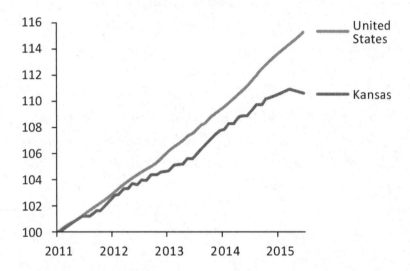

State Coincident Indexes
Kansas vs. United States, 2011-2015

U.S. recovery under Obama vs. Kansas under tax/budget
experiment of GOP governor Sam Brownback
Source: Manzie D. Chinn, Federal Reserve Bank of Philadelphia Data

more typically applied to capital expenditures. One GOP state representative compared this practice to using a credit card to pay a credit card bill. The net effect of this policy has been the postponement of infrastructure maintence that, over the long run, could lead to higher spending as roads and bridges require more costly repairs.

On the other side of the economic spectrum, the two states that fared best in the five years after Obama's policy was enacted were two most associated with the crisis in American industry—Michigan and Ohio. When the recession began, Michigan was in the worst

shape of all the states, with the highest unemployment and an economy shrinking at an alarming 9 percent annual rate. Ohio was in
similarly difficult straits. Both wound up at the top of the recovery
in part because of the stimulus and in part because of Obama's
remarkably successful initiatives that rescued the American auto
industry.

Nationally, the challenge of creating jobs, and in particular jobs
that paid well, was the most difficult for the country to overcome. In
September 2016 the census Bureau reported that median household
income grew by more than 5 percent between 2014 and 2015. This
was the first time the bureau reported an increase since before the
Great Recession. At the same time, the official poverty rate declined
by 1.2 percent. This mean that 3.5 million people left the ranks of
the poor in 2015. Good as this news was, the data did not reflect
the value of social-service benefits for lower income Americans or
the fact households are smaller than they once were. If these and
other factors had been included, the picture would have been even
brighter.

2

AUTO INDUSTRY RESCUE

"The Doomsayers Were Wrong"

In a moment when signs and symbols shaped economic reality in a most immediate way, the chiefs of America's Big Three auto companies arrived in Washington from the Detroit area aboard separate private jets. Their mission: to beg the Senate Banking Committee for a $25 billion taxpayer bailout. The carmakers were in deep trouble caused, in part, by their own blunders and in part by the Great Recession, which had made consumers so frightened that sales of cars and light trucks had dropped 20 percent in a year. Chrysler and General Motors would soon be unable to pay their workers. But what were senators and members of Congress to think as these men of Chrysler, General Motors, and Ford spent about $15,000 apiece—or fifteen times *first-class* airfare—just getting to Capitol Hill?

Once the foundation of middle-class prosperity in dozens of communities, America's car companies had long struggled against nimble foreign competitors. Outflanked on price, fuel economy, and quality, they had failed to offer models that would sustain market share and profits over the long term. Instead GM, Ford, and Chrysler had bet on trucklike sport utility vehicles, which generated higher profits per vehicle but were rejected by consumers every time fuel prices were increased. GM had sold fewer cars every year since 1999. Ford's decline had been almost as long, and Chrysler's had been steeper. Nevertheless, the companies, their suppliers, and other related businesses accounted for more than 3 million jobs. To let any one of them disappear would be devastating to the national economy.

Conventional wisdom held that labor union demands had gone a long way toward ruining the companies. In fact, the so-called union premium, which included all wages, benefits, and pension expenses, added up to only 3 percent of the Big Three's cost of manufacturing a car. The blame for the companies' troubles lay more with managers who conceived, engineered, and produced failed models. Over the years, Pintos, K-cars, Cimarrons, and PT Cruisers had been just the worst of many cars that seemed to prove that Detroit couldn't meet global standards for quality. As manufacturing expert Susan Helper of Case Western Reserve University found, this difference allowed Toyota to charge $10,000 more than GM for larger cars. Consumers thought they were that much better.

Dressed in expensive suits and seated together at a table where they faced the Senate panel, the three executives looked so much alike—they were trim-looking, middle-aged white men with light-brown hair—they could have passed as brothers. They each fixed blame for their predicament on other parties. Robert Nardelli of Chrysler referenced "the devastating automotive industry recession caused by our nation's financial meltdown." G. Richard "Rick" Wagoner of GM insisted, "What exposes us to failure now is not our product lineup, or our business plan or our long-term strategy. What exposes us to failure now is the global financial crisis, which has severely restricted credit availability and reduced industry sales to the lowest per capita level since World War II." Ford's chief executive, Alan Mulally, backed up his mates, citing "the turmoil in the financial markets" as the prime cause of the crisis. Ford might not need federal help, he added, but he was certain the industry as a whole needed it to protect many billions of dollars in business activity and hundreds of thousands of jobs.

The collapse of the financial industry *was* a factor in the Big

Three's crisis. Lenders had so tightened credit requirements that many applicants who would have gotten money in 2007 could not qualify for car loans in 2008. Would-be buyers were also restricted by the decline in home values, which left them unable to tap real estate equity. Finally there was the lack of consumer confidence. People who worried about job security and whether the recession would turn into a depression didn't buy new cars. They invested, instead, in maintenance and repairs to keep their old ones going. All of this had contributed to losses growing at a rate of $4 million per hour at GM alone.

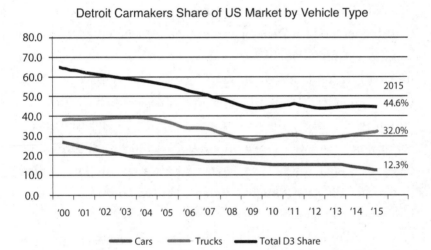

Detroit Carmakers Share of US Market by Vehicle Type

Senators who heard the reasoning of the auto execs understood the context of their troubles but did not want to hear excuses. Republicans, perhaps taking a cue from then president Bush, were generally opposed to giving the car companies the kind of aid the financial industry had gotten. They believed that the firms should endure the judgment of the marketplace, even if that meant a calamity for workers, investors, and communities. Democrats, who knew that President-elect Obama wanted an auto industry rescue, were wary of the political ramifications of bailouts. Voters had noticed that the lords of finance had been rescued with no admission of their own role in wrecking the economy. They would be skeptical of any deal to save another industry led by executives who seemed oblivious of their own failures.

Proof that executive leadership mattered could be found at Ford. Although Alan Mulally stood solidly with his fellow CEOs at the Senate hearing, his company was not in the same straits. Ford had outpaced GM and Chrysler in the race to update its lineup, and Mulally had done a better job than his peers when it came to cutting costs and financing his firm's operations. Although Ford lost money in 2008, the company would end 2008 with $13 billion in cash reserves and a $10 billion line of credit.

After the car men finished testifying, committee chairman Christopher Dodd, a Democrat from Connecticut, noted, "They're seeking treatment for wounds that, I believe, are largely self-inflicted." (Later Dodd would say Wagoner "has to move on" from GM.) Republican Robert Corker of Tennessee doubted that $25 billion would satisfy the companies. "I think, to all of us in this committee, that twenty-five billion dollars was sort of thrown up on the wall and it stuck. There has not been any real thinking behind that number. It is what might be attained today. I think we all know if that occurs, they are going to be back."

On evening broadcasts TV news correspondents delighted in reporting on the private jets the executives had used to get to Washington. Opponents of the bailout stressed the kind of doctrinaire economic view people take when considering someone else's predicament. Alabama senator Richard Shelby, a Republican, said the car companies were "a dinosaur in a sense" and should be allowed to fail and perhaps be replaced by competitors. (Shelby's state was home to three new plants operated by foreign car companies.) Columnist George Will advocated that Washington "do nothing that will delay bankrupt companies from filing for bankruptcy" because the courts would then allow for labor contracts to be canceled. *The Wall*

Street Journal editorial page inveighed against "nationalizing Detroit" as it attacked unions and blamed environmental protection rules, which all carmakers were required to meet, for the Big Three's troubles.

In Washington, Democrats in Congress felt pressure from unions and communities that were desperate to save jobs. Many Republicans saw an opportunity to oppose aid as a violation of capitalist free-market principles and also stick Barack Obama with the responsibility for the whole mess. However, even the most ideologically driven opponents from districts without auto plants had to consider the pleas of constituents who were auto dealers and were eager for a rescue plan. Within the Bush administration, officials were coming to accept that something had to be done to help GM and Chrysler meet their payrolls and pay suppliers in the coming few months.

With public skepticism rising partly due to the symbolism of their private jets, Mulally, Wagoner, and Nardelli traveled in hybrid cars when they returned to Washington two weeks later. They made what they touted as a more realistic request, upping the bailout figure to $35 billion, and expressed themselves with more modesty. "It used to be that our goal was simply to compete. Now we are absolutely committed to exceeding our customers' expectations for quality, fuel efficiency, safety, and affordability," Mulally, of Ford, told the committee. "You were clear that the business model needs to change. I could not agree more." Nardelli of Chrysler pledged similar improvements. GM's Wagoner promised prompt repayment of federal loans and recommended an overseer be appointed to protect taxpayers.

Soon after he made his second bailout pitch, Nardelli supervised the shutdown of every Chrysler plant in the country, which idled forty-six thousand workers and drained the money they would have been paid from thirty local economies scattered across the

United States. At the same time General Motors laid off another two thousand workers, and Rick Wagoner published a letter of apology on behalf of his company:

"At times we violated your trust by letting our quality fall below industry standards and our designs become lackluster. We have proliferated our brands and dealer network to the point where we lost adequate focus on our core U.S. market. We also biased our product mix toward pick-up trucks and SUVs. And, we made commitments to compensation plans that have proven to be unsustainable in today's globally competitive industry."

In the kind of passive corporatese that revealed it to be a product of the GM bureaucracy, Wagoner's letter was both a plea for his firm and a response to calls for his ouster. It was also a departure from the blame-deflecting behavior of financial industry executives, who had, to date, accepted no responsibility for the risk-taking that had created the economic crisis. Marketing expert Jack Trout praised Wagoner for heeding the "law of candor" by speaking openly about mistakes. Others credited the letter as an effective public relations strategy because it separated GM, which needed to please consumers who were also taxpayers, from the financial companies. However, it was not enough to win over the US Senate, where sixty of one hundred voters were required to overcome a filibuster. As the proposal for a bailout failed, GM hired a team of bankruptcy lawyers.

For months Republicans in Washington, led by the Bush White House, had opposed government aid to the car companies. In November of 2008, Mitt Romney, whose father had been a Detroit auto exec, had published a *New York Times* opinion piece titled "Let Detroit Go Bankrupt." Bush had shared Romney's point of view on government and business, but when faced with the Christmastime bankruptcy of one, or perhaps two, of the iconic car companies, Bush lost faith in the free market. He foreshadowed his decision in a speech to a conservative think tank where he said that "under ordinary circumstances" failing firms should be allowed to die and added, "I have concluded these are not ordinary circumstances." Days later the White House announced it would make a kind of first-installment payment on the bailout—$17.4 billion in all—which would be paid out of the Troubled Asset Relief Program fund.

Although the program was envisioned as a rescue for the financial system, the TARP legislation had given administration officials great leeway in how they used the money. Considering the ripple effect of job losses in the auto industry, a case could be made for shifting resources to GM and Chrysler. At the White House, press spokesperson Dana Perino said, "A precipitous collapse of this industry would have a severe impact on our economy, and it would be irresponsible to further weaken and destabilize our economy at this time."

The bailout, which Ford ultimately did not need, came with strings attached. GM and Chrysler would be required to get cost-cutting concessions from unions, dealers, suppliers, and those who owned the companies' securities. Pay caps would be imposed on top executives, and the companies would have to sell their private airplanes. The government would also take nonvoting shares in the companies as collateral. For their part, unions would have to agree to renegotiate labor contracts and close a "jobs bank" that allowed some idled workers to be paid full wages. The Bush White House also envisioned the bailout as a bridge to an orderly or "planned" bankruptcy that would bring creditors, executives, labor, and the government into the reorganization of the companies in the least disruptive way.

In Detroit, Rick Wagoner appeared before the press at GM's downtown headquarters building, where he was flanked by a pair of shiny Chevrolets, one painted red and one painted silver. As he expressed gratitude to various public officials, workers, business partners, and the taxpayers, he seemed visibly relieved, like a sick man who had just gotten some good news from his physician. Although

GM was a global company, and its business abroad would become increasingly important, Wagoner waxed patriotic in the glow of Uncle Sam's rescue: "Our industry helped build this country. Today our mission is to help lead an economic recovery in America."

No place needed a recovery more than the community outside the GM headquarters complex, which was an island of glass and steel isolated in a sea of urban decay. The decline of Detroit had been gradual but inexorable. In 1950, thanks to the auto industry, Detroit was one of the world's most prosperous cities, with a population of 1.8 million and a reputation for industrial might. The first blows to the city's standing came as middle-class residents moved to suburbs that sprouted, ironically, because cars made life there easy. Freeway construction accelerated the hollowing out of the city, as urban neighborhoods were cut off from each other. After 1960s race riots, more middle-class whites departed, and a population decline was accelerated.

By the twenty-first century, Detroit's population had fallen to half its 1950 peak. Unemployment had risen to 20 percent. As violent-crime rates had declined nationwide, Detroit's rose until it was almost three times the national average, and it became the most dangerous city in the country. (In 2008, Detroit saw 418 murders.

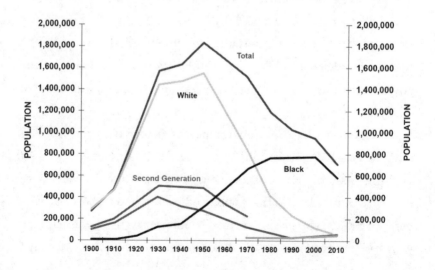

In the same year American deaths in the Afghanistan War totaled 314.) With people fleeing the mayhem, Detroit real estate prices collapsed, and so many houses were abandoned that the city couldn't keep up with bulldozing the remains of those that had been burned by arsonists and vandals. Grand old buildings such as the Michigan Central Railroad Station and the Lee Plaza Hotel were left to vandals and squatters. The crumbling Michigan Theater, once a four-thousand-seat movie palace with huge crystal chandeliers, was gutted and used for indoor parking. Tourists, including many from overseas, came to gape at a landscape that evoked the dystopias seen in films about a postapocalyptic future.

It was hard to believe that this place and its people, so long associated with American superiority, had fallen so far. However, the devastation was undeniable, and little Detroits—smaller communities that also depended on the Big Three—could be found in Ohio, Texas, Illinois, Michigan, Minnesota, and other states. Some, such as Flint, Michigan, were already enveloped in despair, with blight spreading across neighborhoods and violent crime rising at terrifying rates. These cities were, no doubt, on President-elect Obama's mind as he directed his transition team to develop a rescue plan for the industry. But with opinion polls showing the public to be skeptical on this, Obama said federal aid should come with conditions. Referring to auto companies seeking bailouts, he placed a burden of responsibility on key executives: "If this management team that is currently in place doesn't understand the urgency of the situation and is not willing to make the tough choices and adapt to these new circumstances, then they should go." He also tied a bailout to his energy and environmental agendas, adding that the companies should be "retooling for energy efficiency."

Although Obama's push for more efficient, less polluting cars aligned neatly with his campaign themes, it was also good business. Ford CEO Alan Mulally emphasized this point when he announced that his company would both expand and accelerate its sales of electric and hybrid vehicles. Hybrid sales had been a bright light in the US market, increasing by more than 400 percent between 2004 and 2007. Most of this business had been captured by foreign-based companies, but the Detroit-based manufacturers had made up ground with the Ford Escape and GM's Saturn Vue. But as promising as the Saturns were, GM faced problems that were so immediate that they could not be solved by the sales of new models. Like Chrysler, GM was facing a plunge in its stock price and the prospect of running out of money to pay its bills. As President Obama took office in January 2009, things got worse. Chrysler's monthly sales dropped by 55 percent compared with the same month in the previous year. GM's sales declined by 49 percent, and its stock price tumbled to lows not seen since the Great Depression. The two carmakers seemed to be in their death throes.

The good news, for the new president and for GM and Chrysler, was that their balance sheets held considerable assets, including the value of their brands, a wealth of talent, far-flung dealer networks, valuable foreign operations, and more than $100 billion worth of factories. The CEOs at GM and Chrysler also helped their case by forgoing their salaries, which made them seem like true patriots compared with the managers at bailed-out financial firms, who took big end-of-year bonuses. The bad news was that even with assistance, GM and Chrysler would need the protections of bankruptcy to negotiate with bondholders, workers, and others who were owed money by the big carmakers. Chrysler execs were planning to sell their firm to Italian automaker Fiat, which had been remade and reenergized under the leadership of Sergio Marchionne. GM's leaders were not going to turn to outsiders for help. They pinned their hopes instead on a huge rebound in sales, which seemed unrealistic.

Inside the Obama administration, the officials assigned to the auto industry's problems were quickly realizing that a rescue would require at least $75 billion more from the federal government. This figure was confirmed when the group considered GM's long-term viability. In recent years the quality of the company's vehicles, as measured by the authoritative J.D. Power and Associates, had steadily risen. (GM's Saturn division had surpassed most brands in consumer surveys.) Many of these well-made cars were offered at prices below comparable models built by competitors such as Toyota.

Chrysler was in much worse condition than GM, especially in the quality of its cars. In the year just passed, J.D. Power had found that Chrysler's most successful division, Jeep, had the worst record for quality of all American makes. Given Chrysler's long-standing problems, the Obama auto team debated whether saving it was even a good idea. The company's loyal customers were not the type to buy Toyotas, which meant that GM and Ford would gain sales if Chrysler died. Their factories would be powered up to meet new demand, and their balance sheets would improve that much more quickly. However, the political fallout from Chrysler's demise and the loss of three hundred thousand jobs—counting its suppliers—would be a shock to the economy. And then there was the blow to the national morale that would come as a company that could be traced back to the Maxwell Motor Company and the year 1904 disappeared.

Steven Rattner, who had been chosen to lead the Obama auto team, would later write that his group realized that letting Chrysler go under would not be cost-free. Taxpayers would still be on the hook for the unemployment benefits required by all the workers who lost jobs. Demand for social services would increase. Tax revenues would be lost. "Given the uncertainty," Rattner would write, "it was better to invest $6 billion for a meaningful chance that Chrysler would survive than invest several billion in its funeral." This decision to try to save Chrysler did not mean the rescue would take place. All the parties, including Chrysler's potential buyer, Fiat, would have to accept the conditions of the deal, which would include a demand that the government loan be repaid before the Italians could take a majority stake in the company.

As the bailout plan took shape, the president pored over economic data, and reports on the auto industry's condition. On Thursday, March 26, 2009, he held morning and evening sessions with Rattner and advisers. At the second meeting, in the Roosevelt Room of the West Wing, the president heard Secretary of the Treasury Timothy Geithner argue that the government wasn't in a position to provide all the aid that Chrysler, the sickest of the companies, needed to survive. Obama pushed his advisers to tell him all the things that could possibly go wrong with the auto rescue plan, especially if companies filed for bankruptcy. He was concerned about layoffs, bloated inventories of unsold cars, and the burden the bailout would place on taxpayers. In the end he told Rattner and the others to let the car companies know that they were running out of time and that bankruptcy was a possibility. Obama also made it clear that Wagoner would have to leave GM.

As Detroit teetered, Obama's chief economic adviser, Lawrence Summers, urged Rattner to consider policies that would push Americans to buy new cars. The German government had seen some success with a government-funded rebate program that encouraged people to give up old, polluting, gas-guzzling cars for new, cleaner-running cars that ran with much better fuel efficiency. The program, which came to be called Cash for Clunkers, was worked out the night before the president was to deliver a speech outlining his stand on the auto rescue. In that talk he would impose a thirty-day deadline on Fiat, Chrysler, and the United Autoworkers. They would get a $6.7 billion loan if the parties agreed, in that short time, to the terms that would create a new company. GM would get loans to permit it to run for another sixty days while it planned a restructuring under a new CEO. Wagoner had been informed by Rattner that he must resign. In eight years he had improved quality, slashed costs, and established new lines of business, but the crisis had come while he was in charge, and Washington's help was conditioned on his departure.

On March 30, the president addressed the car industry's crisis in brief remarks to the press: "We cannot, and must not, and we will not let our auto industry simply vanish. This industry is like no other—it's an emblem of the American spirit; a once and future symbol of America's success. It's a pillar of our economy that has held up the dreams of millions of our people." However, he added, "We cannot continue to excuse poor decisions. We cannot make the survival of our auto industry dependent on an unending flow of taxpayer dollars. These companies—and this industry—must ultimately stand on their own, not as wards of the state."

Besides Wagoner, the parties who were most aggrieved by the president's approach would include union autoworkers, who would be expected to accept pay and benefit cuts, and GM's bondholders, who stood to lose on their investments. The workers, who had previously made similar concessions, signaled that they would cooperate. However, at moments the administration was forced to intervene to keep talks going. The bondholders protested the losses they were expected to accept. Some of the bigger investors, among them hedge funds, universities, and extremely wealthy speculators, banded together and hired expensive lawyers and consultants. They then went to the press to complain about their potential losses. On a superficial basis their argument about the injustice of bond values cut to pennies on the dollar made sense. However, many of these bond owners had scooped up these securities at severely discounted prices. They were not long-term backers of the Chrysler company, but rather more like gamblers hoping that a resolution to the crisis might give them a windfall.

Much of the maneuvering by the car companies, the government, unions, and creditors was done with the notion that GM might be spared the indignity of bankruptcy. Chrysler's bankruptcy was inevitable and came on April 30, 2009, just thirty days after Obama described the terms for the auto industry rescue. Although one hedge fund lawyer almost spoiled the deal by demanding special treatment for his clients, under the terms of the reorganization plan debtors stood to receive 30 percent of what they were owed. This would be far more than they would have received if the company was liquidated. The UAW's concessions, brokered by the Obama administration, were unprecedented. The union accepted a two-year wage freeze and an increase in the number of new workers who could be hired at half the regular pay rate. Most important, the UAW pledged to forgo the option of calling a strike for the next two contract cycles. This concession would give Fiat more than four years of labor peace. Suppliers were guaranteed full payment on their invoices, which meant they would continue to send parts, and consumer warranties were also guaranteed. To do otherwise would mean no one would ever buy a Chrysler again.

The legalities required to bring the new Chrysler into existence took just forty-two days, which was a remarkably short span for such a complicated arrangement. The process was completed when the US Supreme Court turned away efforts to stop the deal. On June 11 the government transferred $6.7 billion to the new company, and it was off and running.

An embarrassing bankruptcy was preferable to liquidation, and Chrysler's rapid rebirth was proof that a major auto company could remake itself in the courts. A group of GM executives, including an expert named Jay Alix brought in for this purpose, had been considering bankruptcy options for many months. Their plan called for sharp cuts in GM's expenses, including the sale or closure of the divisions that made Saturns, Pontiacs, Saabs, and a bulky, gas-hogging spin-off from military vehicles called the Hummer. These cuts remained in the plan when it was approved by Obama's team in April 2009. The UAW agreed to cuts in starting salaries of new workers and reductions in health and retirement benefits. When implemented, the arrangement would free up an additional $30 billion in federal loans. With roughly $50 billion invested overall, the government would become 60 percent owner of the new GM.

Filed as the company's share price fell to twenty-seven cents, GM's bankruptcy proposal sought to achieve the largest industrial reorganization in history, aided by the government, in ninety days. The company owned $82 billion in assets but was burdened with $173 billion in liabilities. The latter would be greatly reduced by the courts, and the new GM would be born, forty days later, as a more streamlined carmaker. In Sweden, Saab would be taken over by a smaller local car company and continue operations. A Chinese firm would acquire Hummer and make those cars in the United States. The demise of long-struggling Pontiac was eased when the company shifted work on other models to the dying division's plants. This left Saturn, its workforce, and the community of Spring Hill, Tennessee, with the terrible distinction of facing a near-total shutdown. This fate was all the more painful because this GM division had been created, in 1990, as GM's bold answer to the challenges posed by foreign competitors.

Built in the late 1980s at a cost of $3.5 billion, the Saturn plant that dominated the countryside south of Nashville began operating in 1990 and began making profits in 1994. It produced 3.7 million cars of such high quality that they inspired a cult of admirers. Nearly one hundred thousand of them drove their cars to "homecoming" barbecues at the plant. With no-dent plastic body panels and high-tech drive trains, the Saturns of the 1990s were consistently ranked in the top three cars in J.D. Power's customer satisfaction scale and in one of these years placed second to the Lexus luxury car. Flexible work rules and constant consultation between labor and management affirmed the company slogan, which declared Saturn "A different kind of car company."

Naturally others in GM's vast and varied manufacturing

network worried that Saturn's success had come at their expense, and to a degree they were right. Managers at plants that made Chevys, Pontiacs, Buicks, and more resented that investments in factory upgrades and new models had been slowed at their GM divisions as Saturn was created. Workers at these other facilities feared the less restrictive contract that governed laborers at Saturn would set a precedent that might spread. When executives in Tennessee sought to expand Saturn's offerings from a basic compact, as originally planned, they met resistance. GM's leaders were inclined to invest elsewhere in the company. Hungry for more profits, they pressured Saturn to abandon its original mission of building an entirely new kind of car and instead use some of the parts incorporated in other GM cars. When the new division finally got a minivan, it was a copy of a Pontiac and was built in Georgia. A Saturn roadster was made in Delaware.

By June 2009, when Saturn's workers in Tennessee got the news that their plant was to be closed, they had recognized that their newfangled division was no longer special. The machinery that had been used to make the special plastic body parts had been replaced with old-style metal stamping equipment, and headquarters had said they wanted to make Chevys in Spring Hill. With bankruptcy, that work would be moved to Michigan. Spring Hill would either be sold or shut down.

The workers who had gathered in a meeting room at Spring Hill to hear news of Saturn's demise were shocked into silence. Some couldn't keep the tears from streaming down their faces. Years later, the head of the United Auto Workers local would recall the moment. "You could have heard a pin drop," said Tim Stannard. "Everybody was just in shock. It was kind of like a death—it took a little while to sink in."

As word spread through the community, so did the sense of disbelief. In barely two decades Saturn had transformed a two-traffic-light "blink and you miss it" town of a thousand into a bustling city of thirty-five thousand. Spring Hill's police force went from two officers to fifty. The two-man volunteer fire department turned into a paid force of forty-nine. With Saturn's modern methods and efficiency, locals had believed the division would thrive, and so would they, despite the Great Recession and the auto industry crisis. Suddenly both of these assumptions were shattered. This was the human side of the auto crisis.

In Washington, DC, the bankruptcy filing and plant-closing announcements touched off loud criticisms. Representative John Boehner, a Republican from the automaking state of Ohio, said, "Does anyone really believe that politicians and bureaucrats in Washington can successfully steer a multinational corporation to economic viability?" Senator Richard Shelby said, "It's basically going to be a government-owned, government-run company. . . . It's the road toward socialism." Congressman Lamar Smith of Texas called the auto company rescue "the leading edge of the Obama administration's war on capitalism."

Capitalism *was* threatened by the Great Recession, but it had been made vulnerable, in large measure, by the risk-taking and incompetence of the men and women who were supposed to be the system's best. Wall Street speculators and financial engineers had inflated the housing bubble and presided over the collapse of the credit markets. Executives and board members at GM and Chrysler had failed to make their companies competitive in a global economy despite decades of trying. And no administration in recent memory had been more pro-business than the Bush team, which had consistently sought to roll back laws regulating business and had reduced enforcement of the laws that couldn't be changed. As economist Joseph Stiglitz noted, "You can't overestimate what happens when you encourage regulators to believe that the goal of regulation is not to regulate."

Having inherited a capitalist economy driven into a ditch by capitalists, Obama had picked up the crisis management strategy set by Bush. However, the conditions attached to the aid offered auto companies on behalf of the taxpayers were tougher than Bush had proposed. The companies were forced to cut costs. The UAW was forced to concede pay and benefits. The government also took ownership stakes in the new firms so that at least some of the taxpayers' investment could be recouped.

The effects of the rescue would depend, in large part, on public confidence in the manufacturers. GM and Chrysler were already using their own methods to draw people to their showrooms and send them home with new cars. Both promised to make the monthly payments for new buyers who were laid off after making a purchase. Customers were also being lured with rebates paid by manufacturers and by price reductions. While still low, GM's sales actually perked up in May, improving by 11 percent over April. Overall, Chrysler sales suffered because no cars were delivered to rental companies, but dealers did see an uptick in retail sales. Ford, its reputation buoyed by its not taking bailout money, did even better, surpassing rival Toyota.

In June, Obama and Congress added fuel to the flicker of improvement in car sales as they began the Cash for Clunkers program. The program would pay rebate checks of up to $4,500 to anyone who gave up a gas-hogging old car—eighteen miles per gallon or worse—for a new one that could go twenty-two miles or more on a gallon of fuel. (Rebates were greatest for the most fuel-efficient cars.) To qualify, buyers had to show they had owned their trade-ins for at least a year. The old cars would be taken off the road permanently. Overall highway pollution would be reduced as would demand for gasoline, much of which came from imported oil. Presidents of both parties had talked of cutting America's dependence on foreign petroleum supplies since 1970s, but except for Jimmy Carter, every one had left office with oil imports higher than when he arrived.

Predictably, Cash for Clunkers was dismissed by the editorial writers at *The Wall Street Journal*—"Cash for Lunkheads" they called it—and by Republicans on Capitol Hill, where just five in the House and four in the Senate gave it their votes. GOP critics complained that the idea was bad because it added to the federal budget deficit or because it was too small to have any lasting effect. However, the party didn't fight the idea so hard that it might be killed. Republicans, too, represented car dealers, who were running out of space to park unsold cars and were desperate for some good news.

The dealers were not disappointed. So many Americans had put off purchasing cars they wanted that when the rebates program opened, they rushed to buy. In just four weeks Cash for Clunkers

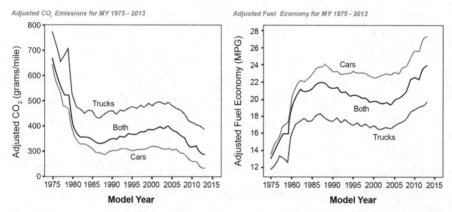

Adjusted CO_2 and fuel economy values reflect real world estimates and are not comparable to automaker standards compliance levels. Adjusted CO_2 values are on average about 25% higher than the unadjusted laboratory CO_2 values that form the starting point for GHG standards compliance and adjusted fuel economy values are about 20% lower on average than unadjusted fuel economy values.

drove 250,000 additional purchases. July sales at Ford were so good that the company actually made a small profit. In August, total sales across the industry increased 26 percent over July. GM and Chrysler still lagged, primarily because their inventories didn't include enough qualifying cars. However, the increased sales prompted by Cash for Clunkers marked the start of a sales recovery. The number of autos sold in 2009 would still be the lowest in more than fifty years. Sales would bump up in 2010 and rise much more strongly in 2011. Accelerated improvements in both fuel efficiency and emissions were also made in this time.

Most important of all, where the government and the national economy were concerned, would be the recovery of GM and Chrysler as profitable corporations. Here the good news came faster than most observers expected. In May 2010, GM reported its first quarterly profit in nearly three years. The $865 million was even more impressive when compared with the $11 billion lost in the first three months of 2009. In the second quarter the company improved further, making $1.3 billion. In the same period the company paid back $7 billion of the roughly $51 billion it had received from the government. It also planned a stock offering, which would give the government a chance to get out of the car business and recoup much of its rescue investment.

GM's success was not just a matter of the government's dollars. It also depended on the demands made by the president and negotiated by his team. The industry's crisis had created an opportunity for these outsiders, who represented the American people, to require GM to kill off divisions that were dragging it down. The administration also used its credibility with unions to push the UAW into concessions. Add the moves made to manage the old GM's creditors, and the government's role in the recovery becomes obvious. Obvious, too, was the answer to the question John Boehner asked about the prospects of "politicians and bureaucrats in Washington" steering "a multinational corporation to economic viability."

Boehner did not acknowledge that the rescue operation succeeded, but others who criticized the effort did. Always pro–free market, *The Economist* had opposed the Obama auto intervention and argued that "GM deserved extinction." One year later, in August 2010, the editors wrote that they had been wrong: "An apology is due to Barack Obama: his takeover of G.M. could have gone horribly wrong, but it has not. Many people thought this bail-out (and a smaller one involving Chrysler, an even sicker firm) unwise. Governments have historically been lousy stewards of industry. Lovers of free markets (including *The Economist*) feared that Mr. Obama might use G.M. as a political tool: perhaps favoring the unions who donate to Democrats or forcing the firm to build smaller, greener cars than consumers want to buy. The label 'Government Motors' stuck, evoking images of clunky committee-built cars that burned banknotes instead of petrol—all run by what Sarah Palin might call the socialist-in-chief." These were the alarms raised at the time, but, the writers concluded, "The doomsayers were wrong."

They were wrong, too, about Chrysler. Although the smaller company could not match GM in the race to profitability, it did report that 80 percent of its dealers made money in the first three months of 2010. A year later the company would break the profit threshold, making $116 million compared with a loss of $197 million in the same quarter of 2010. Some of this profit was generated by the sales of Fiat 500s, which were assembled in Mexico with Michigan-made engines. The company would sell more than forty-three thousand of these subcompacts, which made the US market for this car the biggest in the world. *Car and Driver* magazine judged it to be a stylish, "largely trouble-free" car that would be embraced by many Americans.

With sales recovering, manufacturers, parts companies, and all the businesses that supported them began to hire again. In Spring Hill, where unemployment had spiked to 17 percent, dust-covered equipment remained in place and idled workers hoped for a revival. In November 2011, GM announced that the old Saturn line would be restarted to produce the Chevrolet Equinox. A small sport utility vehicle, the new Equinox went 30 percent farther on a gallon of gas than its pre-bailout version. The car did well in crash tests, and consumer reviews and sales were so brisk the company could not make them fast enough to meet demand.

The restart at Spring Hill would come with more than $200 million in plant improvements that would make it capable of fast retooling to produce many different types of vehicles, depending on sales. Hundreds of workers would immediately be hired under a companywide drive to eventually add twenty thousand to its payroll. Spring Hill would soon be assigned a second car line, the Cadillac SRX, and its engine-manufacturing department would produce power plants for a range of GM cars assembled around the world. The total number of people working on cars in Spring Hill was expected to reach thirty-five hundred in 2016.

The new generation of Spring Hill workers included Amanda Hopkins, whose mother had lost her job there when the plant shut down in 2009. (She found a spot at another GM plant in Kansas City, Missouri.) Amanda was working at the retailer Bed Bath & Beyond making $500 every two weeks before she joined the Equinox team as a lead welder. Soon she was earning triple her previous salary, and when she gave birth to her first child, her benefits package covered the medical expenses and provided her with a month of paid leave.

In early January 2015, President Obama went to Michigan to bask in the industry's remarkable turnaround. US automakers had sold 16.5 million cars in the previous year, which was the most since before the economy crashed. So much of the GM and Chrysler bailout money had been recouped that as the government sold all its remaining shares in General Motors, the final price for saving both firms with TARP money was less than $10 billion. At a Ford assembly plant in Wayne, Michigan, Obama told applauding workers that the rescue had helped save the American economy. "Now this is the heartbeat of American manufacturing. Right here," Obama said as he recalled his momentous decision to help GM and Chrysler emerge from bankruptcy. "It was not popular. Even in Michigan it wasn't popular. But that bet has paid off for America, because the American auto industry is back."

By 2016, the last year of the Obama presidency, the industry had reached new heights. Sales had reached a record annual rate of 17.5 million, and the big American companies held 45.4 percent of the market. GM held first place in sales, followed, in order, by Toyota, Ford, and Fiat-Chrysler. Demand for some GM vehicles made in Arlington, Texas, was so high that fifteen hundred workers were added and the company began a $1.2 billion plant expansion. Ford announced a $4 billion plan for electric cars, and Fiat-Chrysler announced it would invest $5.4 billion in its US plants by 2020.

3

HEALTH CARE REFORM

Saving Spike Dolomite

A low, brick-faced building trimmed to look like a friendly cottage, Lulu's café squats between a Wendy's and a Home Depot on Roscoe Boulevard in Van Nuys, California. It seems an unlikely setting for a miracle, yet Spike Dolomite considers her arrival for dinner to be one. Four years after discovering a lump and learning she had advanced breast cancer, fifty-two-year-old Spike, an artist, wife, and mother, was glad to be alive, and she gave much of the credit to President Obama's health care initiatives. She considered herself proof of the president's success. "The guy saved my life" is the way she puts it.

In fact, Spike might not have survived without the Affordable Care Act, as the president's biggest and most controversial achievement was called. Before the ACA, others like Spike, who had no health insurance, got cancer treatment with the help of charity and by incurring enormous debts. But the act, which created the system nicknamed Obamacare, made it possible for her to receive cutting-edge care without bankrupting her family. "Before I got sick, I was quite critical of the president," adds Spike. "Afterwards I sent an op-ed piece that was basically an apology to the *Los Angeles Times,* which they published. I was glad to say I'm a mom, I got cancer, and I was helped."

Spike Dolomite's cure, accomplished without ruining her

family's finances, proves the success of Barack Obama's most consequential domestic policy achievement. Many previous presidents, including Truman, Nixon, and Clinton, had sought but failed to expand health care insurance on a similar scale, and others had stumbled while attempting lesser reforms. Obama's success in pushing his program through Congress depended on maneuvers and compromises that exasperated both his supporters, who wanted something bolder, and his detractors, who fought it with predictions of financial ruin for America and specious claims that elder and disabled Americans would suffer and die at the hands of "death panels" empowered to decide who would receive medical care.

The main promoter of the death panel canard—the law would *not* permit them—was former Alaska governor Sarah Palin, who was the vice-presidential candidate on the GOP ticket that lost to Obama and Biden in 2008. In July 2009, Palin wrote, "And who will suffer the most when they ration care? The sick, the elderly, and the disabled, of course. The America I know and love is not one in which my parents or my baby with Down Syndrome will have to stand in front of Obama's 'death panel' so his bureaucrats can decide, based on a subjective judgment of their 'level of productivity in society,' whether they are worthy of health care. Such a system is downright evil."

At its frenzied peak, the hysteria over health care reform brought crowds of angry citizens to public meetings where they mounted protests that were often noisy and incoherent. Typical was a town meeting in San Diego where about a thousand people packed into a school gymnasium to question Representative Susan Davis, a Democrat. Some people stood and cheered a woman who rose to say, "I am opposed to socialized medicine." Outside, forty sheriff's deputies watched over two hundred protesters, many of whom identified themselves as so-called Tea Party activists, picketing and shouting their opposition. Although some Tea Party groups were locally based, much of the movement's organizing and activity would eventually be traced to national political activists funded by major corporations.

In San Diego, where one of their number was felled by hundred-degree heat, the protesters were generally older, white, and male. The signs waved at passing drivers read THE BIGGEST POWER GRAB OF ALL and NO CZAR! One man rested an American flag on his shoulder and screamed, "Dirty thieves! Dirty thieves!" Another said health care reform was "a takeover by communism and he's [Obama] a basic Muslim." Nearby a woman explained to a videographer conducting interviews, "This health care bill to me is very scary because I know what happened in Germany under Hitler."

The fear of Obama generally, and health care reform in particular, provided the main sources of energy for the protesters. But they also talked about their opposition to abortion rights, the need to recognize God's authority in all things, and the prospect of a civil war. But the word they used most to describe Obama's plan was *socialism*, which they obviously considered one step away from totalitarianism. Thus their protest echoed the terms used in the 1960s against the Medicare program, which provides health care for Americans over age sixty-five. Back then, the American Medical Association distributed a record titled *Ronald Reagan Speaks Out Against Socialized Medicine*, which the future president recorded to help the failing effort to defeat the legislation that created one of the most popular and successful government programs in history—Medicare.

Although subsidized, government-run Medicare had long guaranteed a more secure and healthful life for older Americans, it did not make them eager to see the rest of the country aided in the same way. When Obama proposed his plan to improve the health care system, polls showed that support was highest (77 percent) among young adults and lowest (35 percent) among the old. Some of the difference could have reflected that younger Americans tended to be more liberal and supported Democrats, while older Americans were more conservative and more likely to be Republicans. More important, though, was the fear of older Americans that the cost savings Obama hoped to achieve through health care reform would be accomplished by cutting their Medicare benefits. This concern was based on distorted interpretations of one of the elements of the Obama plan, which would regulate payments made to private insurers. People on Medicare would not be affected, but this got lost in translation. One result of this problem was the oft-quoted Tea Partiers' complaint—"Keep the government's hands off my Medicare"—which, while ridiculous, was a genuine expression of how many people felt.

The anxiety that drove thousands of people to take up placards and jam public meetings drew strength from the direct effect health care reform could have on people's relationship with their doctors and other caregivers. Although the status of physicians had declined somewhat since the days when they made house calls, they were still revered because they met people when they were at their most vulnerable. People who belonged to generous health insurance programs and liked their doctors feared losing these relationships. Also, membership in a good health care program made a secure, middle-class existence—and the belief that they were self-sufficient—possible for many people who, without insurance coverage, could be impoverished by just one serious illness.

Complex and fragmented, the American health care system was unique in the industrialized world, where the norm was government-run systems available to all. In the United States, the poor, the elderly, and veterans received various forms of government-managed and government-funded care. The rest of the population depended mainly on employer-based insurance plans, and policies they bought themselves, which came in hundreds of varieties.

The main thing people understood about health insurance was that its price was increasing at a rate far greater than inflation and earnings, which meant that premiums paid by both individuals and employers became a bigger burden every year. Add increases in deductibles (amounts patients paid before insurance kicked in) and the insurance bureaucracy's efforts to cut costs by controlling care, and you begin to understand why the word *crisis* was often used to describe the condition of the health care system.

Frustrated as they may have been, the insured still had it better than the 49 million Americans who had inadequate coverage or no insurance at all. These people tended to defer care and, when sick, could rack up enormous bills that they could not pay. Hospital collections departments pursued these debts with varying degrees of vigor, but it was not uncommon for patients to lose their homes when they were sued for payment. Remarkably, more than three-quarters of those who were bankrupted by medical expenses actually had *some* form of insurance when they got sick. Their problems arose when claims were denied, they lost coverage, or the portion they were required to pay themselves grew too costly.

Overall, the US system was unmatched it its ability to deliver technologically advanced treatments, and as a result wealthy people from across the globe often came to medical hubs such as Boston, Houston, and New York for care they could not get at home. This phenomenon supported the argument that American health care was the best in the world. However, when combined with other factors including insurance company profits and the cost of caring for the uninsured, the US system became the most expensive by far. In 2008 the United States spent 17.7 percent of its gross domestic product on medical care compared with 9.3 percent for other economically advanced countries. Government health care programs also contributed more than any others to projected increases in the federal deficit.

What did Americans get for all the money spent? In general they got the best cancer treatment, as measured by five-year survival rates, but lower-quality care in many other respects. American infant mortality rates were higher and life expectancy was lower.

Patients in the United States were more likely to experience a mistake in their treatment, such as receiving the wrong drugs or

US Spends Two-and-a-Half Times the OECD

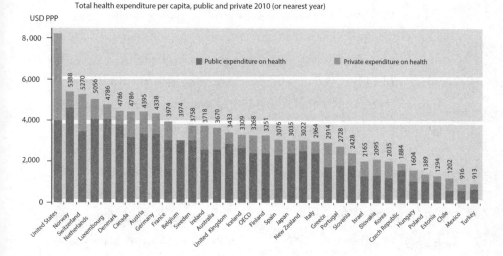

Total health expenditure per capita, public and private 2010 (or nearest year)

USD PPP

■ Public expenditure on health   ■ Private expenditure on health

1. In the Netherlands, it is not possible to clearly distinguish the public and private share related to investments.
2. Total expenditure excluding investments.

improper doses of a medication. This problem had much to do with all the different information systems used by health care providers, which made sharing data difficult. Similarly, the wide range of experiences people had as they sought care made it hard for anyone to judge the whole system. Consequently, a great many people believed America was doing better than, say, the United Kingdom, where medicine was nationalized in 1948. In fact, when the Commonwealth Fund of New York studied the quality of care in eleven developed countries, the UK came out first and the United States last. This was achieved by the British at less than half the US cost.

Although the big-picture data guided policy debates, the suffering behind the numbers could only be understood with a more fine-grain analysis. When a professor at the Massachusetts Institute of Technology studied car-crash victims, he discovered that people lacking insurance coverage were 40 percent more likely to die of their injuries. Other researchers found that the uninsured were less likely to survive cancer, even when they were diagnosed at the same stage of the disease as people with insurance. With death more certain for the uninsured, it was hard to argue that the country didn't have a health care problem.

The problem of a costly system buying not-so-great outcomes had occupied politicians, bureaucrats, doctors, and patients for decades, but insurers, physicians, and others who benefited from the status quo had blocked all efforts at sweeping reforms. In his campaign for president Barack Obama had tried to accommodate the opposition with promises to preserve existing insurance schemes for those who wanted them. The cornerstone of his plan was a requirement that all Americans sign up for some kind of insurance, which suggested a possible bonanza for the insurers. In exchange the companies would have to cover a set list of illnesses and preventive care and end the practice of denying benefits to those with "pre-existing conditions." Obama also proposed creating Internet-based, government-run marketplaces where individuals could shop for insurance plans or choose a so-called government option that would be the equivalent of the Medicaid program provided to lower-income Americans.

As the election drew near and the financial crisis became the Great Recession, the economic emergency became a higher priority than health care. However, Obama had made a point of campaigning as a candidate who would follow through on his promises, and he continued to promote health care reform as part of a larger economic fix. Health care costs were such a burden, he argued, that bringing them under control would benefit everyone. Also aware of the issue, Republican opponent Senator John McCain had countered with a plan for expanding private insurance through deregulation and an end to the tax breaks provided to companies that offer insurance to their workers. By some estimates this change would have caused employers to drop coverage for as many as 20 million people. After they cast their ballots, voters told pollsters that the economy was their main concern. Second came health care. Voters said they favored Obama over McCain on health care, with Obama's call for greatly expanded insurance coverage winning over many self-proclaimed political moderates. His health care proposal was most popular with younger voters, who were more likely to be un-insured. Unusually high turnout among the young, who favored Obama by a margin of 66–31, played a huge role in the outcome of the election.

Obama took office with a Democratic majority in both the House and the Senate and a mandate from voters who expected him to make good on his promises. At no other moment in his presidency would he enjoy such comparable support in Congress and so little opposition. Shortly after he took office, during one of his first Oval Office meetings on health care, the president clarified his view of the project he would undertake. White House communications director Dan Pfeiffer told the TV program *Frontline* that Obama said, "It's about health care, but it's not really about health care. It's also about proving whether we can still solve big problems in this country."

As the administration put together its sweeping economic Recovery Act and moved to save the auto industry, it also took up the health care reform Obama had pledged to accomplish. An ambitious reform of the health care system had been attempted once before, by the master politician President Bill Clinton. He had entrusted the task to his wife, Hillary, who met fierce opposition from Republicans determined to deny him a victory. Mrs. Clinton's mistakes, especially work done in secret, which alienated many law-makers, aided the intense campaign of opposition that defeated the plan.

Years later, many in both parties would recall the fictional couple Harry and Louise, who aired their fears about health care reform in a TV commercial financed by an insurance industry group that saturated the airwaves with it. Harry and Louise may have done more than anyone else to kill the Clinton plan and instill anxiety in those who imagined changing the system. This interest was rooted in softhearted concern for people who lacked access to care or faced financial ruin due to illness and in hardheaded worry about runaway costs. Access could be improved by bringing all Americans into the insurance system. Quality and cost could be addressed by improving basic and preventive care so that fewer people would become so sick they needed expensive, high-tech interventions.

Informed by Clinton's experience, Obama sought to avoid alienating Congress by asking key committees and their leaders to write the provisions of the reform. That effort reached its first milestone with the thousand-plus page document—a bill proposed in the House of Representatives—that sparked the protests that greeted members of Congress when they met with constituents in the summer of 2009. This apparent groundswell made it easier for Republicans to stand firm in opposition, and Obama soon found that almost no one in the GOP would talk about his proposals. Iowa Republican senator Charles Grassley, who had participated in early negotiations on Obama's plan, encountered the protests back home and wound up voicing his concern that the bill would create Sarah Palin's imaginary "death panels." Seemingly won over by an argument already disproven, Grassley backed out of discussions on the reform plan. His departure left just one Senate Republican, Maine's Olympia Snowe, willing to deal with the president on the health care issue.

Snowe, who had formed a friendship with Obama when they were both senators, would meet often with the president to seek common ground. She was especially interested in adding restrictions on spending to any plan, and the president expressed support for her ideas. Increasing access to health care had been a kind of Holy Grail for Democrats ever since the creation of Medicare and Medicaid in the 1960s, and Obama saw his plan as an essential element of any legacy he might establish. He was willing to make deals to win votes in Congress and to lobby the American people. With this in mind he made a speech on health care to a joint session of the House and Senate.

Obama began with the softhearted elements of his argument, noting that fourteen thousand people lost their health insurance, and the access to care it provides, every day. "We are the only democracy—the only advanced democracy on earth, the only wealthy nation—that allows such hardship for millions of its people," he said. A system that allowed insurers to cancel policies too readily and ended coverage for people as they left their jobs created too much insecurity even for those with coverage, he added, before he turned to the problem of health care costs. "If we do nothing to slow these skyrocketing costs, we will eventually be spending more on Medicare and Medicaid than every other government program combined. Put simply, our health care problem is our deficit problem."

Talk of deficits and costs would appeal to the few Republicans such as Senator Snowe who remained open to supporting the reform plan. Obama tried to ease the concerns of others when he pledged that no one participating in employer-based plans would be forced to leave them, and that people receiving health care via the federal government would also see no change. Then, halfway through the talk, he addressed the "bogus claims spread by those whose only agenda is to kill reform at any cost." After dismissing the death panel claim as false, he turned to the argument that he planned to insure illegal immigrants. As Obama addressed this point, he was suddenly interrupted by a voice in the chamber. The moment went like this:

"This, too, is false," said the president. "The reforms—the reforms I'm proposing would not apply to those who are here illegally."

"You lie!" came the cry from a male voice.

"It's not true," continued Obama, seemingly unfazed. "And

one more misunderstanding I want to clear up—under our plan, no federal dollars will be used to fund abortions, and federal conscience laws will remain in place."

The content of Obama's speech won praise from independent, mainstream media sources, but the shouted "You lie!" became the dramatic moment that commentators returned to again and again.

The president's chief of staff, Rahm Emanuel, was seated near the heckler, and as the president left the House chamber, Emanuel sought out Republican leaders to ask that they identify him and address the breach of protocol. The voice was quickly given a name—Representative Joe Wilson of South Carolina—and he became the object of much postspeech commentary.

On the CNN cable network, broadcaster Larry King named him as "the gentleman, if you can call him that, who yelled out." King was interviewing John McCain at that moment, and the senator termed the outburst "totally disrespectful." Reporters immediately discovered that in the previous month Wilson had published a newspaper column on the death panel issue. He wrote that end-of-life counseling "has been correctly highlighted by Alaska governor Sarah Palin as a program which could lead to seniors being encouraged to seek less care in order to protect the government's bottom line." This distortion would likely have gone unnoticed but for Wilson's eruption. As members of Congress tried and failed to recall any similar incidents, Wilson, who seemed most rattled of all by what had occurred, hurried out of the Capitol. *The New York Times* reported that later in the evening he called the White House to offer an apology, which was accepted on the president's behalf. Response from Democrats included the charge, by former president Jimmy Carter, that Wilson's act of disrespect, for both the office and the man, "was based on racism." In a TV interview Carter added, "I think an overwhelming portion of the intensely demonstrated animosity toward President Barack Obama is based on the fact that he is a black man." Carter said that it reflected an "inherent feeling" that African-Americans "are not qualified to lead this great country."

Although race had nothing to do with health care and quite possibly Wilson felt no conscious racial animosity, Obama's presidency was destined to provoke nearly constant commentary on Americans' racial attitudes. In the spring of 2009 a *New York Times/CBS News* poll had noted more optimism on this issue, with the number of people who felt race relations were "bad" declining from 37 percent to 22 percent.

In the summer of 2009, when Obama tried to soothe tensions after the mistaken burglary arrest of a black professor entering his own home, pollsters found that white Americans disapproved of his effort. He hosted the professor and the officer at the White House for what was called the Beer Summit. (Vice President Joe Biden joined them.) Presciently, the president complained, "As we've discussed this issue, I don't know if you've noticed, but nobody has been paying much attention to health care."

Opinion polls provided only the crudest measure of public sentiment, but they confirmed that the first African-American president would always be the focus of speculation about racial attitudes. The burden of his office would be increased by his symbolic role and by the indisputable fact that some of his fellow citizens were racists and would reject him on that basis. The president's election, and eventual reelection, would encourage people to be hopeful, but this hope would be blunted by the shadow of racism evident in his critics who, with sad regularity, veered into bigotry. This problem would be noted by political scientist Norman Ornstein, who, in 2014, noted, "The hostility toward Obama grew dramatically, and so did racist statements." Obama helped "reduce tensions while being exploited by partisans and racists to exacerbate them."

Joe Wilson's outburst deprived Obama's ideas on health care reform of some of the attention they deserved, but his administration pushed ahead. The president appeared at a meeting of the American

Medical Association, the nation's largest organization of doctors, and won applause as he said they represented health care to most people and "I will listen to you and work with you to pursue reform that works for you." Other administration officials appeared to win over the powerful health insurance companies as their lobbying group endorsed the plan.

In cooperating with the insurers, Obama earned criticism from those who considered the companies to be part of the problem in health care. However, some in his administration believed they needed the industry's cooperation and even aid if they were to overcome the claim that the president was trying to put the system under direct government control. Eventually the *National Journal* would reveal that the companies secretly gave the Chamber of Commerce $100 million to spend in its effort to defeat the reform proposal. Why the duplicity? The insurers didn't like a provision that required them to spend 80 percent of premiums on patient care.

Obama also negotiated to win support from pharmaceutical companies and the American Medical Association, which preferred compromise to a confrontation with a president whose party, if unified, could change the health care system in any way they chose. Congressional Democrats were key, because as a final vote on the plan neared, the lone GOP supporter in the Senate, Olympia Snowe, joined the opposition. Obama would need every single senator of his party to avoid a filibuster. Democratic senators Ben Nelson of Nebraska and Mary Landrieu of Louisiana, who represented rather conservative constituencies, saw opportunity in the president's predicament and pressed for special treatment for their states. They wanted the federal government to pay for the expansion of Medicaid indefinitely. Other states would see federal aid for this aspect of the program gradually reduced. Nelson and Landrieu initially prevailed as Senate leaders signaled the two would get what they wanted in exchange for their votes, but the deal was removed from the legislation when House Democrats discovered it. Landrieu and Nelson

wound up supporting the measure, but the uproar over what
came to be called the Cornhusker Kickback cast the process in a bad
light.

Throughout the intense debate over the health care plan, Republicans sought rhetorical advantage with terms such as Cornhusker
Kickback and by calling the president's program Obamacare. Intended as a pejorative alternative to the formal Affordable Care Act
(ACA), the term echoed the word Medicare, which was, second to
Social Security, the most popular government program ever devised. The president would embrace the term and use it himself. He
also continued to search for some common ground with Republicans in Congress.

In January 2010 the president decided to engage in the health
care debate more directly and went to the Baltimore hotel where
House Republicans were conducting their annual retreat. Broadcast
on television as it occurred, this encounter resembled the Question
Time British prime ministers regularly endure in Parliament, but it
may have been unprecedented for a US president. (President Bush
had visited the Democrats in 2001, but that event was not televised.)
Obama began by welcoming the input of the "loyal opposition"
and noting ideas he had adopted at the suggestion of Republicans.
(Indeed, much of his health plan copied the health care law enacted
in Massachusetts under GOP governor Mitt Romney.) He discussed
his economic policy and then invited the members of Congress to
ask questions.

House Republicans complained about health care industry lobbyists who had been welcomed to the White House and urged
the president to consider limiting the legal liability of doctors in
malpractice cases. (The latter had long been a staple of GOP policy
proposals.) Representative Marsha Blackburn of Tennessee asked,
"When will we look forward to starting anew and sitting down
with you to put all of these ideas on the table, to look at these
lessons learned, to benefit from that experience, and to produce a

product that is going to reduce government interference, reduce cost, and be fair to the American taxpayer?"

In responding, Obama seemed politically receptive, but cautious. He told Blackburn that if she could show that her ideas would cut costs, expand coverage, and make insurance affordable for small businesses, "I'm game." However, he added that he would not abandon his reliance on economic and medical experts, a hallmark of his approach, just to make a deal. He insisted that proposals be vetted by "people who know the system and how it works, including doctors and nurses," before they be written into law.

As he fielded questions, the president smiled and joked, saying, "You know, I'm having fun," but he also stood his ground when representatives complained that he hadn't incorporated their ideas in his various policy proposals. He noted a host of compromises made as the economic recovery program was developed, and that in the end not one House Republican supported it. In the case of health care reform, he said, "If there's uniform opposition because the Republican caucus doesn't get one hundred percent or eighty percent of what you want, then it's going to be hard to get a deal done. That's because that's not how democracy works."

Unscripted and polite, the president's session with House Republicans was widely hailed in the press. *The New York Times* observed that Obama used the trappings of the presidency to his advantage, dominating the cameras' attention and the allotted time. The performance, said the paper, allowed him to "reclaim a more bipartisan image and reach out to disaffected independents." The members of Congress benefited, too, as they showed that they were engaged in serious policy debate. For a moment the president's optimism about the possibility for a centrist agreement between the two parties in Washington, something he had spoken of before taking office, seemed to be affirmed. He decided to try to keep the momentum going with a follow-up gathering a few weeks later.

In February, Obama hosted Republican leaders and congressional Democrats at Blair House, the presidential guest quarters that had been established by Franklin Roosevelt during World War II. (The setting signaled Obama's willingness to abandon the symbolic power he could wield at the White House.) With Mitch McConnell and John Boehner both in attendance, Obama opened the session with a reference to the daily packet of letters from citizens, ten in all, that he receives from his staff after they have reviewed the tens of thousands that arrive with every postal delivery:

> I can tell you that at least two, sometimes five, of the ten letters relates to the challenges that people are experiencing in health care every single day. I'll get letters from parents who—whose children have preexisting conditions and maybe those children were able to get health insurance when they were young but now they're growing up, they're about to move out, and they can't get insurance no matter what job they find.
>
> I hear from small businesses who have just opened up their new rates from their insurance company and it turns out that the rates have gone up twenty, thirty, in some cases thirty-five percent. I hear from families who have hit lifetime limits, and because somebody in their family is very ill, at a certain point they start having to dig out of pocket and they are having to mortgage their house and in some cases have gone bankrupt because of health care.
>
> So this is an issue that is affecting everybody. It's affecting not only those without insurance, but it's affecting those with insurance. And when you talk to every single expert, and you just talk to ordinary people, and you talk to businesses, everybody understands that the problem is not getting better, it's getting worse.

For seven hours the men and women at Blair House debated both the grand concepts of health care reform and surprisingly specific details. Early in the day, for example, Senator Tom Coburn of Oklahoma, a Republican who was also a medical doctor, asked Obama why his antifraud measures didn't call for the deployment of "undercover patients" who could report suspected fraud to authorities. Others discussed ways to protect the doctor/patient relationship and methods for protecting doctors from frivolous lawsuits. But in the end nothing of substance was offered by the president's political opponents, and the "summit" amounted to a seven-hour display of Obama's mastery of health care minutiae and GOP intransigence.

Before he could finalize his plan, the president had to negotiate with members of his own party, who understood how much he needed them and, politics being politics, used that leverage to win adjustments to benefit their constituents and backers. The final plan was the product of so many compromises and calibrations that it disappointed liberal partisans, many of whom would have preferred a single, government-run insurance scheme. Instead Congress approved a hodgepodge of changes that would be phased in over six years so that people and institutions could adjust. The negotiations to reach this outcome were at times confusing and Byzantine, and the result was messy. However, both the product and the methods revealed that Obama, a cool character whom many consider too aloof, was actually a skilled politician who understood what he could achieve. In this regard he was more successful than the gregarious Bill Clinton, who had failed when pursuing the same goal.

The highlights of the plan Congress adopted included:

- Outlawing the denial of insurance on the basis of illness or preexisting conditions.
- Mandated insurance for all citizens, with penalties for those who do not obtain coverage.

- Eliminating lifetime limits on benefits.
- Tax credits for small businesses that offer insurance.
- Free preventive care.
- Extending the period children are covered on parents' plans to age twenty-six.
- Expanding Medicaid.
- Cost-cutting estimated to save $100 billion in a decade.
- Creation of online state insurance marketplaces.
- Subsidies, based on income, for insurance purchasers.

Obama's political acumen was evident in the timing of the reforms, which would begin with the elements most people liked, such as expanded coverage for dependent children, and delayed reforms such as the mandatory insurance requirement until after his campaign for reelection. Congress finished work on the bill on the first full day of spring 2010. In the House, where the Democrats enjoyed a large majority, thirty-four of them voted against the plan, mainly out of concern about how they might fair in the autumn election. On the day Obama signed the bill, he said it represented "not radical reform" but "major reform" that proved "we are still a people capable of doing big things." The top Republican in the House of Representatives, John Boehner of Ohio, said, "The American people are angry" about Obamacare. "Shame on us."

The anger would be inflamed by Boehner and his colleagues, who would continue to rail against the Affordable Care Act even as it transformed the health care landscape. In the states, many Republican governors refused to create the insurance marketplaces envisioned in the law. Some turned down the federal funding that would have paid the entire expense of expanding Medicaid. Twenty-six states joined a business association in challenging the constitutionality of the ACA in court. The case went all the way to the Supreme Court where the challenge was turned back.

Defeated in the judiciary, opponents made repeated failed efforts to overturn Obamacare in Congress, voting on more than fifty proposals. Those who pinned their hopes on Obama's defeat in the 2012 election by a challenger who would reverse the reform would be disappointed by the president's reelection. Equipped with veto power, Obama could confidently follow through on the rollout of his reforms. The only major hitch would come in 2013 when the federal insurance exchange Web site crashed. Improvements would require interventions from outside experts. Acknowledging the mess, the administration loosened regulations on those required to buy insurance. By April 15, 2014, sign-ups exceeded the 7 million originally estimated to represent success.

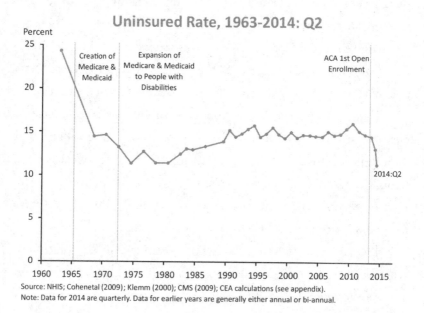

Source: NHIS; Cohenetal (2009); Klemm (2000); CMS (2009); CEA calculations (see appendix).
Note: Data for 2014 are quarterly. Data for earlier years are generally either annual or bi-annual.

Obamacare's positive effects were seen long before the exchanges opened as the percentage of Americans without insurance began to drop in 2010 and continued downward.

In addition to expanding the number of insured Americans, the reform seemed to reduce inflation in health care spending:

Rising Health Care Costs, Then and Now

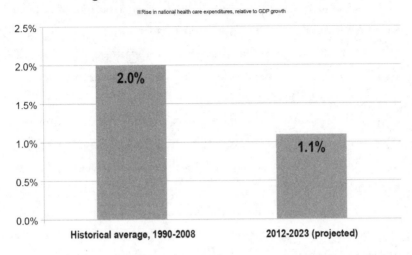

Rise in national health care expenditures, relative to GDP growth

2.0%

1.1%

Historical average, 1990-2008   2012-2023 (projected)

Source: Center for Medicare and Medicaid Services.

The cost of Obamacare turned out to be less than expected, according to the nonpartisan Congressional Budget Office. The CBO estimated that the program's reduction of federal budget deficits would be even greater than first estimated.

Comparison of CBO's 2010 and 2011 Estimates of the Net Budgetary Impact of All Provisions of the Affordable Care Act

(Billions of dollars, by fiscal year)

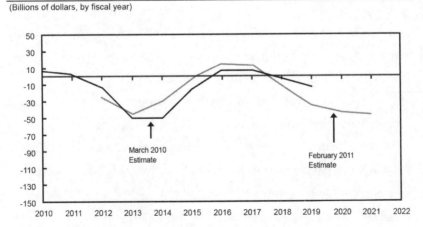

March 2010 Estimate

February 2011 Estimate

Sources: Congressional Budget Office and the staff of the Joint Committee on Taxation.

Although much of the news that followed the implementation of the reform program was good, such as that employers did not stop providing coverage as opponents had predicted, it was not all positive. First, the president did not keep his oft-repeated promise that "if you like your health plan, you'll be able to keep your health plan." In fact, 2.2 percent of the people who had bought plans found they could not keep them, mainly because they didn't comply with new regulations. That the law actually required better coverage than most of these policies didn't make a difference to people who felt they had been misled.

Individual experience with Obamacare varied greatly and was affected by where Americans lived. In states where officials created insurance marketplaces and/or enacted federally funded increases in Medicaid, the number of people who lacked access to health care dropped the most. Fewer people reported that they had delayed getting care they needed, and fewer said they had trouble paying medical bills. In other states, where Republican governors refused to expand Medicaid and declined to create insurance exchanges, more people lacked insurance and more people experienced difficulty getting care and paying for it. Indeed, a divide opened up between states governed primarily by Republicans (so-called red states) and states governed primarily by Democrats (blue states). In red states such as Texas and Florida, health care reform's impact was muted. In blue states such as New York and California, more people gained health insurance and, their well-being improved.

No place did better than very blue California, where an effective state-run exchange enrolled so many people, including many who were healthy and used fewer benefits, that cost savings came even as more people got coverage. In 2015, monthly premiums paid by those who purchased their own care remained below $300 in the southern half of the state and below $400 in the north. These rates were well below national averages. But while policy experts welcomed the economic benefits of the reforms, the human experience of life before, and after, Obamacare was what mattered most, which brings us back to Lulu's café and Spike Dolomite, cancer survivor.

"I filled out a three-page application, that was it, and I provided proof of citizenship," recalled Spike. "I had cancer, which was, after all, a preexisting condition, but I got coverage right away and my premium was $320 per month. The deductible was $2,500, but after that I was covered for imaging, treatments, hospitals, doctors, everything."

Spike opted for a mastectomy followed by chemotherapy, which, she said, "knocked me out. I also lost my hair. But the insurance even covered a $3,000 shot that boosted my red blood cells, and I got better." An artist, Spike made her own bumper sticker, which read OBAMA CARES, and stuck it to her car. For a while she was a bit wary about how her message would be greeted by others "because of the backlash" against health care reform. "But I'm alive because he put everything on the line. I am alive because he did care."

The story told by Spike Dolomite could have been repeated by countless Americans who received vital health care thanks to the Obamacare reforms. But set the anecdotes aside and you can still find evidence of the ACA's ongoing success in data. According to Kaiser Permanente, the big health care provider, every year 10,000 premature deaths are prevented for every one million additional people insured. In 2016 the percentage of uninsured continued to drop and other important benefits of the act came into focus. Hospital re-admissions, which constitute a measure of quality in care, were reported to have declined by roughly 125,000 per year, every year, between 2010 and 2015. This was a case of a less-heralded aspect of the law, which focused on improving the performance of health care providers, produced tangible results.

4

ENERGY

Sun, Wind, and Market Forces

Mayor Rex Parris is a Republican who didn't vote for Barack Obama in either 2008 or 2012. Nevertheless, his sun-drenched city of Lancaster, in California's Antelope Valley, is proof of Obama's energy policy success. On the edge of town Parris can point to some of the world's largest arrays of solar panels, built with federal help, which feed electricity into the state's power grid. In the center of the city a Chinese company named BYD assembles electric buses and is developing the world's largest energy-storage facility, to preserve the sun power generated by day and deliver it at night. All over Lancaster, city-owned solar setups supply a municipal utility, and every new house built must, by local ordinance, generate 850 kilowatt hours of power per year from the sun or the wind.

"I don't have my eyes closed," explained Parris in 2015. "I'm aware of the dystopian future we face if we don't do something about energy and climate change. We looked at one of our major resources, which is our sunshine, and we thought we could create a city that is a center for alternative energy, and also net zero in terms of energy consumption and carbon emissions."

Pragmatic to his core, Parris will use any means necessary to advance his city of 160,000 souls. In true GOP style he cut the red tape in the building department so that solar installation permits can be approved in fifteen minutes. He courted BYD and others for the jobs they could bring, and he aligned Lancaster with the Obama administration's energy agenda. "My main concern is the overall well-being of our people," said Parris. "I want us to have a higher quality of life, and I want us to thrive into the future." In 2016 his city was well on its way. Unemployment was in decline. A sleepy downtown was starting to sprout new businesses, and solar installations were being completed at a rate that would soon make Lancaster a net power exporter, all without consuming a bit of fossil fuel.

The Lancaster story depends on its special location in the Antelope Valley, where the sun shines almost all day, every day, and the high desert offers thousands of square miles of flat, empty terrain perfect for solar panel arrays. However, the city's success is not unique. Thanks to President Obama's policies, which supported and exploited new technologies, solar energy production more than tripled between 2008 and 2012 and then doubled in the next four years. Wind technology, which already generated more supply than solar, increased almost as fast. At the same time, global competition and scientific breakthroughs pushed the cost of power generated by

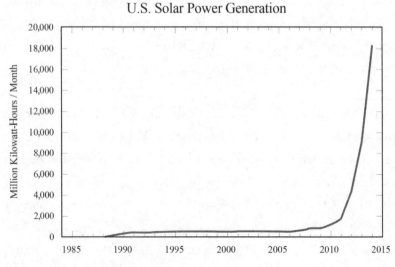

U.S. Solar Power Generation

Source: U.S. Energy Information Administration

these sources ever downward. In 2016 a report issued by the investment company Lazard noted that in Obama's time wind power
got 60 percent cheaper. Solar power generating costs dropped by
80 percent.

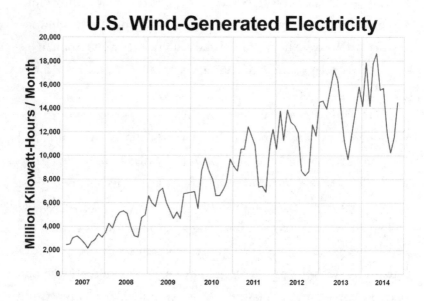

The rise of wind and solar power during the Obama years, after
decades of promise, was just one of the successes notched by the
administration. The Obama team's energy record is one of promises made and kept with remarkable consistency. It is also a demon-
stration of the value of persistent effort and measured risk-taking in
the pursuit of a long-standing national goal.

As Barack Obama campaigned for the presidency, gasoline prices
crossed $3 per gallon and then topped $4. This was a national average. In some places gas cost $6 per gallon, and heating oil followed
a similar track. Much of the increase was caused by roaring demand
in China, where new factories and cars soaked up huge portions of
the global oil supply. The markets may also have been inflated by
speculators, who held futures contracts to sell oil at ever-higher

prices. The oil price shock of 2007–8 joined with the effects of the Great Recession to cause hardship for the American people and worsen the prospects for economic recovery. High prices pinched family budgets, which in turn reduced consumption and demand for goods and services. With consumer spending accounting for 70 percent of the gross domestic product, the economy wasn't going to improve until consumers felt less concerned about buying fuel and more willing to spend on other things.

Candidate Obama calibrated his energy policy to advance his agenda on related economic and environmental issues. He stressed the reduction in pollution that would come as alternative power sources grew, and he argued that central to restoring the economy "is the question of what we will do about our addiction to foreign oil." This line was included in the energy policy speech Obama made in August 2008 at Michigan State University in East Lansing. This was one of several addresses the candidate delivered to explain the promises he was making to the nation as he sought the White House. These pledges were offered to distinguish his priorities from those of his opponent and to build trust with voters who had lost faith in politicians.

If Americans were exasperated with politicians, it may, at least in part, have been due to their experience with candidates who talked about such problems as the country's addiction to foreign oil and failed to address them effectively. Republican presidents had tended to emphasize domestic oil production, while Democratic presidents had promoted alternatives to fossil fuels, but the country received mainly a muddled approach that achieved little. Imports rose from four million to twelve million barrels per day between 1985 and 2007, with much of it coming from countries such as Saudi Arabia and Venezuela, which many Americans viewed as unreliable trading partners.

In his energy speech Obama described three decades of failure and placed his opponent in the middle of it, noting that Senator

McCain had been in Washington for twenty-six of those thirty years. In that time, said Obama, McCain had "done little to reduce our dependence on foreign oil." Willing to spread the blame around, Obama also said that Democrats had boosted alternative technologies that were not ready. But in 2008, he said, the energy future had arrived at "research labs of this university and in the design centers of this state's legendary auto industry. It's in the chemistry labs that are laying the building blocks for cheaper, more efficient solar panels, and it's in the reborn factories that are churning out more wind turbines every day all across this country."

As the first major-party nominee with real tech savvy, candidate Obama had made a point of doing campaign events at places where research and production of new energy technologies were being done. In Toledo, where solar- and wind-power equipment were manufactured, he spoke of a federal investment to promote these industries. Alternative-energy industries needed the help. Although big technological breakthroughs were being made as more companies competed to lower the price of sun and wind power, the economic crisis had frozen their financing. Some venture capital firms were making bets on "green energy" schemes, which suggested their time had come. However, even the capitalists were pushing for a government role, which would help level the playing field with oil companies, which had enjoyed special tax treatment, and other government benefits, for many generations. In his Michigan energy address Obama said:

> If I am president, I will immediately direct the full
> resources of the federal government and the full energy
> of the private sector to a single, overarching goal—in ten
> years, we will eliminate the need for oil from the entire
> Middle East and Venezuela. To do this, we will invest
> $150 billion over the next ten years and leverage billions
> more in private capital to build a new energy economy

that harnesses American energy and creates five million
new American jobs.

The second step I'll take is to require that ten percent
of our energy comes from renewable sources by the end of
my first term—more than double what we have now. . . .
I'll also extend the production tax for five years to encourage the production of renewable energy like wind
power, solar power, and geothermal energy. . . .

. . . Finally, the third step I will take is to call on
businesses, government, and the American people to
meet the goal of reducing our demand for electricity
fifteen percent by the end of the next decade. This is by
far the fastest, easiest, and cheapest way to reduce our
energy consumption—and it will save us $130 billion on
our energy bills.

The energy agenda Obama ticked off in Michigan included not
just incentives for fossil fuel alternatives but also a pledge to increase
domestic production of both oil and natural gas to help the country in the short term. This included gas produced from fracking of
shale formations, a practice opposed by some environmentalists, and
drilling for petroleum on ecologically sensitive federal lands in
Alaska. These stands deprived McCain and his running mate, Sarah
Palin, who often chanted, "Drill, baby, drill," at rallies, of a major
criticism they might make of the Democrat. However, this wasn't
just politics at work. By remaining open to all options, even a role
for nuclear power plants, Obama also gave himself maximum room
for maneuvering in the event that he won the election and had to
make his promises work.

In the eight years prior to the Obama presidency, Washington's energy policy focused on oil, gas, and coal production. This approach
began in the first weeks of the Bush presidency as Vice President

Richard Cheney convened a secret energy task force that met with oil and coal company executives to devise policy. (At the time he was tapped to run on the Bush ticket, Cheney was head of the oil-services giant Halliburton. As he left the company, he received a severance package worth more than $30 million.) In 2003 the Bush administration pushed through Congress legislation that canceled royalty payments due the government on millions of barrels of oil pumped in the Gulf of Mexico, and also subsidized the expenses companies paid to comply with environmental standards.

One hallmark of the Bush-Cheney approach would be reduced enforcement of regulations, including those covering coal-mine safety and the permitting of oil wells. The administration fast-tracked more than a thousand driller applications for new oil wells by exempting them from the usual environmental review process. One of these exemptions was for the Deepwater Horizon rig operated by Halliburton in the Gulf of Mexico. In 2010 an explosion on the Deepwater Horizon killed eleven workers, sank the rig, and, after emergency equipment failed, led to the biggest oil spill ever seen offshore.

What did Bush and Cheney get for all their effort on behalf of the fossil fuel industries? As prices paid by consumers rose, domestic oil production actually decreased by 15 percent, reaching the lowest level in more than fifty years. Natural gas and coal production rose, but only slightly. In the meantime the administration did almost nothing to deal with climate change or encourage energy conservation, which Vice President Cheney termed "a sign of personal virtue" but "not a sufficient basis for a sound, comprehensive energy policy." Efficiency standards for the average new car, unchanged since 1990, remained at 27.5 miles per gallon throughout the Bush years. In comparison, the European Union had required increasing performance from car manufacturers, mandating fuel economy that would exceed 40 miles per gallon in 2005.

Instead of urging efficiency, which even utility companies promoted to cut demand, Cheney said that the United States should plan to build thirteen hundred new electric generation stations in the coming twenty years to meet demand. The Bush administration actually rolled back some efficiency rules (on new air conditioners) and delayed enforcing others. As a result of all these policies, the US contribution to fossil fuel pollution that caused climate change peaked at 1.6 billion tons annually during the Bush years.

Designed to reverse many of the trends established by his predecessor, Obama's energy initiatives began with $90 billion tucked into the economic recovery act. Some of this money would pay for unexciting items such as home insulation and tax credits to encourage the installation of wind and solar equipment. (Lancaster's solar revolution got a boost from these funds.) Other investments made from the $90 billion fund suggested bolder thinking. The Recovery Act included $18 billion for high-speed rail transportation, a $4.5 billion down payment on improvements to the electric supply grid, $3.5 billion for "clean coal" technology, $2.4 billion to support electric vehicle development, and a loan-guarantee program to backstop private investments in new energy technologies.

The mundane aspects of the energy policy produced the desired results with little fanfare. By 2012, a million low-income households would be helped with insulation and other energy-saving improvements that cut consumption and saved families money. The money dedicated to upgrading the power grid was less than one-fourth of what would be required to modernize the whole system, but it was spent effectively. Utilities across the country gained huge improvements in substations and an advanced early-warning network to signal disruptions in supply. The "smarter" grid also streamlined repairs when storms knocked out power. These programs, and many smaller ones, also put people to work and reduced both energy consumption and carbon emissions.

The splashier elements of the Obama energy strategy, including high-speed rail, electric vehicles, and loan guarantees for technology companies, generated far more attention from the press. The high-speed rail effort—some boosters talked of "bullet trains"—was resisted by Republican governors, who declined to move forward on projects in Wisconsin, Ohio, and Florida. However, reports that the whole endeavor was bogged down proved wrong. Construction would require substantial planning, mapping, public hearings, and time for property acquisition and contracts to be developed and awarded. All of this would take years.

Nevertheless, construction did begin in many places where existing railroads such as Amtrak were ready to proceed and in states such as California, where officials were eager for the kind of fast train travel widely available in Europe, China, and Japan. Beginning in the state's Central Valley, the California High-Speed Rail Authority used both federal and state funds to build bridges, underpasses, and rail beds. As generally happens with huge infrastructure projects, the effort to link nearly all of the state, including a station close to Mayor Parris's city of Lancaster, fell behind schedule. However, the investment, which became the largest infrastructure project in America, created jobs and business activity, which helped California lead the nation's economic recovery. Upon completion, the state's advanced rail system will alleviate traffic congestion, reduce pollution, and speed passengers from Los Angeles to San Francisco in three hours. It will also make a state with enviable advantages in climate, higher education, and technology resources an even more attractive place for investment and development than, say, Florida.

Although critics would bash the rail initiative, and many would misstate the actual pace of spending on the program (it fell far short of the sum appropriated by Congress), the most pointed attacks on Obama's energy policy would be reserved for the support the administration gave to technology companies through the Department of Energy. Long involved in basic science related to energy, the department provided grants and loan guarantees to more than thirty companies developing and commercializing cutting-edge technologies, including high-capacity batteries for vehicles and cheaper, mass-produced solar electric panels to compete with equipment made in China, South Korea, and other lower-wage countries. The funding was intended to finance projects that banks and other private lenders considered too risky, especially in a time of tight credit. Government has played this role, as a kind of public venture capital fund, for generations, subsidizing everything from medical advances to smartphones and the fracking techniques used in the oil and gas industries.

The first well-publicized failure in the administration's energy program involved a solar-equipment manufacturing start-up called Solyndra, which received $535 million in loan guarantees. Based in Fremont, California, the company made a lighter solar panel that was easier to install than competing panels and could be used on roofs that wouldn't support heavier ones. The concept had moved venture capitalists to invest in Solyndra, and it had received praise from experts at MIT and from *The Wall Street Journal*. However, in 2009 the company found it couldn't compete as the price of Chinese panels dropped 30 percent in a year. Unable to boost sales, Solyndra went bankrupt.

Other loan-guarantee failures included a battery company called 123 Systems, an experimental energy storage company called Beacon Power, and an electric-car start-up called Fisker. The costliest, Solyndra's fall was also the most consequential failure of the loan-guarantee program because the company had employed more than a thousand people in the "green tech" jobs that Obama had touted as part of his economic recovery plan. The president had even made a widely publicized visit to Solyndra's manufacturing facility. He noted that similar factories were being built by competitors around the world: "These countries recognize that the nation that leads the clean energy economy is likely to lead the global economy. And if we fail to recognize that same imperative, we risk falling behind."

Solyndra's failure gave Obama's critics an opening and they seized it. In the House of Representatives, Republicans on the Energy and Commerce Committee conducted numerous hearings on the loan guarantees given the company, which led to a report titled simply "The Solyndra Failure." The report described the approval for the company's guarantee as a hurried process that was influenced by political considerations. Among them were a desire to show progress in the pursuit of alternative energy successes, and that one of Solyndra's private investors was an Obama campaign donor. It concluded that the administration "should never have issued the loan guarantee."

An independent probe by the Government Accountability Office confirmed that some energy loans had been rushed and that the administration "treated applicants inconsistently, favoring some and disadvantaging others." The GAO report didn't attach political motives to the process, nor did it name the companies that benefited. However, reports in the press confirmed that Solyndra was one. The agency, which is independent of Congress and the White House, also noted that the problems in the program dated back to the previous administration, which had set up the loan-guarantee process and received Solyndra's original proposal, and that the Department of Energy was working to fix what was wrong with the program.

Republicans in Congress pressed their case against Solyndra for three years, seeking to make the company's demise into a scandal. Senator Ron Johnson of Minnesota likened the Solyndra experience to "the lessons of the Soviet Union." In 2012 the firm's failure became the subject of a campaign commercial loosed on the nation's airwaves by GOP presidential nominee Mitt Romney, who, in speeches, described the loan guarantee as an example of "crony capitalism." The advertisement insisted, "Obama is giving taxpayer dollars to big donors and then watching them lose it."

In many of the attacks lurked the suggestion that something criminal may have occurred within the administration as it dealt with the Solyndra project. However, no evidence of criminality emerged in testimony or in the million pages of documents turned over to Congress by the White House. (They did show that the administration was eager to make energy loans, in part to spur the economy, and had acted in haste.) As time passed and committees equipped with subpoena power failed to unearth evidence that any laws had been broken, even the most determined congressional critic, Representative Darrell Issa of California, lost enthusiasm for the cause. "Was there criminal activity? Perhaps not," he mused in March 2012. "Is there political influence and connections? Perhaps not. Did they bend the rules for an agenda not covered in the statute? Absolutely."

This was weak stuff coming from a man who had acted as a grand inquisitor on this issue, hectoring witnesses from his elevated perch as committee chairman and demanding e-mails from the private accounts of Department of Energy employees. Throughout his effort to make Solyndra into a true scandal, Issa had generally struggled to demonstrate that the investigation was much more than an attempt to score political points. His Republican colleague Representative Jim Jordan of Ohio confessed as much in the spring of 2012, explaining, "Ultimately, we'll stop it on Election Day, hopefully." Before then Issa would tell the press that Solyndra could cost taxpayers an additional $300 million, although he offered no information to support this idea.

After the election, which Obama won handily, Solyndra ceased to be a topic of interest in Congress. The firm's demise would ultimately cost the government a little less than $530 million. The other investments made by the program proved to be quite successful. When the GAO reviewed the program in 2014, it discovered that five out of thirty funded projects had failed at a cost of less than $1 billion. When Congress approved the program, it noted that defaults could total as much as $10 billion and planned for such losses. By 2014, nineteen of the high-risk energy projects were completed, and the remainder were still being finished. In 2015 the Federal Bureau of Investigation and the Department of Energy reported that Solyndra executives had misled federal officials when they reported on their company's condition. Among the deceptions was the false claim that they had booked $2.2 billion in purchase orders for their product. The administration had supported the company based on these illusory orders.

While the president's critics struggled to turn Solyndra into an indictment of his entire energy policy, other initiatives turned out well. As candidate for president, Obama said he would push for improvements in car and truck fuel efficiency, which had not changed since 1990. Once in the White House, he used his executive power to raise the requirements for cars sold in the United States. The administration also helped car companies with federal loans to retool factories to produce the more efficient cars and trucks. Ford got $5.9 billion to improve more than a dozen models. Nissan North America received more than $1 billion in financing for a battery plant, and the new electric-car company Tesla got $465 million.

Based in Palo Alto, California, Tesla was created to produce all-electric vehicles that could quickly be charged by the power grid. Private investors had funded the development of its first car, an expensive ($109,000) roadster, which was intended to prove the technology and design. The company's founders envisioned making cars for a mass market, but needed much more funding to make that leap. The loan guarantee supported the Model S, which was priced at less than $60,000. Introduced for sale in 2012, the car was a hit, selling more than seventeen thousand in a year. The company represented the kind of high-tech, entrepreneurial spirit that the president found attractive, and its founder, Elon Musk, had supported Obama's campaign for the White House. This connection would be raised by GOP presidential candidate Mitt Romney in his failing campaign against Obama. Romney would call Tesla a "loser" like Solyndra. However in 2013, the company would repay its federal loan, ten years early. At the end of 2015, Model S sales totaled one hundred thousand. The company planned to sell a true mass-market car, with a sticker price of around $35,000, by 2016. Employment at the company exceeded six thousand. Tesla leased the former Solyndra factory for more production capacity, and it moved into the energy-storage business, building batteries to save power generated by solar panels. Designed to put fossil fuel power plants out of business, the batteries would be made in the sprawling Gigafactory, which Tesla began building in the Nevada desert. With fewer than ten thousand Tesla batteries, a city of one hundred thousand could be powered entirely by the sun.

As the company used both public and private backing to reach for ambitious goals, Tesla became an emblem of the Obama administration's highest aspirations. The president sought similar results, with less gee-whiz technology, from other vehicle manufacturers. The centerpiece of this strategy was steadily rising mileage standards for gasoline- and diesel-powered cars and trucks. If achieved, the goal would save roughly 1.8 billion barrels of oil and reduce carbon emissions by nearly a billion metric tons in four years.

Past efforts to get vehicle makers to up their game on fuel efficiency had met fierce resistance from manufacturers, who said they were concerned about the cost of making more efficient vehicles, which would be passed on to buyers. However, decades of experience had shown that people were generally willing to invest a little more in the purchase price to save more, over time, in fuel expenses. In 2014, when the president moved to increase standards for heavy trucks, no cry of opposition arose from the industry as experts estimated that the $8 billion increase in the price of various vehicles would be offset by $50 billion in savings for their operators. Reductions in pollution would be substantial because transport accounted for 28 percent of the greenhouse gases produced in the United States, and these larger vehicles, which made up just 4 percent of the nation's highway fleet, produced a quarter of all emissions.

Between 2009 and 2014, the higher standards worked, improving the gas mileage of cars sold in the United States by 10 percent. This improvement played a role in the overall reduction of US carbon emissions, a decline in petroleum fuel consumption, and a dramatic reduction in fuel prices.

More significant when it came to energy costs were factors beyond the president's control. The Great Recession suppressed growth in world demand for oil while countries eager for revenues continued to pump. The result of this steady supply and slumping demand was lower prices. At the same time a method for extracting oil and gas from the ground called hydraulic fracturing or fracking, which was developed with the help of tax subsidies and research done by the Department of Energy, came into wide use. In fracking, water and chemicals are pumped underground at high pressure to pulverize rock formations that contain oil and gas, which can then be extracted. When combined with recently developed methods for horizontal and deep drilling, fracking can produce oil and gas in fields previously deemed unprofitable. This oil is known in the industry as tight oil. The gas, which resides mainly in shale deposits, is called shale gas.

After a 2005 act of Congress exempted fracking from many environmental regulations, gas and oil companies began testing the method across the country. Soon thousands of permits would be granted, and production would begin in fields from California to Pennsylvania, where a huge rock formation called the Marcellus Shale held the largest store of natural gas in the United States. The fracking boom came with a price, as both the injected chemicals and the released gas have been found in the well water of neighbors and in the air they breathe. In 2008, salt-laden waste from wells in Pennsylvania fouled the Monongahela River near Pittsburgh. The risks of fracking have prompted bans in certain communities and opposition from some environmental groups. The Obama administration responded to this concern with guidelines for safer fracking, which states and other local authorities could use as they considered applications for drilling permits. (More on this in a later chapter.)

For many Americans the debate over the environmental effects of fracking would remain a puzzle, but all experienced its impact on energy supplies firsthand. Tight-oil production, which was almost nonexistent prior to 2005, ballooned to a volume roughly equal to the amount of oil produced by conventional means. At the same time natural gas production increased by 25 percent between 2008 and 2014. Much of this additional volume came from areas where little or no gas had been produced before. (The Marcellus Shale alone produced 14 billion cubic feet of gas per day in 2015.) And many of these new sources were closer to urban populations

Figure 1 U.S. petroleum and other liquid fuels supply by source, 1970-2040

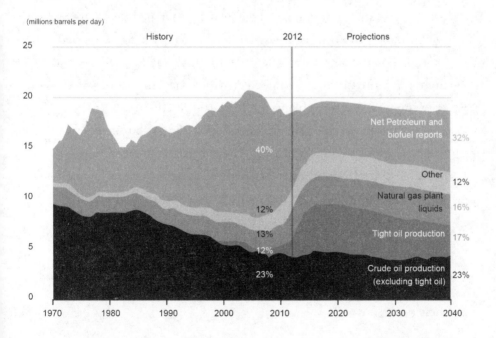

(millions barrels per day)

that needed the fuel. Thanks to fracking, the price of natural gas, which millions of households used for cooking, heating, and hot water, declined to the lowest point in thirty-five years. Industries that relied on the fuel reaped similar benefits, and dozens of electric utility plants that were scheduled to close were converted to run on newly available supplies of gas. These conversions extended the functional lives of some generators and permitted others to continue operating without the expenses of pollution-mitigation equipment required for coal-fired plants.

The oil obtained by fracking contributed to the kind of reduction in America's foreign oil "addiction" that previous presidents had imagined but never realized. Imports declined throughout the Obama years as domestic crude oil production increased from 5 million barrels per day in 2008 to more than 9 million six years later. In 2014 the United States eclipsed Saudi Arabia as the top oil producer in the world, and in 2016 a forty-year ban on exports of American crude oil was lifted. The first shipment sailed from Texas to Europe in January. Days later a US oil company announced that the state-run Chinese oil refiner Sinopec had placed its first order. All of these developments signaled a shift in petroleum power, which made America seem less vulnerable to market moves made abroad. For the first time since the 1990s the United States was pumping more oil than it imported, which made the domestic energy supply less vulnerable to foreign manipulations.

Although the dramatic shifts in the oil and gas businesses were driven mainly by market forces, the Obama administration was about as friendly to oil interests as its predecessor, granting thousands of well permits. The economic benefits of this abundant supply went mainly to consumers as the price of gasoline, which peaked at about $4 per gallon in 2012, declined to below $2 in early 2016. This change was worth $660 per year to the typical American household. Similar savings were seen by people who paid for oil to heat their homes.

In addition to the immediate financial gains realized by consumers, the improved energy markets, including the greater diversification of supply, were good for local economies where the wind, solar, electric-car, and gas and oil companies operated. The green jobs that candidate Obama had discussed in his first campaign actually developed. In 2015 the Bureau of Labor Statistic reported that 209,000 people worked in the solar industry, which was more than the number employed in oil and gas production. The government didn't track all jobs held by people producing the kind of clean energy and technology that might be considered "green," but federal reports put the figure at 3.4 million in 2013. This was below the 5 million Obama had in 2008 hoped for, but nevertheless a significant number.

The one big energy business that lost ground in the Obama years was coal, which continued a decline that actually began in the Bush years. Between 2005 and 2015, the number of active coal mines in the United States fell by 40 percent, and the volume of coal burned to make electricity dropped almost 20 percent. The coal industry had lost about ten thousand jobs as of 2014 (the last figures available), which explains to a major degree the fierce fight waged against Obama by Republican Senate majority leader Mitch McConnell, whose state, Kentucky, is a coal producer.

The president's critics regarded his energy policies as an outright assault on communities that depended on mining jobs. In 2016, as the giant Arch Coal joined three other major American mining companies in bankruptcy, editorial writers at *The Wall Street Journal* said the Obama administration was willing to destroy jobs in coal regions of Wyoming and Montana because they leaned Republican and were not politically important to Democrats. The pro-business journal writers also complained that higher royalties, to be paid to the government, would erode profits.

Outside of coal country, where consumers enjoyed lower energy prices and concern about the environment was likely greater,

Obama's effort to reduce pollution from fuels such as coal won praise from health organizations such as the American Academy of Pediatrics and environmental groups, including Friends of the Earth. The president's policies halted the rise in carbon emissions by the US energy sector and then prompted a decline. For some the change wasn't fast enough. However, the president took a step further in this direction and won more praise when he announced at the start of his final year in office that no more new leases would be granted to allow coal mining on federal lands.

The ban on new leases wasn't expected to have an immediate effect on coal production because much of the American supply was mined on private property and existing federal permits covered tracts that could be exploited for twenty years. However, the administration was moving to cut coal burning over the long term to reduce pollution and address the looming problem of climate change. For communities where the shift away from coal would eventually and inevitably bring economic pain, the administration prescribed economic development programs. This effort, funded through mining royalties paid to the government, wouldn't replace what coal towns would lose, but it was an acknowledgment that the stakes in the policy struggle were more immediate for some Americans.

5

ENVIRONMENT

Saving the Planet

On Christmas Eve 2015, New Yorkers flocked to Central Park where ornamental trees, deceived by seventy-two-degree warmth, had begun to blossom. Young men pulled off their shirts and threw footballs. Women in bikinis lay on blankets and soaked in the sunshine. The warmth felt good, even to those who were unnerved by its arrival in a season for sweaters and scarves. Some politicians would say that the heat wave was an artifact of *weather* patterns, and not proof that something was amiss with the *climate*. True, no single weather event proved anything about the climate. However, when added to data gathered over preceding decades, the Christmas Eve heat wave did suggest a more serious problem.

Measured globally, the year 2015 was the hottest recorded since reliable data became available in the 1880s. Taken alone, the year's weather could be seen as a matter of chance, the kind of anomaly to be expected in any record stretching back more than a century. The trouble was that the previous year, 2014, had also been a record breaker, and thirteen of the fourteen hottest years had occurred since 1990. Based on the best models available, 2016 promised to be even hotter still.

First described as global "warming," rather than "climate change," the problem of pollution causing a rise in temperatures was widely recognized in the 1980s. In 1988, James Hansen of the National Aeronautics and Space Administration said he had a "high degree of confidence" that "it is already happening now." One of the senators who listened to Hansen testify at a public hearing said Congress needed to adopt policies to halt the trend and search for ways to help people cope "with the changes that may already be inevitable."

In the political scrum that arose in Washington, the problem of planetary warming was reframed as "climate change." For those who resisted taking action, the term suggested something less immediate and menacing. Those sounding the alarm could be dismissed as save-the-planet zealots who had appointed themselves earth's heroes. On the other side of the debate, where people believed the planet *should* be saved, the phrase captured all the extreme effects—droughts, wildfires, floods, etc.—caused by rising temperatures.

For roughly eighteen years, from the time of Hansen's testimony in 1988 to 2006, critics of the scientific consensus used the possibility of credible doubt, slight as it was, to block meaningful responses. During this time, denying the evidence of climate change became an article of faith among Republicans. The issue finally became a global cause célèbre with the release of a documentary film called *An Inconvenient Truth*. Narrated by former vice president Al Gore, the 2006 film showed that the earth was growing warmer due to pollution that produced a "greenhouse" effect that prevented the dissipation of the planet's heat. The emissions responsible include, in descending order, water vapor, carbon dioxide, methane, nitrous oxide, ozone, and various chlorofluorocarbons. Water vapor falls from the atmosphere in days. The other gases, which are produced in great quantities by vehicles, industrial plants, and other human sources, can stay aloft and do harm for years, decades, and even centuries.

Had it come at a time when politics was less divisive and from someone other than the man who had lost the most contested presidential race in history, the alarm sounded by *An Inconvenient Truth* might have been heard and heeded. Instead it energized writers at conservative foundations and think tanks, many of which received funding from corporations that profited from the production or use of the main fuels linked to climate change—oil and coal. Their attacks on established climate science relied on a small number of contrarian researchers, few of whom actually worked in relevant areas, and on the insistence that action could be taken only on the basis of absolute certainty about cause and effect. A plan of "strategies and tactics" for promoting uncertainty was developed by the American Petroleum Institute, an industry trade group, and distributed to lobbyists and apologists. These were the same techniques that had been used for decades to deflect concerns about smoking and cancer and to shield the tobacco industry from litigation and regulation.

Although some oil companies—most notably BP plc, formerly known as British Petroleum—eventually dropped their support for climate-change skeptics and switched sides in the debate, doubt about the science became an article of faith, if not fact, among many political conservatives. In the vanguard of this group were people such as Senator James Inhofe of Oklahoma, who called concern about climate change "the greatest hoax ever perpetrated" and said he wasn't worried about the issue because "God is still up there, and He promised to maintain the seasons and that cold and heat would never cease as long as the earth remains."

By the time of the 2008 presidential campaign, the Gallup poll reported a 50 percent increase in skepticism about the human causes of climate change. This doubt, based on no credible science, was nevertheless required of anyone who would seek the votes of far-Right-wing conservatives, who considered it essential to their identity. Climate-change denial was so important to the Right that the GOP's nominee, John McCain, chose a confirmed skeptic to join him on the ticket. McCain, who had previously acknowledged the cause and seriousness of the problem, found in Sarah Palin a partner who declared, "I'm not one though who would attribute it to being man-made." Palin spoke as the governor of Alaska, a state that was both dependant on oil fields for revenue and more threatened than all others by rising temperatures. Melting permafrost, retreating sea ice, and a spike in forest fires all pointed to the effects of climate change on her state. The island community of Kivalina faced total destruction from rising waters. Palin had started planning to protect citizens, but would not support a reduction in emissions of greenhouse gases. She also opposed efforts to protect her state's polar bears and beluga whales because regulations intended to help them could interfere with drilling for oil and gas.

That McCain needed Palin on the ticket was evidence of how far the party had moved on climate change. In 1997, 52 percent of Democrats and 48 percent of GOPers told pollsters that the effects were already evident. McCain was so concerned about a warming

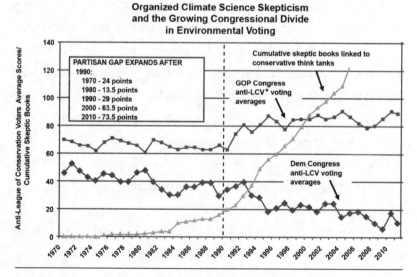

Courtesy Theda Skocpol, Harvard University

*LCV=League of Conservation Voters

earth that he advanced legislation to cap carbon pollution and allow companies that obtained permits for emissions to trade them on an open market. Cap and trade, as the policy was known, would empower the government to set an overall limit on carbon but let the free market determine how the country would meet the goal. It was conservation with the least government intervention.

No one could deny that cap and trade was a Republican policy idea. It had been used by the Reagan administration to phase out lead in gasoline, which was known to cause intellectual disabilities and other health problems in children. Cap and trade was also employed by the first president Bush, who had said he wanted to be the "environmental president," to reduce the sulfur dioxide emissions that caused acid rain. However, by 2008, despite mounting evidence of a climate crisis, the GOP was abandoning its concern about climate change. Only 42 percent of Republicans polled said they thought global warming had begun, compared with 75 percent of Democrats. In Congress the gap was even wider, with 80 percent of Republicans in the skeptics' corner and just a handful of Democrats expressing doubt about the science.

This change was consistent with the increasing partisanship in politics, but also reflected the success of the concerted effort to persuade the public that the science was not settled. Frank Luntz, a political consultant, laid out this strategy in a memo that encouraged this approach because "the scientific debate is closing [against us] but not yet closed." Luntz recommended a campaign to persuade with narratives instead of data, writing, "A compelling story, even if factually inaccurate, can be more emotionally compelling than a dry recitation of the truth."

The "story" was told in a spate of books that offered little data but a strong political critique.

Emotion worked so well that cap and trade, once a mainstay for GOP leaders who favored free markets, became a liability for Republicans seeking campaign donations and party support. As it had during the health care debate, the GOP would repudiate ideas it once originated, in its drive to deprive Obama of an achievement.

With the economy crashing, environmental policy had not been a lynchpin issue for voters in 2008. After Obama swamped McCain at the polls, the Pew Research Center reported that in addition to the economy, voters cared more about the war in Iraq, the threat of terrorism, health care, and energy. However, the president-elect kept the problem of climate change at the top of his agenda. Just days after the election he recorded a speech that was played at an international conference convened in Los Angeles by California governor Arnold Schwarzenegger. Obama promised new leadership from Washington "that will start with a federal cap-and-trade system. We will establish strong annual targets that set us on a course to reduce emissions to their 1990 levels by 2020 and reduce them an additional eighty percent by 2050. . . . Delay is no longer an option. Denial is no longer an acceptable response."

Obama's predecessor, George W. Bush, had acknowledged the problem of climate change as a candidate and even pledged to reduce carbon emissions. However, he abandoned this promise shortly after taking office and also withdrew from the so-called Kyoto Protocol because he thought it "would affect our economy in a negative way." In 2004, the same NASA scientist who had sounded the alarm about global warming in the Reagan years, James Hansen, accused the administration of trying to block publication of data that showed that climate change was accelerating. Before his time in office ended, Bush would also reduce protections for animals covered under the federal Endangered Species Act and move to weaken long-standing regulations on air and water quality. He did this through executive rule-making authority, a practice employed by every president since Jimmy Carter. In Bush's case, the "midnight regulations" would be better described as "deregulations," and many amounted to favors for specific industries and even individual corporations.

In the beginning of his presidency, Barack Obama pursued his priorities for the environment mainly through his green energy initiatives. By funding development of electric and hybrid vehicles, he built a partnership with auto companies and eventually won their support for substantial increases in fuel economy. However, he wasn't able to get congressional approval for legislation to reduce carbon pollution. This failure came into sharp relief at the end of his first year in office when Obama traveled to Copenhagen to attend a summit on climate change that produced no real progress toward lowering world carbon output. (The top "achievement" of the summit was an agreement to keep on working for a meaningful carbon-reduction treaty.) This lost opportunity seemed all the worse to the green wing of the Democratic Party when compared with the president's success in other areas.

In 2010, climate scientists determined that the earth's temperature had been the hottest on record that year. Nine of the ten hottest years had occurred since 1998, and extreme weather events—floods, droughts, heat waves, cold snaps—had also increased. Many of these anomalies were traced to the melting of polar ice, which had historically moderated climate. The implications of these events were not lost on those who stood to pay the price of lost property and revenues. Insurance companies began considering climate change in their estimates of future claims from policyholders, and governments made contingency plans for the effects of rising sea levels. At the Pentagon, planners added the effects of climate change to their studies of national security risks and future conflicts. Drought was already a factor in the conflict in Sudan, where deserts were expanding, and water supply was becoming a strategic concern across the Middle East.

The facts of climate change were so well established and

Obama's struggle to address the problem directly was so halting that Al Gore published a long essay asserting, "What we are doing is functionally insane." Gore acknowledged the challenge Obama faced was "a ferocious, well-financed and dishonest" opposition to any effort to reduce greenhouse gases. Nevertheless, "President Obama has never presented to the American people the magnitude of the crisis," argued Gore. "He has simply not made the case for action." In addition to calling on the president to lead, Gore implored citizens to demand better from politicians, the press, and businesses.

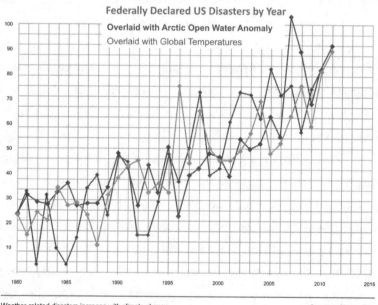

Weather-related disasters increase with climate change　　　　　　　Courtesy Shawn Otto

When considered on a scientific or moral basis, Gore's plea merited immediate action. However, just as the tobacco industry had thwarted antismoking action while thousands died, polluters and their allies had used distortions and leaps of logic to successfully block those who sought to save a baking planet Earth. Blocked by opponents in Congress, Obama gradually let go of the idea that he might make progress on the environment with straightforward legislation. After he won reelection in 2012 and was freed of concerns about ever facing the voters again, he eyed a proposed pipeline for transporting liquefied tar-sands oil from Alberta, Canada, to refineries in Texas. The low-quality petroleum in tar sands would require heating prior to delivery to the proposed pipeline, called Keystone XL, which would cross aquifers responsible for almost one-third of the water used to irrigate US crops. Opponents considered the risk of a spill and the carbon that would be emitted by the use of tar-sands fuel—a 14 percent premium over regular oil—unacceptable.

Canada's participation in the pipeline project made it an international endeavor and added a layer of bureaucratic review of the proposal made by the pipeline company TransCanada. As the State Department worked slowly through this process, energy companies in the Alberta tar-sands business pressed allies in Washington for action. (Among the players in this business were BP, Chevron, ExxonMobil, and Royal Dutch Shell.) Republicans in the House and Senate touted the jobs that would be created by construction of the pipeline, although once it was finished only about fifty workers would be employed in its day-to-day operation.

While the State Department continued its review of the pipeline, the president hinted broadly at his position. Fresh from his reelection he used his State of the Union to announce, "If Congress won't act soon to protect future generations, I will. I will direct my cabinet to come up with executive actions we can take, now and in the future, to reduce pollution, prepare our communities for the consequences of climate change, and speed the transition to more sustainable sources of energy." These lines were little noted at the time, as the press focused more on the president's impassioned plea for action on gun violence. (Much was also said and written about how Florida Republican senator Marco Rubio, who gave his party's official response, nervously gulped water throughout his talk.)

Among the few who noticed that Obama had shifted gears on environmental action was Jonathan Chait of *New York* magazine, who wrote that during the president's first term, greenhouse gas emissions had declined 12 percent. Chait also gave Obama credit for energy initiatives that doubled as environmental protection. Although Chait didn't use the words *midnight regulations,* he described a president who was already using the powers his predecessors had saved for their waning months in office. "The heavy lifting will be, by conventional political terms, invisible," Chait concluded. "There is no need for Johnsonian arm-twisting or Sorkin-esque rhetorical uplift. The fight of Obama's second presidential term— the much-mocked fight to slow the rise of the oceans and heal the planet—requires only the simple exercise of power."

All presidents have exercised power in the way Chait described, and invariably opponents have complained of overreach more worthy of a king or an emperor. Abraham Lincoln's Emancipation Proclamation was an executive order, and so was Harry Truman's directive that integrated the US military. Over the generations administrations had reported executive actions in different ways, labeling some "orders" and others "signing statements," which made comparisons difficult. However, experts who studied the question, such as John Woolley and Gerhard Peters at the University of California at Santa Barbara, found that Obama had issued fewer than any president going back to Grover Cleveland.

In addition to executive action, Obama was free to seek an international strategy on climate change. This option provided him with an opportunity to deal with one of the main criticisms voiced by members of Congress—that industrializing countries such as China and India sought to continue burning cheap dirty fuels while the United States transitioned to lower-carbon energy supplies. As the number one greenhouse gas emitter in the world, China dumped more than 10 billion tons of CO_2 into the atmosphere annually. This was almost twice the amount that the United States, the world's second-biggest polluter, sent aloft. However, on a per capita basis, Americans exceeded the Chinese by a ratio of more than two to one.

If they were to lead in the area of climate change, the two countries would have to overcome their differences, which included a new kind of Cold War being waged mainly in cyberspace. Obama had made an effort to cool the conflict by establishing a closer relationship with China's president, Xi Jinping, who sought a higher profile in global affairs. The leaders found common ground on climate change and set diplomats to work on the problem in April 2013. Within two months they would complete an agreement to sharply reduce the most potent greenhouse gasses—hydrofluorocarbons—and cut carbon dioxide pollution from trucks and buildings.

Obama understood that China's leaders had to balance concern about climate change with the demands a growing middle class made for economic growth, which could be powered by dirty energy. In June 2013 Obama and President Xi met at Sunnylands, an estate in Southern California that had hosted previous presidents for high-level meetings. Except for photos that showed the two men amiably chatting as they strolled the two-hundred-acre estate together, the outside world learned little of what happened at these meetings. (Officials would reveal only that a "new pattern" of world power relations had been discussed.) However, in time Obama's personal touch would be credited with inspiring significant improvements in China's climate change policies.

Later in June 2013, after a record heat wave brought ninety-plus temperatures to Alaska, Obama noted that a pact with China was almost complete, and he tipped his hand on the Keystone XL pipeline. Speaking at Georgetown University, he said he would only permit the pipeline's construction if it "does not significantly exacerbate the problem of carbon pollution. The net effects of the pipeline's impact on our climate will be absolutely critical to determining whether this project is allowed to go forward."

For those environmentalists who had been frustrated in the president's first term and criticized him roundly, the Georgetown speech was a rallying cry. They applauded his call for an end to public financing to help build conventional coal-fired power plants abroad, and he made the problem of climate change a moral imperative: "The question is not whether we need to act. The overwhelming judgment of science—of chemistry and physics and millions of measurements—has put all that to rest. Ninety-seven percent of scientists, including, by the way, some who originally disputed the data, have now put that to rest. They've acknowledged the planet is warming and human activity is contributing to it."

At Georgetown, Obama also announced that the Environmental Protection Agency would soon finalize new standards on carbon dioxide emissions from vehicles and power plants, which produced 40 percent of that pollution from American sources. In 2007 the Supreme Court found that even without specific legislative authority, the Environmental Protection Agency could regulate greenhouse gases, including carbon dioxide, under the Clean Air Act signed by Richard Nixon. Years of subsequent effort to work with Congress failed as representatives from coal states, and others tied to energy interests, blocked progress. When the EPA announced its own rules, court challenges ensued, delaying action even further. As the political battle raged, hundreds of corporations, including the industrial giant GM, had recognized that green policies were good for business—their customers cared about the issue—and joined the call for action on climate change. Like the president, leaders in these companies saw a need to save the planet and an opportunity. "Obviously, we can figure this out," said Obama. "It's not an either/or; it's a both/and. We've got to look after our children; we have to look after our future; and we have to grow the economy and create jobs. We can do all of that as long as we don't fear the future; instead we seize it."

In striving to achieve a solution that was "both/and," the president would consider the State Department's final report on the Keystone XL pipeline. That report found that though Alberta's tar sands were a dirty source of fuel, the pipeline wouldn't have much effect on whether this grade of petroleum was added to the world's carbon burden. Although TransCanada executives saw victory in sight, officials in another branch of government, the EPA, noted that the report was based on oil priced at $75 per barrel, which made tar-sands crude competitive in the marketplace. But with global petroleum values in steady decline, tar sands became less attractive as an energy source with every passing week.

As with the development of the natural gas boom, Obama was aided on Keystone by market forces beyond his control. Due mainly to a glut in supply, oil fell below $75 per barrel in December 2014 and kept dropping. In a year's time the price would pass $50, on its way to $28 in January 2016. Tar sands was so much more difficult and expensive to process into fuel that it was sold at a $20- to $30-per-barrel discount. However, it was still too costly, as American refiners found they could purchase all the high-grade oil they needed at lower cost. Some tar-sands producers cut back their investments in new facilities, other suspended projects, and the case for the new pipeline fell apart.

On November 6, 2015, Obama formally rejected TransCanada's application to build the pipeline, saying it "would not make a meaningful long-term contribution to our economy" and that the oil it would have delivered was not needed to improve the nation's "energy security." In addition to these energy arguments, Obama noted that approving the pipeline would harm the country's position in the world effort to address climate change: "America is now a global leader when it comes to taking serious action to fight climate change. And frankly, approving this project would have undercut that global leadership. And that's the biggest risk we face—not acting."

As he had in other policy areas, Obama had approached the Keystone proposal with patience and sophistication. He balanced a complex mix of related concerns—economic, environmental, diplomatic, political—and worked on many of them simultaneously.

The massive effort made to save the auto industry, which came with increases in mileage standards, made executives at companies such as GM into allies on climate change. Similarly, Obama's outreach to Xi Jinping had produced progress that showed that other nations were willing to help deal with climate change. Finally, by delaying his decision and weathering complaints from his own supporters, Obama bought the time that permitted conditions to change. In the end he didn't have to kill Keystone XL, but, instead, merely presided over its natural death.

Obama's multilevel, long-game leadership style was evident, too, when he unveiled a big environmental initiative called the Clean Power Plan, in August 2015. Appearing in the East Room of the White House, where he was joined by scientists and lawmakers, the president noted that the level of carbon dioxide in the atmosphere was the highest it had been in eight hundred thousand years. Asthma rates in the United States had doubled in thirty years, and so much ice had melted at the north and south poles that maps were being redrawn. Unwilling to wait for Congress, the president announced the first national limits on carbon pollution by power plants, including those long in operation. The rules would reduce CO_2 emissions by 32 percent by the year 2030. States would be given the authority to manage these reductions, and federal money would be paid to those that developed ambitious projects to generate power from nonpolluting sources.

The context for Obama's proposal included news reports of extreme weather issued almost daily, and a papal encyclical issued weeks before that made a moral case for action to address climate change. (In this remarkably technical document, Pope Francis, leader of the world's one billion Catholics, discussed science, economics, and politics as he narrowed the question to a matter of morality.) The European Union had adopted an assertive plan for reducing greenhouse gasses in its twenty-eight member states, and more than a thousand mayors of American cities had signed an agreement to reduce the carbon emitted in their communities.

Environmentalists, such as the leader of the Natural Resources Defense Council, welcomed the Clean Power Plan with the kind of enthusiasm one might show when meeting a long-lost friend. (NRDC president Rhea Suh called it "the greatest national advance ever against the central environmental challenge of our time.") The response from Obama's political opponents, and certain business groups, was just as predictable. The Heartland Institute, which had received substantial funding from ExxonMobil, issued a statement saying that the president's plan "poses a far greater threat than terrorism to America's prosperity." Not to be outdone, Senator Mitch McConnell of Kentucky, who could have been called the senator from the coal industry, termed it an "attack on the middle class" that was "likely illegal."

One would be hard-pressed to find a single example of a modern health, safety, or environmental regulation that was not opposed on the grounds that it was bad for the economy and middle-class people. Industrialists and their political supporters had made similar claims when lead was removed from gasoline in the 1980s, and when power plants were required to cut sulfur dioxide pollution by 80 percent in the 1990s. In both of these cases, and many others, the alarms were false. Nevertheless, McConnell was certain that jobs would be lost and energy prices would rise with little benefit to anyone other than a president who is "concerned with his legacy" and who "prioritizes symbolism over substance."

McConnell's critique, which was published in *The Washington Post,* referenced an upcoming UN conference on climate change where, he seemed to fear, the president might actually achieve something. This sentiment was consistent with his party's hardened skepticism about climate science. In the world's democracies, the GOP was perhaps the only major party that held so firmly to the notion that no real action was required. This conviction had made it impossible for Obama to find common ground with Republicans in Congress and left him no alternative but to use the power of the presidency to confront what amounts to an existential global threat.

As the president prepared to attend the UN climate conference in Paris, McConnell and others in Congress sought to undermine him with legislation to repeal the Clean Power Plan. Since Obama could dispose of these threats with a veto, this was a symbolic effort. Nevertheless, the opposition would make things difficult for American negotiators, who needed to assure other nations that the United States would keep any promises it made in Paris. The goal of the talks was to create an agreement on pollution controls that could be accepted by the countries attending. Much of the work had been done in advance, as individual nations devised strategies to cut greenhouse gases by 2020. However, few would commit to these efforts if they believed that others couldn't be trusted to fulfill their promises. In this way the climate talks were similar to arms control negotiations, where trust was the central concern. The difference was that while arms control talks might involve, perhaps, a dozen parties, the climate conference was attended by thousands of people from 195 nations.

Besides trust, the climate treaty would depend on verification, and here China had recently presented a problem. An official energy audit issued just prior to the summit announced that China had been burning 17 percent more coal than previously reported. (The updated figure took into account smaller industrial facilities that had not previously been monitored.) The news emboldened those who questioned whether climate change could ever be addressed globally and who suspected that some countries would seek the economic advantage of cheating any regime put in place. Those hoping for better out of the summit observed the ecological problems present around the globe, including the air, water, and soil pollution in China, and saw ample reasons for leaders to act. For them the conference provided a kind of cover, in the form of inter-national consensus, for those facing opposition at home.

The report from China confirmed data developed by scientists in the United States who had studied the country's industrial out-put. The one bright element in this picture was evidence that China would reach its coal-burning peak sooner than expected. In fact, the 17 percent increase was based on revised data for 2013, and it ap-peared that China's coal consumption had leveled off or perhaps de-creased slightly since.

A month after the Chinese reported the new coal figures, the government in Beijing pledged to reduce carbon pollution from the country's coal-fired electricity plants by 60 percent by the year 2020. China's cabinet, which issued the promise, timed it to coincide with the climate summit, which maximized their country's role in the negotiations. (China had also been encouraged by US officials, who had capitalized on President Obama's relationship with President Xi.) However, the country's leaders were doubtlessly motivated, too, by the damage done to its citizens by pollution levels that often ex-ceeded safety levels by as much as 1,000 percent.

In Paris, negotiators began with the hope of limiting future planetary warming to two degrees Celsius, which was the limit most scientists endorsed to avoid catastrophe. Among the experts who offered findings at the conference were those who connected cli-mate change to the refugee crisis in the Middle East. The flow of people fleeing fighting in the region had become a torrent, creat-ing a vast humanitarian crisis. Many of the people seeking asylum were coming from Syria, where a water shortage caused by a long drought was one cause of a civil war. "Climate-related displacement is not a future phenomenon," said Marine Franck, of the office of the United Nations High Commissioner for Refugees. "It is a real-ity; it is already a global concern."

As the meeting progressed, representatives from the most

vulnerable nations, including small island countries, made strong arguments for a stricter limit on pollution that would hold the increase in the world's temperature to 1.5 degrees. Every one degree Celsius increase in temperatures was calculated to produce a seven-foot rise in sea levels. Some of these nations were already building seawalls to stave off destruction. However, funds for these efforts were limited and fear was increasing. "Maldives itself has over three thousand years of history," said Ahmed Sareer, the country's representative at the talks. "The location, the culture, the language, the traditions, the history, all this would be wiped off" if a more serious effort wasn't made.

Although scientists and government officials had spent years working on the outlines of a possible agreement, the sessions in Paris were not pro forma. The meetings produced real conflict as poorer countries pushed richer ones to create a larger fund to pay for the poorer countries' efforts to both cut emissions and accommodate climate change. The United States was contributing more than $430 million per year to this effort, and the president offered to double this amount by 2020. Developing countries also argued for rich ones to do far more to reduce global greenhouse gases because they had already reaped the economic benefits of cheap dirty energy. Gradually the pleas from vulnerable countries and the argument over which nations would cut emissions most sharply produced a consensus. Industrialized countries agreed to do more, but poorer ones were also required to stem the flow of greenhouse gases.

The talks that pushed the conference toward a final agreement were led by the Americans and the French, who were determined to see the conference, which they hosted, succeed. Although much of the negotiating was done behind closed doors, the content of these talks was quickly revealed, which created a cycle of rising and falling hopes. Eight years before, when the Bush administration was widely viewed as obstructionist, delegates had actually booed America's chief negotiator. This time, when word of a final deal spread through the main hall, American diplomat Todd Stern was cheered. Stern and Secretary of State John Kerry had pressed developing countries, particularly India, to commit to reductions in their emissions in exchange for aid. Here again Obama's effort at building personal relationships had paid off. He had met frequently with Prime Minister Narendra Modi, and when the Indian leader was named one of the world's most influential people by *Time* magazine, the president published an essay in which he called him "India's reformer in chief." During the climate treaty negotiations Obama telephoned Modi to urge compromise. Eventually the Indians would give up their fight against limits on their use of hydrofluorocarbons, which caused far more damage to the environment, pound per pound, than other pollutants.

In Paris, India had stood first as the chief advocate for the interests of poorer countries, pressing the needs of people who did not yet have access to a modern standard of living that included something as basic as electricity. After making some gains, the Indian delegation signed on to a draft agreement, signaling a host of countries that had been following their lead. When the oil giant Saudi Arabia dropped its opposition, approval was assured. On the night before the final vote the Eiffel Tower was illuminated with the message NO PLAN B. Before the conference, UN secretary general Ban Ki-moon had said of the task before it, "There is no plan B."

The signatories to the agreement pledged to slow the growth of greenhouse emissions and eventually reduce them. Each nation was required to develop a plan to do its part, which would be updated and improved at five-year intervals. More a voluntary framework than a binding treaty, the Paris Agreement took into account that the Republican Party was likely to deny the US president ratification of a binding treaty. This arrangement was considered too weak by advocates such as writer/activist Bill McKibben, who wrote that the same pact "might have worked" had it been approved years earlier. However, even McKibben could see benefits in the document. He wrote, "With every major world leader now on the record saying they at least theoretically support bold action to make the transition to renewable energy, we've got a new tool to work with."

With most of the world's nations agreeing on the central facts of the climate change problem—that fossil fuels were largely to blame and must be curbed—the Paris conference further isolated those who denied the science. Not surprisingly, the loudest sour note sounded in response to the agreement came from the editorial board of *The Wall Street Journal,* which saw trouble in such a broad agreement and no role for government in addressing the problem, if it actually existed. "What will help," said the editors, "is human invention and the entrepreneurial spirit."

Nothing in the climate accord barred inventors and entrepreneurs from developing energy sources and technologies to replace fossil fuels or to make them cleaner. Previous generations of businesspeople had profited from selling catalytic converters for cars and chemical scrubbers for industrial smokestacks. If the rapid decline in solar panel prices that doomed Solyndra proved anything, it was that enterprising people of the sort *The Journal* favored would find ways to wring profit out of changes in policy and technology. *The Journal* editors offered another complaint about the climate deal as they mocked what they called Obama's "familiar modesty" because he had said it "can be a turning point for the world" and is "the best chance we have to save the one planet that we've got." Few scientists expert in the field would have taken issue with the president's tone or his claims. The planet was in danger and the climate treaty signaled the first real response to an imminent threat.

Obama's triumphant tone revealed his delight at having achieved one of the major goals of his presidency. When joined with his energy program and initiatives such as the Clean Power Plan, it proved that when it came to the environment, he was the most successful president since Nixon created the Environmental Protection Agency in 1970. Perhaps more important, the climate agreement gave the world hope, something like the kind of hope that had accompanied Barack Obama's election in 2008. The people of the earth sorely needed this encouragement, especially in light of events that had occurred in the same city of Paris, one month before. On that day, November 13, the world was confronted with the other great international challenge of the day and learned yet another lesson in tragedy.

6

FOREIGN POLICY

Obama's World

On a searingly hot day in July 2015, the temperature reached 105 degrees and the streets of Tehran were all but deserted. Then, at sundown, the evening call to prayer echoed across the city, and people spilled out of homes, shops, and offices and into the streets. Spontaneous celebrations erupted to mark not the breaking of the Ramadan fast, but a nuclear arms agreement with Western powers led by the United States. This breakthrough would establish the high point in Obama's foreign policy efforts, which would move the world to greater stability than it had known since the terror attacks of September 11, 2001.

In Tehran's Vanak Square people cried, "Freedom! Freedom!" A group of girls, blasting loud music from their car, shouted, "It's another revolution! Be happy!" On fashionable Valiasr Street authorities ignored the men and women who appeared in Western-style clothes and danced on the sidewalks in defiance of religious regulations. South of Tehran, in the four-thousand-year-old city of Isfahan, Bahar Ghorbani took to her computer and Facebook, writing, "This is a first step to becoming a friend with the world. I think the biggest achievement of the nuclear deal is the victory of logic and dialogue over war mongering and violence."

Logic and dialogue had prevailed, and Iran had made a step away from pariah status. But Iranians celebrated mainly because the agreement ended sanctions that had crippled many sectors of their country's economy and made everyday life more difficult, more expensive, and less secure. This was no small change. Declining oil production and bans on trade had led to bank panics and spikes in inflation. Increasingly isolated from the world, Iranians were blacklisted from the global banking system, which made even the purchase of approved items, such as medicines, difficult. In a few documented cases sick people had died from lack of medicines. Many more, including tens of thousands of hemophiliacs, suffered long waits for access to care. Everyday life was constrained by shortages and price gouging that allowed a black market to flourish.

The first sanctions had been imposed by the West in the wake of the 1979 Iranian Revolution and the seizure of the US embassy in Tehran. Lifted briefly when American hostages were released in 1981, the sanctions had been reimposed and strengthened through five American presidencies. Iran's support for Islamic terrorists and its pursuit of nuclear weapons had prompted the most severe international response. Imposed by the United States, the United Nations, and the European Union, these bans on trade cut Iranian oil exports by two-thirds and caused Iran's economy to contract. Although political opponents depicted him as weak on the matter, President Obama had strengthened enforcement of the various embargoes. Banks and petroleum refiners, who were shipping gas into the country, came under greater pressure to reduce their dealings with Iranian entities.

Iran's nuclear history began when it was a US ally and America aided the development of a research reactor. Efforts to build a nuclear electric power plant were begun by a West German company in 1975, halted by an Israeli air strike and other events, and then resumed in 1995 by a Russian firm. When it went online in 2011, it was the first nuclear power plant in the Middle East. A concurrent weapons program, at first aided by Pakistan, proceeded in secrecy. In 2002 documents leaked by a dissident group confirmed the effort. It was scaled back under criticism from the Bush administration, but not halted. By the time Bush left office, Iran maintained thousands of centrifuges to produce weapons-grade uranium and had built a complex of facilities to create and support a nuclear arsenal. In the first month of the Obama presidency UN officials confirmed that Iran had continued to work on weapons small enough to fit on a missile warhead.

A nuclear-armed Iran represented a much greater threat than the other rogue nuclear state, North Korea, which had conducted a successful bomb test in 2006. One of the poorest countries in the world, North Korea was grossly underdeveloped and more politically isolated. Iran, in contrast, occupied a strategic location in the Middle East, fielded a competent conventional military, and possessed both an educated workforce and valuable natural resources that could support a conflict. These elements made Iran's nuclear ambitions rival terrorism as the world's leading security concern as Obama took office.

More than a year before he was elected president, Obama had announced his intention to reverse Bush-era policy and talk with the Iranians. He said he would not set preconditions for talks at the highest level and said that Iran could be rewarded with certain economic benefits for "good behavior."

This approach reflected Obama's preference for practical problem-solving, which he described as hitting "singles" or "doubles." Although such deliberateness might disappoint those who expected sweeping achievements to match his rhetoric, it was consistent with the man's personality and cast of mind. His approach also called for recognizing the complexity and interrelatedness of various policy objectives. As George W. Bush's disastrous invasion of Iraq demonstrated, it was easy for a superpower to stumble into a quagmire. Hence the president's oft-quoted admonition, "Don't do stupid shit." However, those who belittled this theme didn't consider the other element of the Obama approach, which called for acting in ways that would yield greater advances by considering how seemingly disconnected policies—on the environment, the economy, foreign affairs—could be developed in concert.

Soon after he was elected president, Obama sent US diplomats to European-led negotiations with Iran. He also made a New Year's Day video greeting to the Iranian people and, more important, their government, which was posted with a Farsi translation. The message included a quote from the Persian poet Saadi—"The children of Adam are limbs to each other, having been created of one essence"—and a personal plea:

"In this season of new beginnings, I would like to speak clearly to Iran's leaders. My administration is now committed to diplomacy that addresses the full range of issues before us, and to pursuing constructive ties among the United States, Iran, and the international community. This process will not be advanced by threats. . . . The United States wants the Islamic Republic of Iran to take its rightful place in the community of nations."

The president's overture made the bellicose words about American intentions by Iranian hard-liners, whose policies had brought their citizens both hardship and isolation, less useful than ever. Obama was the first president to acknowledge that Iran was, by its lights, an "Islamic republic," and even his name, Barack Hussein Obama, signaled to the world that he was a different kind of American leader. The president put more pressure on Iranian leaders when he revealed the existence of an underground uranium enrichment plant near the city of Qom in September 2009. Under pressure from Israeli allies, who possessed their own atomic weapons but saw in Iran an existential threat, American officials also began to discuss the possibility of military action to halt Iranian progress toward a bomb.

In the complex dance of diplomacy, the Israelis expressed true concerns but also played the convenient role of an insistent ally pressuring the United States to take ever-tougher stands. Domestically the president's Republican critics served a similar purpose, as their attacks on Obama's approach also suggested that Iran would never find a better bargaining partner. In 2007, Senator John McCain was recorded singing a Beach Boys' parody called "Bomb, Bomb Iran." His singing was televised and caused a minor uproar. In 2012, GOP nominee Mitt Romney repeatedly called on Obama to be harder on the Iranians. Romney was aided in his effort to undermine Obama by Israeli prime minister Benjamin Netanyahu, who criticized the administration even after he was given a guarantee that the United States would intervene militarily to stop Iran from developing a nuclear weapon.

On the Iranian side, America was confronted with a leader, President Mahmoud Ahmadinejad, whose regime supported terrorist groups, tortured dissidents, and curtailed human rights. However, Ahmadinejad was not a singular leader. He ceded certain authority to the country's supreme religious leader, Ayatollah Ali Khamenei. The ayatollah wielded control over nuclear policy in particular and had even issued an order forbidding an Iranian nuclear weapons program. In a realm filled with danger and intrigue, any effort to determine realities on the ground was futile without independent verification. The United Nations had attempted to accomplish this through International Atomic Energy Agency (IAEA) inspection, but their effort, conducted in stop-start fashion beginning in 2002, had been largely unsuccessful.

A chance to end the impasse seemed at hand as Ahmadinejad's time in office neared its end and Iran prepared to elect a new president. About a year prior to the election, when a moderate named Hassan Rouhani seemed to be gaining popularity, Obama opened secret diplomatic talks with Tehran. (This was done at the suggestion of an Omani sultan.) Few Iranians possessed a better background to deal with the United States than Rouhani. Exiled during the shah's reign, he had returned after the Iranian Revolution to serve as a religious, military, and political leader. In the 1990s he earned postgraduate degrees in law at Glasgow Caledonian University. Prior to Ahmadinejad's election, Rouhani had been his country's principal negotiator in the nuclear talks. He won the 2013 election with three times the number of votes as his nearest rival, sweeping to victory with promises to restore Iran's relationship with the West and begin an era of "rationality and moderation . . . peace, stability, and hope."

Again acting on a personal basis, Obama wrote to Rouhani as he assumed his office, telling him the United States was ready to resolve the nuclear issue in a way that would let Iran show the world that its scientific and technological intentions were peaceful. Obama expressed urgency about the need to reach an agreement, noting that the chance for a breakthrough would not last indefinitely. After hearing back from the Iranian leader, Obama told an interviewer that he was under the impression that "there is the potential for resolving these issues diplomatically." He added that with a "credible threat of force" and a "rigorous diplomatic effort," the chances for a deal were good.

In Rouhani and Obama the world could recognize leaders who might reduce the nuclear threat and ease the sanctions that caused so much pain in Iran. Iranians sought, in addition to an end to their isolation, a level of respect, which meant they wanted to be trusted to keep some of their nuclear facilities. (The Bush administration had insisted that every centrifuge be dismantled.) The United States sought to protect Israel, nearby Arab states, and the wider world from an Iran with nuclear capabilities. Like their Iranian counterparts, American officials also saw some benefit to a normalization of Iran's status in the community of nations. As a major Muslim power, Iran held sway with parties America could seek to influence.

Decades earlier, the idea of Iran/American cooperation might have been unthinkable. However, conditions had changed. Both countries were led by men who seemed willing and able to break from the past. Second, America's painful experiences in Iraq and

Afghanistan—both could be called quagmires—had shown the limits of military power. In Iran, a 1980s war with Iraq left an estimated 1 million dead and had produced a population that was so young that most people had not been alive during the revolution. The United States had backed Iraq during the war, and the younger generation had heard America described as the "Great Satan" but did not know, firsthand, the moments of conflict. A 2009 poll found that 77 percent of Iranians favored normalization of relations. America was viewed as a potential ally, and the idea of international inspections of nuclear facilities, in exchange for economic benefits, was acceptable to 70 percent.

The two sides' secret negotiations led first to an agreement that halted Iran's development of new nuclear facilities and began the diluting of materials that had been refined to near-weapons-grade quality. The Iranians got to keep intact the major buildings and certain pieces of equipment, to demonstrate they hadn't sacrificed too much. Held mainly in Lausanne, Switzerland, the intense negotiations featured two key players, American secretary of energy Ernest Moniz and Iran's top atomic energy official, Ali Akbar Salehi. Physicists who had been at the Massachusetts Institute of Technology at the same time, the two men seemed well suited to lead the talks. (Moniz enjoyed the confidence of a president who had promised to "restore science to its rightful place" and felt comfortable with high-level experts.)

As the talks neared their end, the parties moved to the Palais Coburg hotel in Vienna and higher-level officials, including US secretary of state John Kerry and Iranian foreign minister Mohammad Javad Zarif, joined the delegations. The effort produced a document that required the Iranians to give up two-thirds of their eighteen thousand ordinary centrifuges and every one of the more than one thousand machines that were essential to making plutonium. Iran would be forced to give up its stores of dangerous, moderately enriched uranium and reduce its stockpile of low-enriched uranium by nearly 95 percent. Other elements of the agreement hobbled the Iranians' ability to violate the deal and convert facilities to military uses. A "snap back" provision allowed for a return to sanctions in the event of such violations, and the IAEA would conduct full and continuous inspections to certify compliance with the deal. Economic and diplomatic sanctions imposed on Iran for its dealings with terror groups and its development of conventional weapons were left in place.

The lifting of economic embargoes and sanctions would open vast markets for Iranian oil and give Iran access to both consumer and industrial goods that it sorely needed. Normalized trade would ease shortages, shutter black markets, and, most likely, help alleviate inflation, unemployment, and underinvestment. Many foreign companies were prepared to start buying and selling with Iranian interests, and Iranians were eager to access both Western products and culture. Finally, but perhaps most important, Iran would be able to tap as much as $100 billion in cash and other assets that had been "frozen" abroad when sanctions were imposed. Iran could also look forward to an improved status in the international community. Long an influential power, Iran could better advance its own interests and perhaps help stabilize the region if it enjoyed better relations with the United States and the other powers included in the treaty—France, the United Kingdom, Russia, China, Germany, and the European Union.

Reaction to the agreement ranged from the street celebrations in Iran to condemnations from Israeli prime minister Benjamin Netanyahu and some corners of the American Jewish community and a host of Barack Obama's political opponents. (Conservative elements in Iran were also unhappy about it.) Months before the agreement was completed, Netanyahu had taken the extraordinary step of speaking against it in an address to a joint session of Congress. In a breach of protocol the speech had been scheduled by GOP leaders in Congress who did not notify the White House of their plans. Although the negotiations were months from completion, Netanyahu nevertheless declared, "This is a bad deal. It's a very bad deal. We're better off without it."

Aimed not just at Congress but at voters in Israel, where he faced an election in two weeks, Netanyahu's talk represented a low point in US-Israeli relations, which had been strained for some years. The problem resulted in part from poor chemistry, as *The Washington Post* observed before the prime minister's speech. Netanyahu had hoped for John McCain to beat Obama in 2008 and had enjoyed a long-standing friendship with the 2012 Republican presidential nominee, Romney. Although US/Israeli security cooperation reached an all-time high under Obama, he had also expressed concern for the conditions in the Palestinian territories. He also said that he could be supportive of Israel without supporting all of the policies of Netanyahu's Likud Party. These positions, and Obama's strong interest in freezing the construction of Jewish settlements in the West Bank, got the two men's relationship off to a bad start. The Israeli leader and his aides openly criticized the administration. Netanyahu cultivated relationships with congressional Republicans and, when candidate Romney visited Israel in 2012, listened to him speak about Iran and declared, "I couldn't agree with you more, Mitt."

When he addressed Congress, Netanyahu drew enthusiastic applause from Obama's congressional opponents and praise from supporters back home. However, it was widely criticized as a diplomatic blunder. One powerful pro-Israeli lobby, which also opposed the Iran deal, declared it harmful to the cause of defeating it. Domestic criticism of the deal ranged from the thoughtful to the hysterical. On the hysterical side, former member of Congress Michelle Bachman compared the president to a Germanwings airline pilot who had purposely crashed a passenger jet, killing 150 people. Presidential candidate and US senator Ted Cruz said, "Any commander in chief worthy of defending this nation should be prepared to stand up on January twentieth, 2017, and rip to shreds this catastrophic deal." On the more considered side, Republican senator Bob Corker of Tennessee said he feared the Americans had pursued a muddled strategy while Iran had achieved an agreement that will "boost and strengthen" its power. Corker also suggested that the agreement might somehow benefit Syrian strongman Bashar al-Assad, whom Iran supported against various factions waging war against his regime.

US public opinion on the agreement was somewhat favorable when it was announced, with one poll finding 47 percent approval and 43 percent opposition. As with so many issues in the age of hyperpartisanship, a finer analysis of the numbers revealed that opinion on the agreement closely matched respondents' views on the president.

Although many in Congress pledged to undo the agreement, a previously established framework gave the US Senate just sixty days to complete its review of the pact and vote on it. Republicans who led the opposition to the pact were unable to muster the votes to kill it. Soon both sides would make moves to implement the deal. Iran so quickly dismantled nuclear facilities that in January 2016 the sanctions were lifted and benefits began to flow. Critics in Congress, and on the political trail, continued to say they intended to reverse the arrangement, but this was a practical impossibility. Besides, as implementation progressed, many skeptics came to recognize the agreement's value.

Writing in *Foreign Policy,* Stephen Walt of Harvard University said that his previous fear that Obama would accomplish little in his second term had proved unfounded. As Walt saw it, as long as the United States refused to talk, Iran could continue to build more nuclear capabilities and muddle along under the burden of the sanctions. This is precisely what had happened during the Bush years, when the centrifuge count went from to zero to five thousand, and in the pre-agreement Obama years, when the number expanded again to almost nineteen thousand. The United States "had come to its senses" when it opened earnest discussions, and the result, Walt wrote, had been an agreement that brought a reversal of developments that had gone on for fifteen years.

After the agreement survived reviews in Washington and Tehran, the Iranians released five Americans, including a journalist and a student, who were being kept in detention. In trade the president either pardoned or commuted the sentences of one Iranian and six people with dual Iranian and American citizenship who were being held in the United States. The two countries also cooperated to avert a military crisis when two US patrol boats with engine trouble drifted into Iranian waters in the Persian Gulf. The sailors on the boats were taken into custody by Iranian forces but were released within twenty-four hours. The quick resolution of the wayward-boat incident demonstrated an unexpected benefit from the Iran nuclear deal. (Prior to the agreement the two nations were less likely to cooperate on such matters.) Some observers held out hope that it would also shift the dynamic in the effort to stop the terrorist group called ISIS (Islamic State of Iraq and Syria), which had seized great swaths of territory and conducted or inspired international terror attacks.

Iran was opposed to ISIS and in December 2015 agreed to join the fight against it with Iraq, its ally Syria, and Russia. Given American concerns about ISIS, which grew out of the failed American war in Iraq, Iran's decision was a positive development. President Obama was eager for Muslim-majority states to do the fighting. By the end of December 2015 the Iraqis would drive ISIS out of the city of Ramadi, which was a major victory. However, progress against ISIS did nothing to resolve the problem of Syria's al-Assad, who continued to wage a brutal war against not just ISIS but also Syrians who had taken up arms against him. Syria, where Obama had not acted when he said he would, represented his biggest foreign policy failure. Years of fighting there had permitted ISIS to establish a base for international terrorism and had produced a humanitarian disaster that included more than 250,000 dead, including roughly 70,000 civilians.

The chaos in Syria also contributed immensely to the tidal wave of refugees that carried more than 1 million people into Europe in 2015. As Europe and the United States struggled to deal with the crisis, ISIS and ISIS–inspired terror attacks in Paris, Nice, Orlando, Florida, and San Bernardino, California, illustrated in horrific fashion the interconnectedness of terrorism, foreign policy, and domestic affairs. ISIS had been born out of the debacle of the Iraq War, which had been fought on the false premise that Iraq had aided the terror group al-Qaeda's September 11, 2001, attacks on America. ISIS had surpassed al-Qaeda as it seized territory throughout Iraq and Syria. It has also terrorized Western populations with attacks that seemed more brutal and difficult to prevent.

As a senator, Obama had opposed the invasion of Iraq and then struggled as president to end the wars there and in Afghanistan. Nevertheless, thousands of troops remained in both countries, and Obama had failed to reach the related objective of closing down the American prison for terror suspects in Guantánamo Bay, Cuba. He had also been the commander in chief who gave the go-ahead to the mission that resulted in al-Qaeda leader Osama bin Laden's death. These developments animated Muslims who considered America an enemy of Islam and proved the limits of any American leader seeking to navigate relations with the Muslim world. However, they did not prove the failure of the Obama administration's foreign policy or security efforts. Among his security initiatives, *besides* the dramatic killing of bin Laden, Obama could count:

- The killing of at least seven possible successors to bin Laden.
- End of ground combat operations in Iraq, which had

resulted in the deaths of nearly forty-five hundred American personnel.

- End of formal fighting in Afghanistan, which had claimed more than twenty-two hundred American lives.
- Destruction of thirteen hundred tons of Syrian chemical weapons, keeping them out of terrorist hands.
- Held American deaths due to Islamic terror attacks to an average of six per year (equal to the number killed by homegrown Right-wing extremists).
- Thousands of lethal drone strikes against terror suspects around the world.
- More than ten thousand air strikes flown against ISIS by US and allied jets between August 2014 and January 2016.
- With American airpower and advisers, local fighters took back great swathes of territory held by ISIS in Iraq.

Critics on the Right would try to paint Obama as weak, complaining that he was too reluctant to talk about the religious aspects of terror attacks carried out by Muslims and insisting, despite the record of drone strikes and killings, that the president was taking a passive approach to security. These critics were also dissatisfied with Obama's response to Russia's seizure of territory in Ukraine, which included minor economic sanctions and a buildup of forces in the region but no direct military intervention.

Obama also failed to please many on the Left, for whom the troops that remained in Iraq and Afghanistan, and Obama's inability to close Guantánamo, proved the president was an abject failure. Finally, people who value privacy rights were alarmed by the revelations of domestic and international surveillance by whistleblower Edward Snowden, who made public documents showing that the government was monitoring the electronic communications of many millions of people. The vast majority had nothing to do with security threats.

Altogether, the Obama record suggested to his critics a president who either failed to deviate enough from his predecessor when it came to foreign affairs or strayed too far. In reality, Obama followed a hard-line approach to security, especially antiterrorism efforts, combined with a realistic and flexible foreign policy that restored international respect for the United States and opened new avenues to cooperation and peace.

One key factor in America's improving reputation was the president's refusal to conflate Islam and terrorism. Although political figures such as human rights activist Ayaan Hirsi Ali wanted the president to say that the Muslim religion was particularly prone to terrorism, Obama would not. This disagreement between the president and critics such as Ali grew more heated over time, but the White House didn't change its approach, which permitted ongoing contacts with foreign leaders who considered the Islam-equals-terror argument an insult. This practice had been followed by Obama's predecessor, who was not widely criticized for separating terror activities and Islam. It was George W. Bush who said, "Our enemy doesn't follow the great traditions of Islam. They've hijacked a great religion."

Bush added to his Iraq debacles a series of unilateral decisions that alienated even close allies. Among them were rejecting a global response to climate change, abandoning the International Criminal Court, torture of terrorism suspects, and failing to engage the Muslim world. These actions and failures reflected Bush's superconfident, faith-based view of the world, which permitted him to act, as he said, based on "my instincts" and left no room for doubt or recalibration. This mind-set was famously described to journalist Ron Suskind by an administration official who expressed it succinctly in response to one of the writer's questions. Susskind wrote:

The aide said that guys like me were in what we call "the reality-based community," which he defined as people who "believe that solutions emerge from your judicious study of discernible reality." I nodded and murmured something about enlightenment principles and empiricism. He cut me off. "That's not the way the world really works anymore," he continued. "We're an empire now, and when we act, we create our own reality. And while you're studying that reality—judiciously, as you will—we'll act again, creating other new realities, which you can study too, and that's how things will sort out. We're history's actors . . . and you, all of you, will be left to just study what we do."

The errors perpetrated by Bush administration officials as history's faith-based actors could be measured in vast amounts of blood and treasure and would occupy historians for generations to come. The effects could be seen in polls that showed a decline in esteem for the United States, even among allies in Western Europe, and

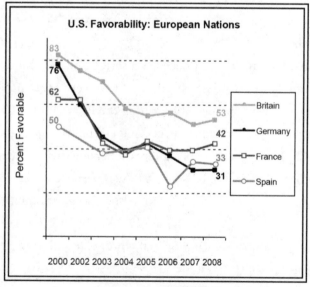

Courtesy Pew Research Center

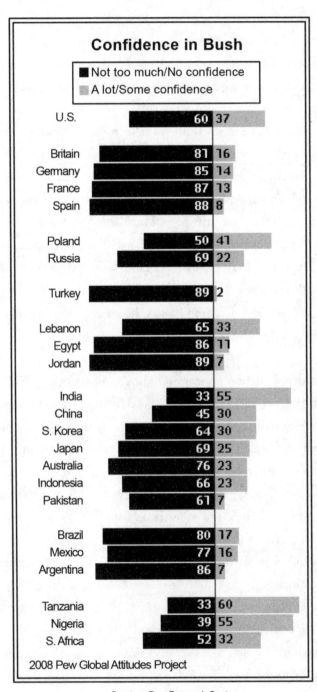

Confidence in Bush

- ■ Not too much/No confidence
- ■ A lot/Some confidence

Country	Not too much/No confidence	A lot/Some confidence
U.S.	60	37
Britain	81	16
Germany	85	14
France	87	13
Spain	88	8
Poland	50	41
Russia	69	22
Turkey	89	2
Lebanon	65	33
Egypt	86	11
Jordan	89	7
India	33	55
China	45	30
S. Korea	64	30
Japan	69	25
Australia	76	23
Indonesia	66	23
Pakistan	61	7
Brazil	80	17
Mexico	77	16
Argentina	86	7
Tanzania	33	60
Nigeria	39	55
S. Africa	52	32

2008 Pew Global Attitudes Project

Courtesy Pew Research Center

such a loss of confidence in Bush that by the end of his presidency a Pew survey of twenty-three nations found he enjoyed majority support in only India, Nigeria, and Tanzania.

Obama's intention, as he contemplated turning the ship of state, would be to make adjustments in ways that would not be so disruptive that they created uncertainty or unforeseen problems. His American constituents would want to be reassured on terrorism, trade, and their country's preeminence in world affairs. However, all presidents also serve a global constituency that includes world leaders and ordinary citizens who expect the United States to serve as a bulwark of economic and geopolitical stability. His global constituents generally hoped for a more inclusive, intelligent, and nuanced style of leadership. Even before he became his party's nominee, Obama expressed toughness on matters of security, and in his one major address abroad as candidate Obama, he struck the tone that his audience, weary of Bush, hoped to hear.

On a golden Thursday afternoon in July 2008, people began streaming into Berlin's Tiergarten park and claiming places in view of the massive Siegessäule, or Victory Column, which was completed in 1873 and looms 220 feet over the grass, trees, and gardens. It was a predominately young crowd—tattooed, pierced, and peaceful— which came bearing guitars and picnic food and turned the blocked-off Strasse des 17. Juni into a festival ground.

As the crowd grew to two hundred thousand strong, Barack Obama had been jetting to Berlin from meetings in both Israel and the Palestinian city of Ramallah. (He also spent time with Benjamin Netanyahu, who was, at the time, not prime minister but Likud Party leader.) A long and packed schedule had left Obama so exhausted that he had told Netanyahu he could fall asleep standing up. On the flight from Tel Aviv he had tried to tamp down expectations, telling reporters that he doubted he would be greeted by "a million screaming Germans." Such was the rock star quality of

Obama's popularity that in less than a year he had gone from an unknown figure on the world stage to a headliner whose biggest problem was the widely held belief that he could draw larger crowds than the Rolling Stones.

When he finally appeared in Berlin, he glided across a pathway carpeted in blue to stand behind a podium that looked out on the crowd where many people wore OBAMA TSUNAMI T-shirts and stood with fellow members of local Obama Clubs that had formed across Germany. The weary Obama's performance was not one of his best. He started slowly, and somewhat quietly, but with a humility that was pitch-perfect for those seeking an anti-Bush. "Tonight, I speak to you not as a candidate for president, but as a citizen—a proud citizen of the United States, and a fellow citizen of the world."

Much of what Obama offered in Berlin would have been considered boilerplate in the United States, but it was fresh to his German audience. He spoke of a great-grandfather who had herded goats in Africa, a black father who split time between the United States and Kenya, and a white mother who shouldered much of the burden of raising him alone. This story affirmed Obama's status as a different kind of American leader and an internationalist who was not limited by the isolationism and exceptionalism that make it difficult for some of his countrymen to appreciate the concerns of people who live elsewhere. He evoked the loudest cheers after he listed a series of problems—the drug trade, terrorism, poverty—and then declared, "No one nation, no matter how large or how powerful, can defeat such challenges alone."

As he spoke of alliances and the burdens of "global citizenship," Obama delivered a nuanced view that included a confession, "I love America," and the admission "I know my country has not perfected itself." He added, "At times, we've struggled to keep the promise of liberty and equality for all of our people. We've made our share of mistakes, and there are times when our actions around the world have not lived up to our best intentions." These words, reflective of Obama's personal experience and education, acknowledged the reasonable doubts his listeners may have harbored about the United States and reassured them that they were hearing from a realist who, while fully American, was capable of considering the concerns of other nations.

Although Obama's break with Bush pleased his listeners, they were more excited by the up-tempo heart of the speech when he used the refrain "this is the moment" eight different times to call for action against terrorism, for peace in the Middle East, and to "save this planet" from climate change. The audience cheered as he encouraged the embrace of the vast majority of Muslims who reject the extremism that leads to hate instead of hope. "People of Berlin—people of the world—this is our moment," he said. "This is our time."

Months later, the world seemed to swoon over Obama's election, recognizing something remarkable in the country's choice of its first black president, and one whose name was not typically American. For those who idealized America as a land of immigration and equal rights, his election amounted to a restoration of faith. "Un rêve d'Amérique"—a dream of America—declared *Libération* of Paris, where French president Nicolas Sarkozy wrote a letter that said, "Your election raises in France, in Europe, and beyond throughout the world immense hope." One politician in Tehran told *The New York Times,* "People around the world look at this development with respect." A clerk at the Arab news service Al Arabiya admitted he was hoping Obama would win election "with ninety-nine percent, like Saddam Hussein." When Obama won, the clerk said, "I am positively surprised. It's great."

Obama encouraged the world's hope in his victory speech at Grant Park in Chicago, where he said, "To all those watching from beyond our shores, our stories are singular, but our destiny is shared, and a new dawn of American leadership is at hand." In his first inaugural address Obama addressed the world's Muslims, promising "a new way forward, based on mutual interest and mutual respect." After the inauguration he granted his first interview, as president, to the Al Arabiya network. He may have disappointed some viewers when he said that Israel's security was his "paramount" concern, but he surely pleased them when he said, "What we will offer to the Muslim world is a hand of friendship."

Born of a Muslim father who became an atheist and clearly not from the place of privilege and Christian piety occupied by George Bush, Obama presented a challenge to anyone who held a limited view of what it meant to be an American leader. This was especially true in the Muslim world, where America had recently struggled to find friends and successes. After he took office, Obama put two Muslim countries, Iraq and Turkey, on the itinerary for his first major trip abroad. (He had previously visited only Canada, for a day.) In Turkey he made his first formal speech in a foreign country, pledging, "The United States is not, and will never be, at war with Islam." He said that US relations with the Muslim world would be based not just on opposition to terrorism, but on "broader engagement based on mutual interest and mutual respect."

Obama's words and deeds reflected his commitment to combining diplomacy and security strategies to blunt Islamist terror groups and promote America's interests in Muslim-majority countries. This effort reached an apex in June 2009, when Obama spoke to three thousand people who had been carefully screened to enter the domed Great Hall at Cairo University and a global audience watching on television and listening by radio. Obama began with the Arabic greeting *as-salaam alaikum,* which means "peace be upon you" and is typically used at the start of sermons or speeches. He then devoted nearly an hour to the task of extending his hand to Muslims and showing himself to possess a different cast of mind from any previous president. He recited a history of "civilization's debt to Islam" and acknowledged the colonialism and interferences practiced by the West in the Middle East and Africa. He also personalized his talk, describing his childhood years in Muslim-majority Indonesia and recalling the Muslims in his father's family.

Although he offered respect at every turn and spoke of an "occupation" of Palestinian territory, Obama did not pander or talk down to his listeners. He also refused to abandon Israel. Instead he defended Israel's right to its homeland, condemned Muslim anti-Semitism, and called the denial of the Holocaust "ignorant" and "hateful." Obama also used the example of the American civil rights movement to urge peaceful and nonviolent tactics upon Hamas as it sought fuller independence and self-determination for Palestinians in Gaza and the West Bank. Titled "A New Beginning," the speech offered no novel policy prescriptions or promises, but it set a tone that was radically new. The feeling created as Obama spoke was the message he sought to communicate. When he finished, the crowd in the Great Hall offered him a standing ovation and scattered chants of "O-bama, O-bama."

The Al Arabiya interview, the visit to Turkey, and the University of Cairo speech, which all came in the first five months of his presidency, extended to the Muslim world the message of hope Obama had delivered in his election campaign. It also inspired such optimism that the Norwegian Nobel Committee decided to give him its 2009 Peace Prize in recognition of "his extraordinary efforts to strengthen international diplomacy and cooperation between peoples." The honor, perhaps the greatest in all the world, had previously gone to such figures as Albert Schweitzer, Martin Luther King Jr., Anwar Sadat, and Menachem Begin. The choice of Obama, who hadn't achieved a single substantive foreign policy goal, was unexpected and could be interpreted as a reaction to the Bush administration's eight-year record. The official announcement noted that "Obama has as President created a new climate in international politics. Multilateral diplomacy has regained a central position, with emphasis on the role that the United Nations and other international institutions can play. Dialogue and negotiations are preferred as instruments for resolving even the most difficult international conflicts."

The Nobel committee's statement described, in a succinct way, the values that Obama applied to foreign relations. Given that global leadership is often a matter of communicating priorities and building relationships, the award was a reasonable honor for a president who had not yet served even a year in office. However, the committee also acknowledged that the honor was as much about the Obama mystique as it was about his diplomatic approach. In a world ever more dominated by the power of imagery, communicated through the media, charisma equals power, and the new president's appeal was powerful indeed. As the committee said, "Only very rarely has a person to the same extent as Obama captured the world's attention and given its people hope for a better future."

As it offered its admiration, the committee also bestowed upon Obama a problem. The president's rapid rise from the Illinois State Senate to the White House in four short years had inspired his critics to complain that he was more style than substance and didn't deserve what he had achieved. Michael Steele, chairman of the Republican Party, used the moment of honor to attack, saying, "It is unfortunate that the president's star power has outshined tireless advocates who have made real achievements working towards peace and human rights. One thing is certain—President Obama won't be receiving any awards from Americans for job creation, fiscal responsibility, or backing up rhetoric with concrete action." Within hours White House officials were noting that the Nobel Prize had created real awkwardness for them. Put in the strange position of responding to an award that many saw as premature, Obama seemed chagrined as he spoke to the press at the White House. In a lighthearted moment he revealed that after he heard about the award, his daughters came to see him and, after saying congratulations, reminded him that it was their dog's birthday and "we have a three-day weekend coming up."

Turning serious, Obama said, "To be honest, I do not feel that I deserve to be in the company of so many of the transformative figures who've been honored by this prize, men and women who've inspired me and inspired the entire world through their courageous pursuit of peace. But I also know that this prize reflects the kind of world that those men and women and all Americans want to build, a world that gives life to the promise of our founding documents."

Such humility would be expected of any honoree, but what Obama said as he accepted the prize was a departure from the norm. Noting that he led a country engaged in two major wars, Obama talked about the concept of "just war" waged as a matter of "last resort or in self-defense." He also worked to diminish the world's expectations: "I do not bring with me today a definitive solution to the problems of war. . . . Evil does exist in the world. A nonviolent movement could not have halted Hitler's armies. Negotiations cannot convince al-Qaeda's leaders to lay down their arms. To say that force is sometimes necessary is not a call to cynicism—it is a recognition of history; the imperfections of man and the limits of reason."

As he refused to renounce war and described the limits of nonviolence, Obama stressed his commitment to a realism that reassured Americans who may have worried about his resolve and gave him leverage in his dealings with leaders of states such as Iran, who approached the United States with hostility. Obama was burdened with the wars his predecessor began, and ending them would be a long and arduous process.

Determined as he was to reduce America's military presence in Iraq and Afghanistan, Obama worked hard to demonstrate his commitment to soldiers serving in these countries. In April 2009 the president made a surprise visit to Iraq, where he met with senior commanders and Iraqi officials and addressed a gathering of troops. Even in this setting Obama's celebrity was evident, as troops

strained to shake his hand and take his picture. At a session where
he was often interrupted by cheers of "Hooah!" he said:

> Under enormous strain and under enormous sacrifice,
> through controversy and difficulty and politics, you've
> kept your eyes focused on just doing your job. And
> because of that, every mission that's been assigned—
> from getting rid of Saddam, to reducing violence, to
> stabilizing the country, to facilitating elections—you
> have given Iraq the opportunity to stand on its own as a
> democratic country. That is an extraordinary achieve-
> ment, and for that you have the thanks of the American
> people. That's point number one.
>
> Point number two is, this is going to be a critical
> period, these next eighteen months. I was just discussing
> this with your commander, but I think it's something
> that all of you know. It is time for us to transition to the
> Iraqis. They need to take responsibility for their country
> and for their sovereignty.

The president's point about Iraqis taking over the mission was
applauded by the men and women who gathered to hear the president. The long war had demonstrated to them, and the world, the
difficulty inherent in any outside power's effort to impose a governing scheme on a state riven with warring factions. In Iraq, Obama
faced the almost-certain prospect that a civil war would occur upon
America's departure, but he had been elected, to some degree, on
the premise that he would end the expenditure of blood and dollars in a fight that was begun on false pretenses. The president would
succeed in reducing America's forces until the last troops devoted
to direct combat were withdrawn in December 2011.

In Afghanistan, where the United States had gone to war in
pursuit of the organization that carried out the 9/11 attacks, the

president faced a situation that was similarly difficult to resolve. In the Taliban the government in Kabul faced an organized and well-rooted armed opposition that maintained a sort of shadow government and enjoyed substantial support in many regions. Obama had campaigned with a pledge to add to the American presence in Afghanistan, where, he said, the United States had waged war on a legitimate basis. In December 2009 he ordered a "surge" of forces

U.S. Troops in Iraq

President Barack Obama has ordered all U.S. troops out of Iraq by Dec. 31. Troop levels and deaths by month since the U.S. invasion in March

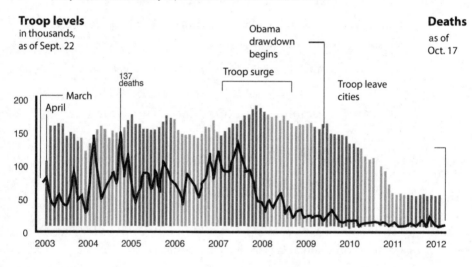

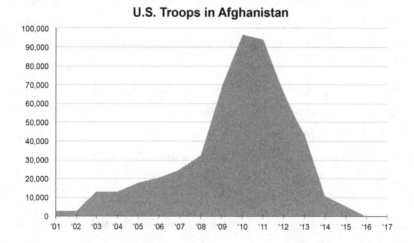

in an effort to gain a decisive military advantage and buy time for training Afghan troops and leaders. By the end of 2013, Afghan forces were leading the great majority of military missions (by one estimate, 99 percent), but their effectiveness varied widely. Troop withdrawals would continue until late 2015, when the president froze the process. Approximately ten thousand American military personnel remained in the country as advisers and occasional combatants. In its fifteenth year, the conflict in Afghanistan was the longest in American history.

Though costlier—a combined $1.6 trillion—and longer, the military engagements begun by George W. Bush did not create the same divisions as the definitive quagmire that was Vietnam. The difference was that Bush had acted mainly in response to the 9/11 attacks on America and that the troops who fought in Iraq and Afghanistan were volunteers and not draftees. With only a tiny percentage of families sending fighters abroad, and combat deaths occurring at a much lower rate, the two wars that Obama inherited did not incite the kind of opposition—massive street protests and riots—that raged during Vietnam. But though he operated under less pressure than Lyndon Johnson and Richard Nixon, Obama had campaigned on a pledge to end US involvement in both conflicts, and by this measure he could not claim a full success.

Although they were partial, Obama's accomplishments in Iraq and Afghanistan largely matched the goals he had set for himself as a candidate. America departed Iraq and, as promised, maintained no bases there. On a closely related issue he had ended the use of torture in the interrogation of terror suspects, as practiced by the Bush administration. And while the Guantánamo Bay prison remained, the population there had been reduced by 85 percent.

Overall, Obama's effort to improve relations with the Muslim world, coupled with his determined antiterrorism efforts, had set the conditions for the breakthrough nuclear agreement with Iran and contributed to the president's continued popularity worldwide.

In 2015 a Pew poll of thirty-nine nations found 69 percent favorable ratings for the president. He enjoyed majority support in countries as disparate as Israel, Indonesia, Brazil, and Japan. Most remarkably, he had reversed America's standing with its most important allies, the countries of Western Europe.

Besides Iran, Obama could count foreign policy successes that included a new arms control treaty with Russia, which cut the number of launchers in half, and a surprise and sudden normalization of America's relationship with Cuba. For more than fifty years, beginning when Fidel Castro nationalized US-owned businesses, the two countries had barely engaged with each other. America had launched a failed invasion. Cuba turned to the Soviet Union for aid and protection. Distrust and antagonism ebbed and flowed. The end of this stalemate had been aided by Pope Francis, who had discussed Cuba with Obama and written to the leaders of both countries. In Cuba the agreement signaled the end of isolation and a promise of beneficial trade and unification with families in the United States. For Americans it marked the start of the gradual resolution of a political issue that had divided Cuban communities, and both political parties.

More controversial than the opening to Cuba was Obama's Trans-Pacific Partnership, a sprawling trade agreement negotiated among a dozen countries of the Pacific Rim. Under TPP, tariffs on thousands of products and services were reduced or eliminated, and standards were established to police child labor, pollution, union rights, and workplace safety. Although it was much criticized by the Left, Obama considered it an essential part of his "pivot to Asia" strategy, which was devised to counter China's influence in the Pacific. China was not part of the TPP and would miss out on the opportunities for trade and closer relations that the agreement fostered.

In his willingness to defy much of his party on the trade agreement, Obama showed, as he had in the Middle East, that he was not merely an idealist or an internationalist. With TPP he sought to advance America's economic interests and maintain US primacy over China, even if it meant disappointing those who viewed the agreement as a giveaway to certain business interests. In this way Obama's approach to foreign policy was similar to his philosophy on domestic issues. In both cases he seemed to recognize an interconnected "whole" rather than a series of disparate challenges. It's relatively easy to see lines connecting Obama's domestic initiatives—on energy, the environment, the economy, and more—with his global agenda. For example, by increasing fuel economy standards on cars at home, Obama enhanced US credibility in the talks that led to the Paris climate change agreement. Similarly, domestic energy policy affected global oil prices in ways that strengthen America's position in dealing with oil-producing states on a host of issues.

The wisdom of Obama's approach, which showed him to be playing the diplomatic game on many different levels at the same time, was explained in the fall of 2015 by Gideon Rose, editor of *Foreign Affairs*. As Rose argued, Obama had coolly pursued America's security agenda, keeping a lid on terrorism and strengthening military alliances, even as he persuaded the Muslim world that America was not an intractable enemy. He cut America's losses in places such as Iraq and Afghanistan and avoided new entanglements. Despite real failures, most notably in Syria, wrote Rose, Obama "will likely pass on to his successor an overall foreign policy agenda and national power position in better shape than when he entered office, ones that the next administration can build on to improve things further." Considering the mess he inherited from the man who had preceded him, this was a considerable achievement.

7

EDUCATION

Racing to the Top

At eight twenty in the morning, bright yellow school buses diesel up to the curb at Murkland Elementary School in Lowell, Massachusetts. This spring day in 2015 is cloudless and warm. Brakes squeal, bus doors swing open, and kids come spilling out like brightly colored gumballs. The sounds made by teachers herding five hundred kids are the same sounds you might hear at any other school. The difference is the setting. Look past the buses and playground and you'll see sterile public housing projects and factories that have been closed for decades. Greater Lowell is poorer than the state average, and Murkland's neighborhood, called The Acre by locals, is poorer still. Fully 97 percent of the kids at Murkland are so needy they qualify to receive subsidized meals.

Poverty here is a given. So is the constant fluctuation of a student population drawn largely from immigrants and refugee families from the Middle East, Africa, Latin America, and beyond. The majority of these children come to Murkland unable to speak English. Most do not possess even a rudimentary understanding of arithmetic.

As one teacher explains it, some Murkland third-graders must be taught the relationship between numbers and objects. For them, the relationship between the symbol 1 and a lone pencil resting on a table is a completely novel concept.

In 2011, poor student test scores meant Murkland was rated a Level Four school by state officials. At Level Five, it would be taken over by state officials, who could dismiss staff, scatter students, and transform the school in any way they saw fit. But instead of failing, Murkland retooled with the help of federal aid. By 2015, more than two-thirds of the school's students were reading at or above grade level. Murkland leaped to Level One status.

The test scores at Murkland show that the educators there could get the job done, but the real proof of their success lies in the hearts of the children. Follow the gumballs from the sidewalks and through the schoolhouse door. Inside, a big whiteboard bears the message "Good Morning Friends, Today is Friday. T.G.I.F.!! We are on vacation next week. We're going to miss you. What will you miss most about the Murkland School next week?" On the space left below the message students have written:

"The amazing teachers."

"Reading."

"I will miss Everybody!"

"Math and my teacher."

"All the teachers."

"I'm gonna miss reading and writing and math so much."

"EVERYTHING!"

Written by small hands in vivid marker ink, the spirit of Murkland is a product of the school's remarkable success, which has brought a stream of curious experts to the school. Each asks the same questions about how the change was accomplished. The answers generally revolve around two factors—money and local control. The cash lowered the number of students taught by each teacher and brought assistants and aides into the classrooms. With students arriving from Uganda, Ethiopia, Somalia, Vietnam, and Cambodia, Murkland needed interpreters, and cultural specialists, just to start educating them. But for teachers the big change has been having the time to reflect, plan, and execute their own strategies. Teacher Marytherese Lenihan explains:

"It's getting together, reflecting on what we're doing, the pluses, the minuses, and then moving forward, which was never really a part of what we were doing before. And this is on a regular basis that we do this. It's putting the money towards teacher preparation, teacher planning, teacher reflection, having the time to look at student work. . . . So it's just a complete turnaround that the teachers are the ones that are making a difference."

The Murkland story illustrates a debate that has raged around American education policy for many generations. Ever since John Dewey began his reform movement a century ago, partisans have debated classroom discipline versus creativity, local standards versus national curricula, and the value of "common sense" versus education theory. At various times the condition of American education has been a source of pride and a cause for hand-wringing. During the Reagan administration, a federal report titled *A Nation at Risk* sounded an alarm and recommended higher standards, testing to determine student achievement, and federal action to help poorly served students. In the years since, schools have been buffeted by politics, with the Right generally criticizing teachers (and especially their unions) and the Left calling for more money to be spent on education.

The meeting point during the George W. Bush administration had been somewhat to the Right of center with demands for frequent testing to measure student performance and a push for ways to make educators compete as if they were businesspeople. This competition concept had prompted a boom in "charter" schools, which were founded and operated by both for-profit and nonprofit groups that received taxpayer money. However, neither testing nor charter schools changed the fact that teachers charged with educating poorer students from communities such as the one near Murkland started several steps behind their colleagues in wealthier, more stable neighborhoods.

The link between wealth and the health of schools is easy to see across the country. In most states schools remain dependent on local real estate taxes for much of their funding, which means poor communities struggle to serve children who actually need more than their peers from privileged backgrounds. At the same time, people looking for homes favor places with good schools, which creates a cycle of rising real estate prices and tax receipts in rich places and a constant struggle for funding in poorer ones. A similar dynamic affects families and their children. Although exceptions abound, children from families with higher incomes generally do better in school, which leads to success in college or university and lifelong advantages in income.

Before he became president, candidate Obama stressed the responsibilities of families to help their children overcome their circumstances. In a well-publicized speech in Chicago he chastised fathers who act "like boys instead of men," and he criticized leaders with low expectations for poor and minority children. However, his education platform acknowledged the valuable role education plays in helping kids rise above their beginnings. He called for increased funding of early education, and improvements to the No Child Left Behind program, which promoted charter schools and linked federal education funding with performance, as measured by tests of student progress.

Though supported by both parties in Congress, enthusiasm for the Bush-era policy had waned as students and educators dealt with the program's demand for constant improvement, demonstrated by tests, and many fell behind. Poor schools that lacked the resources to change quickly and show improvement suffered as they were forced to be restructured, like failing corporations. In Lowell, the teachers and administrators at the Murkland School were unable to get their students' test scores high enough to escape the shadow of the tough-love sanctions that were part of No Child Left Behind. One education expert described the system as "quicksand" for many poor schools.

When then candidate Obama discussed "fixing the broken promises of No Child Left Behind" in a 2008 speech at a Denver school, he had in mind the problem of penalties that added to the burdens of struggling schools. He said, "Labeling a school and its students as failures one day and then throwing your hands up and walking away from them the next is wrong."

When he tried to describe his own education priorities, Obama revealed the difficulty every president has faced. America's schools are primarily a state and local concern, but presidents can use financial aid and the bully pulpit of their office to nudge educators in one direction or another. President Bush had believed he was helping poor schools the most by imposing strict standards on them. This is why Obama told the crowd in Denver, "I believe that the goals of this law were the right ones." However, as the Bush program imposed administrative and educational duties on schools, the funding provided by the program sometimes failed to meet the costs of complying. These shortfalls and the pressure students felt under various testing regimes energized a backlash against the No Child Left Behind law. However, the task of replacing it would be delayed as the administration grappled with the Great Recession.

As Obama took office, the Great Recession was wrecking school budgets and had forced the dismissal of forty thousand teachers. Although education experts disagreed on almost every topic, the central role of the classroom teacher was not in dispute, and in almost every school setting students benefited from smaller class sizes. As teachers were laid off, class sizes increased. Sixty-two percent of districts surveyed at the time reported they were asking teachers to take on greater numbers of students. More than half the districts said they were cutting after-school programs such as sports and clubs and reducing transportation, which would put pressure on working parents to get their kids to and from school.

The Obama administration's education initiatives began with the 2009 Recovery Act, which history would recognize as the

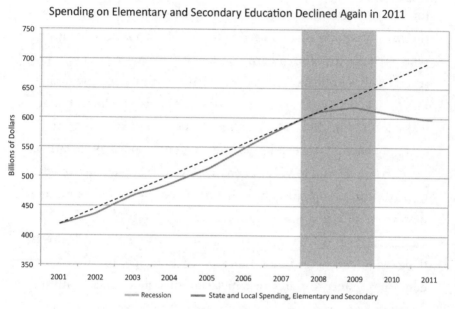

Spending on Elementary and Secondary Education Declined Again in 2011

Dollars not adjusted for inflation. Source: BEA, Table 3.15.5

president's single-biggest domestic policy push. Education was the number three priority in the stimulus bill, with schools getting $100 billion in "stimulus" funds. More than $50 billion in stimulus funds were sent to schools to pay teacher salaries, halt budgets cuts, and repair crumbling buildings. In the prior decade local districts had deferred $500 billion in repairs to school buildings. As a result, students were forced to attend classes in buildings where roofs leaked, mold spores threatened their lungs, and the water from the taps was undrinkable. Typical was the public high school in Biddeford, Maine, where officials estimated $34 million was needed to repair the roof, replace windows, and deliver reliable heat to classrooms. In Los Angeles, unrepaired damage from a *1972* earthquake allowed iron rebar to rust, which caused bricks to crack and crumble. In Rockland, Massachusetts, duct tape held together floorboards that had been weakened by termites.

Administration officials who sent grants to local districts stressed the need to put the money to work quickly so that repair projects would spur local economies and provide immediate employment for construction workers. When the money was used for teachers, the idea was to keep them in their schools to prevent turnover, which studies had shown harmed student achievement. Lowell got several million dollars from this fund. When added to new money for special education, the federal boost to the city's schools budget exceeded $10 million. Murkland got a share of this money, but it was only enough to keep it treading water as a poorly performing, Level Four school. However, more help would soon come from the new administration's most heavily funded education policy push, a new program called Race to the Top.

Tucked inside the massive stimulus act, Race to the Top was designed to encourage innovation and accountability by offering big education grants to states that met certain criteria and submitted winning proposals to federal evaluators. (States would then mete out the funds to localities.) Some of the standards, such as support for charter schools, were drawn from the Right side of the political spectrum, while others, such as increased attention for early childhood education, came from the Left. Perhaps the most controversial element was a requirement that states adopt some version of a new curriculum standard called Common Core.

Developed by the National Governors Association, the Common Core standards reflected the power of those demanding accountability from educators and were an attempt to set a baseline of achievement that would make students prepared for post–high school education or careers. The governors had acted in response to repeated international surveys that had shown that American students lagged behind their peers in dozens of countries. Most states adopted part or all of the Common Core standards for proficiency in math and English and instituted testing regimes to determine whether the standards were being met.

Fashioned to deliver large sums and to create a major impact in states that qualified, the Race to the Top scheme required elaborate proposals that were presented by teams of state officials who trouped to Washington to compete against each other. In Massachusetts roughly one hundred school districts opted out of the pro-

READING			MATH			SCIENCE		
OECD Average:		493	OECD Average:		496	OECD Average:		501
1	Shanghai-China	556	1	Shanghai-China	600	1	Shanghai-China	575
2	South Korea	539	2	Singapore	562	2	Finland	554
3	Finland	536	3	Hong Kong-China	555	3	Hong Kong-China	549
4	Hong Kong-China	533	4	South Korea	546	4	Singapore	542
5	Singapore	526	5	Taiwan	543	5	Japan	539
6	Canada	524	6	Finland	541	6	South Korea	538
7	New Zealand	521	7	Liechtenstein	536	7	New Zealand	532
8	Japan	520	8	Switzerland	534	8	Canada	529
9	Australia	515	9	Japan	529	9	Estonia	528
10	Netherlands	508	10	Canada	527	10	Australia	527
17	United States	500	31	United States	487	23	United States	502

gram because local officials didn't want to get involved with the curriculum, testing, and evaluation protocols. (Local unions, administrators, and school boards were required to give their approval to these moves.) Among those that stayed in, Lowell and its Murkland School received funds from an overall state grant of $250 million. The district used the money to educate sixty-eight teachers to become trainers in their schools, where they then taught new methods to their one thousand colleagues. Teachers were assigned to teams and coaches, and lessons were revised with state standards in mind. Time was taken for meetings attended by the entire faculty. A rarity in the past, the conferences provided a forum where problems could be noted, discussed, and addressed before they became unmanageable.

At Murkland a new principal, Jason DiCarlo, met with every

teacher and described his plan for reviving the school. He offered transfers to teachers who didn't want to be part of the change and welcomed every one who did to stay. Almost every teacher stayed. Their union agreed to increase from one to five the number of days teachers would devote to preparing the school for the start of the year and agreed to add nearly three hours per week to the work schedule without demanding overtime pay. Some of this time would be used for the frequent faculty gatherings, and some of it would be devoted to planning interventions so that children who were strug-gling wouldn't fall too far behind their peers.

As teachers began to coalesce as a team, morale began to rise. Mistakes and problems aired at meetings became fodder for brain-storming without blame. DiCarlo used Race to the Top funds to set up a bonus system that would reward every worker at the school, including custodians and aides, if test scores reached certain targets. The targets were met by Christmas, and every paycheck delivered prior to the break contained an extra $500. This success helped Murkland qualify for a subsequent competitive grant that paid for staff to increase the school day by forty minutes and to add a sum-mer program. "Our summer program actually had two purposes," says DiCarlo. "One was to address an area of need for kids. The other was to let us try things, to say, `Let's try it during the sum-mer program, let's see what we get from it.' And then we will have plenty of knowledge for us to roll it out for the staff for next year."

DiCarlo's plan, and the added funding, put two or three adult assistants into each classroom to assist primary teachers. On a typi-cal day at the school the teacher in one room was surrounded by students, gathered onto a rug, intent on a lesson. Others worked at desks in groups of three or four. They planned projects, debating methods and arriving at steps they would take to complete their assignment.

In another room, second-graders used blunt scissors to cut sen-tences from printed pages and pasted them in the proper order to create a story. The children worked on their own, but were free to consult one another. Some wandered to nearby classmates to ask questions. Others checked the prompts that were written on a big piece of paper set up on an easel. These prompts, displayed in words and pictures, reduced the number of times students needed to raise their hands to ask a question and interrupt a lesson, or to pull focus from a teacher who was working with another student.

Although Murkland students were often free to talk to each other and get up from their chairs, they experienced fewer discipline problems after the reforms DiCarlo instituted with Race to the Top money. This surprising outcome occurred, in part, because of the added staff, but Principal DiCarlo also credited better lesson planning and teaching techniques. Improved teaching engages students' mind and leaves fewer openings for a bored or unhappy child to act out.

For a school with five hundred students, many of whom struggle to speak a shared language, Murkland is remarkably quiet. Students pass in the hallways without much conversation, and teachers don't need to raise their voices in the classroom. Unannounced visitors caused no excitement, perhaps because Murkland has become a destination for educators who hope to discover what works. The only moment when the quiet was defeated came during the principal's daily announcements, which were made via a loudspeaker system. It was Friday, which is also "Dance Day," so DiCarlo played the Pharrell Williams song "Happy" over the speaker system. As the song played, a thousand feet shook the floors.

As a school gaining ground, Murkland is a happy place. Specialized math and English-language teachers give frustrated children extra help before they become discouraged, which also frees classroom teachers for their other students. Administrators walk the hallways wearing fleece vests decorated with the motto MURKLAND, EXPECT THE BESt, and kids sent to the principal's office can pick a picture book from his vast collection to scan as they talk things over.

From the improved test scores to the lighter moods inside the school, Murkland's revival highlighted the success of Race to the Top. Lowell schools superintendent Jean Franco recalls that the school's progress began with the crisis of its Level Four ranking:

"When Level Four comes, you're worried about a lot of things—not just the possibility of the state intervention—but that you're not doing the best, you're not making the best outcome for the kids. Race to the Top allowed us to have a full-time English-as-a-second-language coach and a full-time mathematics coach in this school that was having trouble. It also allowed for an additional social worker."

Most important, the Race to the Top money bought teachers the time to plan, reflect, evaluate, and adjust their work with students who required focused effort. A new culture of teaching, backed by evaluations and adjustments, took hold, and Murkland's improvement continued even after the infusion of funds ended. Franco expected this result because fixing a school is a matter of fostering faculty confidence, professionalism, and cohesion. "School improvement takes `I believe in you' and `You believe in me,'" said Franco. "It's mostly free."

In all, fourteen of the most beleaguered elementary schools in Massachusetts raised their student test scores enough to leave Level Four. The high schools that received money raised their graduation rates and narrowed the gap separating white and minority students. When they were assessed in 2014, Massachusetts schools were judged the best in the country. Nationally, Race to the Top improved schools in every state that received grant money, advanced teacher evaluations, and moved schools toward the Common Core standards. However, a system that permitted state and local control over federal money produced widely varied results. Massachusetts raced to the top, but Hawaii, according to one evaluation, dawdled. In several states educators pushed back against aspects of the program, In New York State, for example, more than one thousand principals signed a petition opposing the program's system for evaluating students, schools, and teachers. Tests and evaluations, inherent aspects of No Child Left Behind and Common Core, were generating a backlash that would grow more powerful every year and demonstrate the limits of federal intervention in the level of government that resides closest to daily life in America, its schools.

For all of its good intentions, which were endorsed by liberal standard-bearer Senator Ted Kennedy, No Child Left Behind introduced a level of standardized testing that Americans had never before seen. Indeed, evaluation by numbers resided at the heart of the sweeping law Bush sought to make schools accountable. Theoretically, testing would allow parents, taxpayers, and officials to compare schools with each other, and to see if schools were making progress, or losing ground, year to year. With a rather vague standard called Adequate Yearly Progress, Bush administration officials believed they could meter federal aid and improve virtually all of the country's schools, even though they had no direct control over what occurred in classrooms.

From the start skeptics noted the difficulty of measuring students from disparate backgrounds and with different skills gathered to be taught by individual teachers with similarly varied abilities. Would high grades show that a particular teacher is better than his or her peers, or just that the students in the room were more ready to learn? What would dips and rises in school performance really show? And what if schools, districts, and states used different tests, as the law allowed?

People who lived in the communities that schools served understood the makeup of the kids who filled their classrooms and developed, over time, a sense of how teachers performed. Public reporting of test scores did permit comparisons, which could be helpful in identifying both excellent and ineffective teachers and schools. However, the vast majority of students were taught by teachers who fell into a middle range. For them, the scores that were published in the local press and on Web sites produced as much confusion as insight. As time passed and students were subjected to more and more testing, complaints about the pressure placed on students and teachers whose lessons were geared to the scores grew louder and more insistent.

Anti-testing sentiment produced campaigns to oust education officials and exam boycotts. (In many states students were permitted to opt out of some tests without penalty.) Similar opposition arose as states adopted the Common Core standards. Though widely assumed to be a federal mandate, Common Core was backed by Republican and Democratic governors and had not been imposed on schools by Washington. However, it was included as a requirement for Race to the Top winners, and the scheme quickly attracted opposition from those who saw it as federal overreach and technocracy run amok. Professor David Kirp of the University of California put it this way in an article in *The New York Times*:

"Public schools have turned into pressure cookers. Teachers are pushed to improve test results. A vanishingly small amount of time is spent on art, music and sports, because they aren't part of the testing regime. Students have become test-taking robots, sitting through as many as 20 standardized exams a year."

In the Obama years, Education Secretary Arne Duncan heard constant complaints about Common Core and the deficiencies in No Child Left Behind. Eventually the Obama administration began granting waivers for states to opt out of the Bush regulations and began devising a law that would address many of the concerns raised by critics of the law. In 2015 the administration and key members of Congress from both parties agreed to gut the old law. States and local schools were freed to use their own methods to help poorly performing schools. Teachers would no longer be evaluated on the basis of how well their students performed on tests. And federal incentives that encouraged schools to adopt the Common Core program were eliminated.

Judged by House Speaker Paul Ryan to be the "biggest rewrite of our education laws in twenty-five years," the new program, called the Every Student Succeeds Act, did not include one of Obama's big education priorities: access to prekindergarten classes for every American child. However, he did get a mechanism for holding states accountable for their worst schools, and for their records on educating poor and minority students. Improving the education of these children had been a major element of No Child Left Behind, and it was one area where it achieved some success, as measured by tests of fourth- and eighth-graders.

As Obama replaced his predecessor's big education plan with something more modest, he demonstrated the limits of his power at a time when his political opponents controlled the House and Senate, and partisanship ran high. However, when added to Race to the Top, this success showed that the president could get things done, even in one of the more hotly contested areas of public policy. Schools have always been an ideological battleground, where partisans fight over child welfare, the nation's economic competitiveness, and moral values. Under these conditions, presidents have tended to work around the margins. In Obama's case this process yielded a variety of little-noticed but nevertheless consequential initiatives.

The most significant of these quiet accomplishments revamped the system for lending money to college students and parents so they can pay tuition and other expenses. Tucked inside health care reform legislation, new rules eliminated the middleman role played by private lenders who made a profit on loans. The interest rate students paid was cut, and repayment plans would be based on income. None would be required to pay more than 10 percent of their income, and roughly $6 billion in annual savings would be recirculated to provide more loans. For families faced with ever-rising college costs, which exceeded $50,000 per year at some elite institutions, the new scheme represented substantial financial relief.

Obama's other under-the-radar achievements in education included:

- An $8 billion program to train an elite corps of teachers in science, math, engineering, and technology.
- $4 billion invested in high-speed Internet for schools.
- A 50 percent increase in Pell Grants to low-income college students.
- A college scorecard system that helps students compare costs and programs online.
- New tax credits for college worth $2,500 per year, per student.
- A crackdown on for-profit colleges found to offer substandard programs (more than a thousand were closed).

Like the rest of his accomplishments, President Obama's education policy successes came despite consistent opposition, even to his least controversial effort. An example of this arose when the president gave a speech addressed to schoolchildren who were returning to classes in September 2009. Obama had made education a primary focus and would often visit schools during his presidency. While his back-to-school address every year began a new practice, he was not the first to make such a speech. President George H. W. Bush did it during his first year in office, taking to national TV and radio networks to encourage children to do their best. "You're in control," said Bush, "but you are not alone. People want you to succeed. They want to help you succeed."

When Obama announced he would make a similar address in 2009, outrage arose among his critics even before the subject matter was revealed. Florida GOP chairman Jim Greer said Obama intended to "indoctrinate" children and that Greer was "absolutely appalled that taxpayer dollars are being used to spread President Obama's socialist ideology." Oklahoma state senator Steve Russell, also a Republican, complained, "As far as I'm concerned, this is not civics education—it gives the appearance of creating a cult of personality."

When he actually spoke, Obama told the students at a high school in Virginia, and millions watching around the country, that his mother gave him extra early-morning lessons when he was a child. When he complained about being tired, he said, "My mother would just give me one of those looks and say, `This is no picnic for me, either, buster.'" He went on to admonish young Americans against playing too many video games and to encourage them to do their homework. He urged them to respect their teachers, find what they were good at, and then dedicate themselves to excelling at it. "I expect you to get serious this year, I expect you to put your best effort into everything you do." He finished his lesson in socialism with the words "Thank you, God bless you, and God bless America."

8

FINANCIAL REFORM

Boring Is Better

In the wake of the financial crisis that spawned the Great Recession, the phrase *too big to fail* seeped into the American vernacular in a way few other financial terms ever would. It was plastered on men's underwear and used to describe the gargantuan payroll of the New York Yankees baseball team. It came to be a ready reference for the kind of excess that endangered everyone except the people responsible. In the case of the financial system, *too big to fail* was shorthand for institutions that had to be preserved, despite their blunders, lest their collapse destroy the foundation of the economy.

Essential to the workings of every industry as well as every layer of government, major financial institutions affect both the well-being of the nation and the prospects of virtually every American citizen. Homes cannot be bought and sold without the financing supplied by these institutions, and businesses cannot function if they are deprived of capital by them. In providing investments as well as credit for everything from infrastructure projects to college loans, banks, insurance companies, investment firms, and hedge funds keep society functioning. This truth, rarely considered when the system operates normally, became painfully apparent even to those with little financial education as a banking crisis became a recession marked by high unemployment, spikes in personal and business bankruptcies, and a tidal wave of mortgage foreclosures. The suffering experienced by families that lost their incomes, their savings, and their homes prompted outrage across the political spectrum as voters and public officials sought to fix blame and find cures.

As Barack Obama sought the White House, the extent of the financial crisis became apparent. Bankruptcies in the mortgage industry were followed by the collapse of Lehman Brothers and the failure of Bear Stearns. Public confidence in banks plunged to its lowest level in generations, and federal officials rushed to save the system with hundreds of billions of dollars. When the economic recovery began, Washington focused on changing the regulatory schemes that governed various elements of finance. This task would be nearly as difficult as the struggle over health care reform. As with health care, the targeted industry contributed huge sums to political candidates and employed legions of lobbyists. It was also so rife with arcane terms and Byzantine practices that it was more baffling to people than healthcare and the system that had grown up to pay for it.

During his first campaign for the White House, Obama said he believed that Congress and President Bill Clinton had set the conditions for the financial meltdown when they repealed the Depression-era regulations that had prevented this type of crisis for more than sixty years. "By the time the Glass-Steagall Act was repealed in 1999, the three-hundred-million–dollar lobbying effort that drove deregulation was more about facilitating mergers than creating an efficient regulatory framework," Obama said in March 2008. "Instead of establishing a twenty-first-century regulatory framework, we simply dismantled the old one."

Repeal of Glass-Steagall permitted greater risk-taking by banks that were federally insured, allowing executives to seek extra profits with the assurance that taxpayers would save them if their bets went sour. The result, said Obama, was "a winner-take-all, anything-goes environment that helped foster devastating dislocations in our economy." One example of this change could be seen in the issuance of "subprime" mortgages, made to borrowers who lacked the income to repay them. In the past, regulations and prudent practices meant that borrowers would not be given loans they couldn't repay. In the new environment, unqualified borrowers got the money they asked for, and future problems were shifted to investors who purchased securities based on the premise that these loans would be repaid.

The subprime problem was the first sign of crisis to gain public notice, and press reports made clear that lenders freed from the old rules had run amok. In October 2008, candidate Obama addressed this issue as he pledged to "put in place the commonsense regulations and rules of the road I've been calling for since March—rules that will keep our market free, fair, and honest; rules that will restore accountability and responsibility in our corporate boardrooms." Two weeks later Alan Greenspan, who had pushed for deregulation when he was chairman of the Federal Reserve, admitted that he had been at least "partially" wrong about that policy and confessed he was in a "state of shocked disbelief" over the transgressions on Wall Street. In time even the GOP stalwart Newt Gingrich would say that "repealing the Glass-Steagall Act was probably a mistake" and call for its return.

In 2008, Obama's election opponent John McCain was burdened with a voting record that included his consistent support for deregulation. He had also made the chief architect of deregulation, former Texas senator Phil Gramm, his top domestic-policy adviser. In a TV interview McCain said, "Deregulation was probably helpful to the growth of our economy." On the campaign trail McCain also questioned the severity the economy's troubles, wondering aloud if a recession was actually under way.

As the financial crisis worsened and voters began to fear its effects, the candidate who blamed deregulation benefited. By September, the Gallup Poll was reporting that "the Wall Street crisis may give Obama a slight political benefit," and the Democrat opened up a six-point lead among likely voters. By mid–October, Obama had a fourteen-point advantage over McCain when people were asked which candidate would be better for the economy. This issue would remain the number one concern for voters and provide much of the impetus for Obama's eventual victory.

Once in office Obama responded first to the immediate economic crisis and then turned to the imposition of regulations that might prevent another breakdown of the financial system. He saw this task as essential to restoring confidence and stability to the financial system. In May 2009 he signed an act of Congress that added mortgage companies under the law covering fraud in the financial industry. The act also created the Financial Crisis Inquiry Commission (FCIC) to investigate the crisis that had spread from housing to Wall Street and then the entire economy.

The president faced a difficult political task as he tried to deal with the financial industry. He needed to support institutions that could sustain the economy through lending, investments, and the everyday business of banking and insurance. But he understood that many Americans were appalled, as he was, by the irresponsible practices that had led to the Great Recession. In late 2009 he vented his feelings of outrage on the TV news program *60 Minutes,* telling correspondent Steve Kroft that he thought that financial executives were still in denial that the recession was "caused in part by completely irresponsible actions on Wall Street." Obama added, "They don't get it. They're still puzzled—why is it that people are mad at the banks? Well, let's see. You guys are drawing down ten-, twenty-million-dollar bonuses after America went through the worst economic year that it's gone through in decades, and you guys caused the problem. And we've got ten percent unemployment. Why do *you* think people might be a little frustrated?"

If anyone harbored doubts about the role bankers played in the economic meltdown, they were resolved by the FCIC hearings, which revealed the misdeeds of executives who loosened standards and practiced complex deceptions in pursuit of ever-higher profits for their companies and bonuses for themselves. Jamie Dimon, head of JPMorgan Chase, blamed "the management teams one hundred percent." Lower-level executives described their struggles to warn disinterested bosses of the impending crisis, and independent experts cited lax regulation as a major factor.

Eventually the FCIC would issue a lengthy report that found the crisis had been the product of "low interest rates, easy and available credit, scant regulation, and toxic mortgages." It concluded that executives, the Federal Reserve, regulators, and politicians had all failed to act to protect the economy, and that "there was a systemic breakdown in accountability and ethics" that damaged the integrity and public trust in "markets [that] are essential to the economic well-being of our nation."

Produced after testimony from more than five hundred witnesses and hearings held all across the country, the conclusions of the FCIC came too late to help the president's financial reform effort. However, the public parts of its investigation and hearings in Congress did focus attention on the industry's excesses and the regulatory deficiencies that resulted in the loss of trillions of dollars of capital. For his part, the president focused primarily on the question "What do we do now?"

The president stated this question aloud at the start of 2010 when he spoke to the press at the White House. He appeared with a group of advisers including former Federal Reserve chairman Paul Volcker, who stood closest to the president and directly in front of a portrait of George Washington. Then eighty-two years old, Volcker was one of the most visible economic figures of his time. He was not prominent because he stood six feet seven inches tall, but because he had tamed the runaway inflation that began in the late 1970s, using draconian restrictions on credit that initially made things worse for many Americans. Protesting farmers shut down parts of Washington with a "tractorcade," and picketing workers blocked the entrance to the Federal Reserve office. However, Volcker stuck to his strategy, and inflation plummeted to below 4 percent in 1983 and has stayed low ever since.

Volcker had backed Obama during the 2008 campaign and chaired the president's advisory board on economic recovery. Unlike others in the administration, particularly Treasury Secretary Timothy Geithner, Volcker advocated strict limits on the risks taken by bankers who could access federal money at discounted interest rates and were insured against failure—and their own bad decisions—by the government. Banks received cheap money and were protected from disaster by the taxpayers because they were vital to a functioning economy. In exchange, they owed the nation prudence.

Financiers, including many big bankers, said that the esoteric and risky investments that had caused so much trouble were innovative and beneficial "products." In a 2009 speech Volcker told a conference of bankers, government officials, and financial experts that he thought these new forms of debt were of no value to the overall economy. These innovations created cash flow for financial companies and funded a rapid run-up in Wall Street pay, but were otherwise little more than "intellectual fun" for those who dealt in them. "I wish that somebody would give me some shred of neutral evidence about the relationship between financial innovation recently and the growth of the economy, just one shred of information," said Volcker. He said that he knew of just one real innovation in banking that actually helped people: the automatic teller machine. "It's useful," he said.

Many members of Obama's economic team considered Volcker's call for a return to Glass-Steagall–style limits on banks unworkable. Well acquainted with banking executives—Geithner had spent much of his adult life working with bankers—they often seemed to channel the arguments made by industry lobbyists. A frustrated Volcker gave press interviews and made arguments in public forums and sharpened his critique, describing the paychecks distributed on Wall Street at the end of 2009 as "grotesquely large." Banks distributed $145 billion in year-end bonuses. Jamie Dimon of JPMorgan Chase got $16 million. As bankers rewarded themselves, they stirred public outrage and betrayed those in Washington who had worked so hard to rescue them. At a meeting in the White House, which was reported by the journalist Michael Hirsh, the president reconsidered the idea of imposing strict limits and said, "I'm not convinced Volcker's not right about this." Vice President Joe Biden said he definitely agreed with Volcker's approach. (The writer Jonathan Alter would report Obama also said, "These guys want to be paid like rock stars when all they are doing is lip-synching capitalism.")

By January 2010 a president who had lost the momentum on financial reform was gaining it back. On a Thursday morning the White House press corps was summoned to watch a dozen or so advisers and officials file into a press conference. Volcker took a spot right behind a podium and next to House Financial Services Committee chairman Barney Frank, who stood a head shorter than him. When the president then spoke, he took notice of "this tall guy behind me" and credited him with the central concept behind a new proposal "to rein in the excess and abuse that nearly brought down our financial system." The heart of this plan was something the president called the Volcker Rule, which would prohibit federally insured banks from the kinds of investments made by hedge funds and private equity companies as they chased greater profits by accepting greater risks.

The president, and the men and women who flanked him, knew that the banks would oppose the Volcker Rule and other elements of the financial reform proposal. But they also understood that the American public was furious with the financial industry. The president said, "So if these folks want a fight, it's a fight I'm ready to have. And my resolve is only strengthened when I see a return to old practices at some of the very firms fighting reform; and when I see soaring profits and obscene bonuses at some of the very firms claiming that they can't lend more to small business, they can't keep credit card rates low, they can't pay a fee to refund taxpayers for the bailout without passing on the cost to shareholders or customers—that's the claims they're making. It's exactly this kind of irresponsibility that makes clear reform is necessary."

In addition to the Volcker Rule, the Obama plan called for regulations to cover exotic securities that had slipped through the old system, for new protections for whistle-blowers who reported potential fraud, and for tougher standards for the credit agencies that certified the quality of bonds and other investments. A new agency was also proposed—the Consumer Financial Protection Bureau—that would have regulatory authority over a wide range of financial companies, from banks to debt collectors. The CFPB would write and enforce rules aimed at guaranteeing fair treatment of consumers.

Although many people would struggle to understand the details of the Volcker Rule, the notion of an agency such as the CFPB, which would be devoted to protecting consumers in a buyer-beware financial marketplace, was easy to grasp. Financial firms enjoyed enormous advantages in their relationships with customers, as anyone who had ever tried to read a credit agreement knew. They also exerted substantial influence in Washington, through donations to political campaigns and lobbying efforts. (In the year before Obama's proposal was made public, financial companies had spent more than $380 million on lobbyists.)

The CFPB was imagined by the president and his team to be a completely independent agency, not beholden to the Congress for its budget or to the White House for its authority. The bureau won support from the man least likely to back any restraints on banks, former Fed chairman Greenspan. The most influential proponent of deregulation in the country, Greenspan had spent forty years pressing for law-of-the-jungle capitalism. Now he said the move to impose more rules on the system was "probably the right decision." He also said that the "intellectual edifice" of his extreme free market views had "collapsed."

Even as they lost their prime intellectual supporter, banks mobilized against financial reform, deploying lobbyists to argue specific policy points and money to make friends with members of Congress. In just one month, March 2010, Goldman Sachs's political action committee gave more than $290,000 to campaign organizations. In the same four weeks the PACs of JPMorgan Chase, Citigroup, and Bank of America dished out a combined $150,000-plus. But even as the bankers wrote checks and argued against regulation, a strange thing happened in their own industry. A number of senior executives, including a former head of Citibank and a man who had served as treasury secretary in two Republican administrations, announced their support for more regulation to save capitalists from themselves. "I can be convinced that we should move back in the direction of Glass-Steagall," said John Reed, former co-chairman of Citibank. Nicholas Brady, the treasury secretary under presidents Reagan and George H. W. Bush, said he'd opt for regulations that erred on the side of toughness: "You draw a line that is too tight, that does not bother me a bit."

Named the "Elders of Wall Street" by *The New York Times,* the gray-haired men (they were all men) seemed to be appalled by the behavior of the generation that had followed them to top positions on Wall Street and feared a future marked by public distrust of the financial system. John Bogle, founder of the massive Vanguard mutual fund group, went so far as to say, "I am a believer that the system has gone badly awry and needs massive reform." Others suggested that Obama might not be going far enough to protect the public from Wall Street, and Wall Street from itself.

The Elders, and everyone else who favored increased financial regulation, would be helped because one of the most demanding reforms the government *could* have imposed was *missing* from the president's program. Nothing in the plan referred to the level of solid capital—shareholders' money and reliable assets such as government bonds—that banks would be required to keep on hand to protect against losses. In the crudest terms, higher capital requirements would limit the risk taxpayers faced should the government be required to aid a failing institution. However, they also limited the banks' lending and investments.

An all-out political battle over capital requirements imposed by Congress could have made financial reform impossible. However, banks were also subject to international rules set by the roughly thirty countries represented on the Basel Committee on Banking Supervision, which was headquartered in Basel, Switzerland. Established at the height of the Great Depression, the committee worked to create a system to support global trade and economic stability. Institutions and countries that adhered to the group's standards enjoyed the kind of trust that made doing business far easier, and less risky. After the financial meltdown of 2007–8 the committee relieved US officials of the chore of setting tougher capital rules by moving to raise the requirement for all banks under its umbrella. By 2012 the eighteen largest banks would double their capital from $400 billion to $800 billion. All of this would be done without political struggle or much public notice.

In Congress the big push for the Obama reforms was led by Congressman Frank in the House and Christopher Dodd of Connecticut in the Senate. (Dodd was chairman of the Senate Banking Committee.) Dodd and Frank, whose names would be on the final version of the legislation, were both Democrats. They were both aware that their party might lose control of Congress when voters cast their ballots in November. Frank was popular in his home district and could be certain of reelection no matter how things worked out. Dodd was not so secure, but he made things easy on himself by deciding not to run for a new term. This freed him from worrying about how his effort might affect voters and campaign donors in a state that was home to a large number of financial industry executives who were quite active in politics.

Although Frank could count on a comfortable Democratic Party majority for reform in the House, Dodd would be buffeted from the Right and the Left as he tried to get enough support to overcome a filibuster threat. Within his own party he was criticized by those who said the new regulations didn't go far enough, because they didn't cut the huge financial players down to size. Many would remain too big to fail, which meant that they would likely be bailed out in a crisis. Republicans, on the other hand, wanted to weaken the reforms in any way they could to please their friends from Wall Street and deprive the president of a success. At one point House GOP leader John Boehner tried to encourage bankers in the fight, telling them, "Don't let those little punk [congressional] staffers take advantage of you. . . . Stand up for yourselves." Congressman Frank responded by distributing to his aides red lapel buttons with the words LITTLE PUNK STAFFER printed on them in bright white letters.

Despite the intransigence of the opposition, Senator Dodd matched the effort Democrats had made to win GOP votes on health care, engaging in long negotiations in hopes of bipartisanship. He ended up talking with just one GOP senator, Bob Corker of Tennessee, who asked for concessions but couldn't deliver votes. As he walked away, Dodd noted, "If it's just he and I agreeing, the compromise isn't worth much."

Fortunately for Dodd, the media continued to reveal the sins of Wall Street and inform public outrage. In March 2010, for example, news outlets reported that Lehman Brothers had used elaborate schemes to move certain transactions to affiliates out of the United States in order to escape regulations. Weeks later two new books, *The Big Short* by Michael Lewis and *The End of Wall Street* by Roger Lowenstein, illuminated both the farcical and the tragic elements of the financial crisis in ways that any reader could grasp. These books created the impression of a system that was rigged to reward a few cagey insiders while it delivered disaster to the nation as a whole.

Near the end of April, as Congress prepared to vote on Dodd-Frank, the president traveled to New York to speak directly to the financial elite, many of whom were invited to attend the speech. During the last great economic crisis, the Great Depression, President Franklin Delano Roosevelt had decided to speak to investment executives and bankers and dramatically declared that "enemies of peace—business and financial monopoly, reckless banking, class antagonism . . . are unanimous in their hate for me—and I welcome their hatred." Obama may not have been so reviled, but he was greeted by a full-page ad in the local papers, purchased by the Chamber of Commerce, which declared, defensively, that "beating up on Wall Street may be good short-term politics—but not if it gets in the way of the right solutions."

In fact, Obama had never been as hard on the lords of finance as FDR. Obama did refer to them as "fat cats," but he was more annoyed than angry. Near the end of his presidency he would tell Andrew Ross Sorkin of *The New York Times* that Wall Streeters complained about his policies as a matter of belief rather than experience. "It has to do with ideology," he would say, "and with their aggravations about higher taxes."

In New York, as Obama began his speech, he could look down at executives from Goldman Sachs, JPMorgan Chase, Credit Suisse, Barclays, and Bank of America. They were all seated in the front rows along with public officials, including the billionaire mayor of New York, Michael Bloomberg, whose enormous fortune had been made delivering information to the financial industry. A week earlier the Securities and Exchange Commission, which oversees Wall Street, had filed fraud charges against Goldman. The suit focused on a failed fund that cost investors $1 billion in losses and alleged that it had been created with direct input from an investor who stood to profit from its failure.

Although he could have selected from countless examples to highlight Wall Street's sins, Obama did not do so. Unlike FDR, he dwelled at length on the value of banks and investment companies: "I believe in the power of the free market. I believe in a strong financial sector that helps people to raise capital and get loans and invest their savings. That's part of what has made America what it is. But a free market was never meant to be a free license to take whatever you can get, however you can get it. That's what happened too often in the years leading up to this crisis."

The most scolding line in the president's speech came after he described the Dodd–Frank reforms and argued that they would be good for Wall Street as well as the nation: "And unless your business model depends on bilking people, there is little to fear from these new rules." Finally the president appealed to patriotism, concluding, "I urge you to join me not only because it is in the interest of your industry, but also because it's in the interest of your country."

In this not especially stirring address, the president's delivery was often hesitating and strained. And the audience was hardly the sort to stand up and cheer his plan. However, the speech was widely reported by the news media, and the public was inclined to favor a president taking the battle to Wall Street. The most recent Harris poll had found that 80 percent of Americans thought the government should do more to police financial institutions, and two-thirds agreed that "most people on Wall Street would be willing to break the law if they believed they could make a lot of money and get away with it."

In the political environment revealed by the poll, Republican senators were trapped between their leaders, who insisted on unanimous opposition to tougher financial regulation, and constituents who considered Wall Street untrustworthy. The president, who sometimes enjoyed poking at his political opponents, joked about the GOP at a Democratic Party fund-raiser in Manhattan. Referring to the economy, he said, "After they drove the car into the ditch, made it as difficult as possible for us to pull it back, now they want the keys back." Obama paused, raised his eyebrows, and added, "No! You can't drive! We don't want to go back into the ditch. We just got the car out!"

The GOP's unity on financial reform began to crack as Senator Corker publicly refuted some of his colleagues' criticisms of the reform plan, and Charles Grassley of Iowa backed parts of it as it was reviewed by the Senate Banking Committee. However, Grassley would eventually turn against the reform plan, in part because he objected to concessions made to win the vote of Scott Brown, a Republican who had shocked Democrats by winning a special election required by the death of Ted Kennedy.

As the senator from one of the most liberal states in the union, Massachusetts, Brown was a likely target for Obama administration officials, who hoped to find some Republican support. In an episode recounted by then treasury secretary Timothy Geithner, Brown expressed overall support for the Obama reforms but said he needed changes to benefit two of his state's financial firms. Brown needed an aide's help to name them—Fidelity Investments and State Street Corporation—but he got the changes he wanted. In exchange, Brown promised to vote in favor of the plan.

Messy political trade-offs, which are almost always part of getting any big proposal through Congress, meant that the reform plan reached a final vote speckled with amendments that Geithner would call "barnacles." These flaws provided arguments that were used by those who would vote against reform and needed to explain their position to constituents, but they weren't significant enough to doom the plan. It was approved by both houses of Congress and signed by the president in mid-July. On that day advocates at the Chamber of Commerce and the Business Roundtable, which served chief executives of major corporations, practically howled with pain. The new law "takes our country in the wrong direction," declared the Roundtable. At the ceremony when the president signed the new law, lawmakers were almost giddy with excitement over what they had accomplished.

In his brief statement the president noted that the "primary cause" of the Great Recession "was the breakdown of our financial system." He elicited a big cheer and standing ovation when he praised the work of Representative Frank and Senator Dodd, who, Obama said, "had worked day and night" to get the bill through Congress. He outlined the many elements of the new regulations, which included more power for shareholders over executive pay, rules requiring plainer language in loan and credit documents, and a reduced risk of future taxpayer-funded bank rescues. After he signed the law, the president sought out Paul Volcker in the crowd and gave him a light embrace and a firm pat on the back. A tall, bespectacled woman named Elizabeth Warren looked on, beaming.

Warren was a sixty-one-year-old Harvard Law School professor. An expert in bankruptcy law, she had been one of the earliest and loudest voices to warn of the financial crisis. She had long advocated for the creation of an agency that would help ordinary citizens in the financial marketplace in the way that the Consumer Product Safety Commission aided them as they bought appliances, clothes, furniture, and other goods. Warren made this point in an article she published in 2007:

It is impossible to buy a toaster that has a one-in-five chance of bursting into flames and burning down your house. But it is possible to refinance an existing home with a mortgage that has the same one-in-five chance of putting the family out on the street—and the mortgage won't even carry a disclosure of that fact to the home-owner. Similarly, it's impossible to change the price on a toaster once it has been purchased. But long after the papers have been signed, it is possible to triple the price of the credit used to finance the purchase of that appliance, even if the customer meets all the credit terms, in full and on time. Why are consumers safe when they purchase tangible consumer products with cash, but when they sign up for routine financial products like mortgages and credit cards they are left at the mercy of their creditors?

Warren's ideas got wider notice when the financial crisis hit, and she was appointed to a congressional commission that monitored the bank bailouts begun under President Bush. She retained traces of the accent she acquired growing up poor in Oklahoma and became somewhat famous through appearances in documentary films and on Jon Stewart's parody of a news program, *The Daily Show*.

Appearing on April 15, 2009, Warren had explained to Stewart that her task was to determine whether taxpayers were getting a "fair deal" in the bailout and added that she had discovered that "for every one hundred dollars we put into it, we got back stocks and warrants that were worth sixty-six dollars. It turns out that we gave away seventy-eight billion dollars."

Warren made a charming interviewee, admitting, "I don't know," when Stewart asked her to decipher an acronym and then waving her hand a bit as she joked, "It's an investment thing."

When an exasperated Stewart discovered that Warren's committee possessed no real authority to compel anyone to reveal information, Warren stammered a bit but then reassured him, "What I can do is I can talk about this."

Warren talked so much about protecting consumers from opaque financial agreements and unscrupulous practices—she even appeared in the provocative filmmaker Michael Moore's *Capitalism: A Love Story*—that by the time Obama's financial reform program became law, she was widely regarded as the leading candidate to run the new agency. She had also made herself a target for those who opposed the new regulations. William Cohan, a Wall Street executive, complained that Warren had peddled a fallacy about the need for consumer protections and bemoaned that the new agency "gives us all yet another excuse to avoid taking responsibility for our own actions. . . . We can now continue to blame others for our own failings. This is not progress."

Cohan's main argument—that individual borrowers were fairly matched against the giant banks—was belied by the efforts those on his side of the argument poured into stopping financial reform, and the CFPB's creation and implementation. In 2010 alone, Cohan's industry dispatched an army of more than twenty-five hundred lobbyists to fight for its cause in Washington. Huge banks including JPMorgan Chase, Goldman Sachs, and Citigroup, which accepted billions of taxpayer dollars to save them from self-made disaster, spent millions to urge friends in Congress to block Dodd-Frank's implementation. In a fight that often turned personal, they also focused on preventing one person—Elizabeth Warren—from becoming the head of the consumer protection agency.

Many in the president's party pushed for Warren to get the CFPB job, but the opposition from bankers and their supporters in Congress became so loud that the president chose, instead, the attorney general of Ohio, Richard Cordray. Although he, too, ran into opposition, Cordray would eventually win confirmation and establish himself as an effective regulator. Under his leadership the bureau began enforcing rules such as Regulation Z, which required that lenders verify a borrower's ability to repay a loan before it is made. This practice was standard before deregulation but became much less so in the run-up to the financial crisis. The agency also took up more than 650,000 complaints of deceptive practices and, as of 2015, helped return more than $10 billion to consumers. In the case of the mortgage services company Ocwen, consumers who had been through flawed foreclosures received $125 million.

As Cordray proved himself to be a male version of Elizabeth Warren, the original bankers' antagonist decided to challenge Senator Scott Brown in the 2012 election. Warren's campaign caught fire after she gave a populist speech in which she called on businesspeople to support the country that allowed them to succeed. "You built a factory out there? Good for you. But I want to be clear. You moved your goods to market on the roads the rest of us paid for. You hired workers the rest of us paid to educate. You were safe in your factory because of police forces and fire forces that the rest of us paid for. . . . You built a factory and it turned into something terrific, or a great idea. God bless—keep a big hunk of it. But part of the underlying social contract is, you take a hunk of that and pay forward for the next kid who comes along."

After Warren's speech, the political director of the Chamber of Commerce declared her the number one enemy of business, saying, "No other candidate in 2012 represents a greater threat to free enterprise than Professor Warren." The title *professor* was no doubt deployed to incite a little anti-intellectual prejudice against Warren, but in a state where colleges and universities form the foundation of the economy, it wasn't an effective slur. Besides, many voters thought she was right about the obligations of the wealthy. The president adopted Warren's populist economic theme, and it helped him win reelection. Warren trounced Brown and in January wound up on the Senate Banking Committee, where she would press for criminal prosecutions of officials at banks involved in fraudulent activity. In the two years following her election Warren became the top fund-raiser for Democratic candidates across the country, and she led the defense of the Dodd-Frank reforms, which Republicans hoped to roll back.

In the years that followed the landmark reforms enacted in Dodd-Frank, the law became a rallying point for Wall Streeters and the GOP, who talked about it as if it were truly unfair to financiers. Republican candidates attacked it in their campaign speeches, but given the way Americans felt about Wall Street, the cause did not rouse the faithful. The reforms became part of President Obama's legacy, as did the CFPB, which had the power to create new rules for the financial marketplace. In 2016 the agency moved to give consumers the right to bring class-action lawsuits against lenders, who had changed the fine print in contracts to deny them this right. The gradual revision in contracts had shifted power in the direction of lenders because individuals were unlikely to undertake costly efforts to recover, for example, an erroneously charged late fee or overdraft charge. As a class, however, thousands of consumers who felt similarly victimized would be willing to join together to challenge a credit card company or other lender. As an independent agency the CFPB could and did act to level the playing field.

In addition to the achievements of the consumer protection bureau, Dodd-Frank made the world economy safer in a number of ways. Obama's reforms gave the government greater ability to monitor the entire financial industry and step in when important players neared failure. The law put more controls on previously unregulated types of investments and reduced the threat to the economy posed by firms that were deemed "too big to fail."

The president's critics on the Left complained that not enough had been done to cut the risk of megabanks' disrupting the economy again and favored breaking up the big financial firms. A breakup would have appealed to a public that was outraged by the scandalous behavior of some financiers, but given the political and legal constraints, it was never a real possibility. Instead the president and his allies in Congress did the hard work of drafting a complex law, filled with boring terminology, that wound up achieving something more effective. The capital held by the major banks increased substantially, making them much safer, and the major financial companies returned to profitability, making them much stronger. That kind of change didn't make big headlines, but when it comes to the financial system, boring is better.

With the passage of Dodd-Frank and with the CFPB formed and in action, the president and his allies in Congress would devote themselves to protecting their achievements from continual attacks and looking for ways to help people navigate the complex and treacherous financial environment. One quiet move came in

Regulatory Capital Ratios at Top 25 Bank Holding Companies

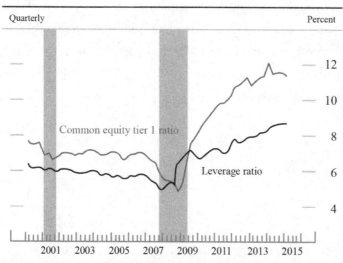

NOTE: Prior to 2014: Ql, the numerator of the common equity tier 1 ratio is tier 1 common capital. Beginning in 2014: Q1 for advanced approaches bank holding companies and in 2015: Q1 for all other bank holding companies, the numerator is common equity tier 1 capital. The shaded bar indicates a period of business recession as defined by the National Bureau of Economic Research.

SOURCE: FR Y-9C (top panels)

2015. With the debt burden of college students soaring past $1 trillion and graduates facing payments stretching far into the future, the president cut in half the amount of income a borrower was supposed to devote to paying certain of these debts. Some borrowers could also have loans forgiven after twenty years. The result was a break for students worth about $22 billion.

In 2016, the benefits of Dodd-Frank were seen in the Federal reserve's mid-year report on the stregnth of major financial institutions. After conducting so-called stress tests, which simulated the effects of a major economic downtown, the Fed issued unconditional passing grades to all but one American-based bank, Morgan Stanley. However Morgan Stanley's performance had improved and it was given a passing grade overall. Two subsidiaries of European banks did not pass. In sum, the review showed the lenders had built up their reserves so well they could weather a crash in the value of equities, a big spike in unemployment, or a sudden rise in interest rates. For the financiers, who put substantial sums of money and executive time into passing the test, the grades signaled their success. For Americans who were outraged by the role banks played in the fianncial crisis, and feared a repeat of the crisis and bailout, the shoring-up was proof that the political system, and the president they had elected twice, had delivered.

9

EQUALITY

Expectations, Limits, Progress

The work was physically demanding, and the overnight shifts, which were twelve hours long, would wreak havoc on anyone's body. Then there was the harassment. Lilly Ledbetter was pawed and catcalled. One boss made it clear that she was to be his next sexual conquest because everyone at the plant expected it. When she rejected him, he told her that her job depended on her agreeing to have sex with him. Even the wives of her male coworkers harassed her. The intimidation included cut brake lines on her car. But not many places in the entire state of Alabama paid as well as the Goodyear Tire plant in Gadsden, so Ledbetter endured. She rose in the ranks, eventually becoming a supervisor. In 1996 Goodyear gave her a "top performance" award. She was, as she said, a "company person. I was true-blue."

Mortgage payments and her children's college tuition bills kept Ledbetter on the job for nearly twenty years. She sometimes wondered if her counterparts—all men—were paid more, but didn't learn the facts until she was close to retirement. Ledbetter discovered then that every one of the men who worked at the same job was being paid more. The difference ranged from $6,000 a year paid to a recently hired coworker to close to $20,000, which was 40 percent more. Ledbetter and Goodyear wound up in federal court in Anniston, Alabama, where a jury agreed that she had been cheated and said she deserved $328,597 in back pay. The panel also concluded that Goodyear should be punished in a way that might discourage future cheating of this sort and added $3,286,000 to the amount to be paid Ledbetter.

Lilly Ledbetter's experience at Goodyear was never in dispute. For nearly twenty years she had been paid less than the men who did the same work. The injustice was obvious, even if you discounted the harassment that Ledbetter endured as she was paid less. But the facts weren't enough to protect Ledbetter from the letter of the law. In its appeal, Goodyear persuaded a higher court to find that while she may have been cheated, the company didn't have to pay. The decision hinged on a statute of limitations that required anyone who had been discriminated against to file a complaint within six months. It didn't matter that the company acted in secret and Ledbetter had no way of knowing what was happening. Goodyear was still protected by this rule.

The Supreme Court took up the Ledbetter case to resolve a dispute between judges who said companies could get away with secretly cheating female workers and those who noted that lawmakers had intended to punish discrimination, not excuse it. Ledbetter lost in a vote that found five conservative-leaning justices lining up against her. In his decision, Justice Samuel Alito wrote, "Ledbetter's policy arguments for giving special treatment to pay claims find no support in the statute and are inconsistent with our precedents. We apply the statutes as written."

A 5–4 decision ended the matter for Lilly Ledbetter, but she could take some comfort and encouragement from the dissent published by four justices. Writing for the four, Justice Ruth Bader Ginsburg took the commonsense view that the type of gender-based cheating Goodyear practiced is "often hidden from sight" and that it caused a cumulative harm that should not be covered by the time limit noted by Justice Alito. The dissenters noted that Ledbetter had proved at trial that she had suffered discrimination, and federal law had been written to address this type of harm. Ginsburg also suggested that what the Supreme Court had done could be reversed by the legislative branch of government: "Once again, the ball is in Congress's court."

In the year that followed her defeat, Lilly Ledbetter toured the country making speeches and giving interviews. Well into her sixties, she spoke with the soft drawl she acquired while growing up in a rural community called Possum Trot. She talked about her children and grandchildren and about how she didn't want to "sound like a whiner and a complainer." Ledbetter recalled that when she asked her husband, Charles, if he would support her if she went to Birmingham to file her complaint, he had replied, "What time do you want to leave?" Ledbetter's tour included a stop in Washington, where the US Senate was about to vote down a bit of legislation that would have overturned the 180-day rule that Goodyear had exploited. (One House Republican said it would be unfair to ask executives to take responsibility for discrimination that occurred in the past under previous managers.) On Capitol Hill, Ledbetter met Barack Obama, then a senator, and made a lasting impression. Months later when her husband died, the senator called with condolences and then asked her to speak at the upcoming Democratic Party convention.

On August 26, 2008, Ledbetter walked onto a brightly lit stage at a twenty-thousand-seat arena in Denver. Billed as a "pay equity pioneer," she told the crowd about how "our highest court sided with big business. They said I should have filed my complaint within six months of Goodyear's first decision to pay me less, even though I didn't know that's what they were doing." Ledbetter added, "My case is over. I will never receive the pay I deserve. But there will be a far richer reward if we secure fair pay for our children and grandchildren, so that no one will ever again experience the discrimination that I did."

A plainspoken woman who had worked extremely hard through

her entire life, Ledbetter was from the same generation as the president's mother. The discrimination Ledbetter had experienced was not much different from the cheating that black Americans had endured forever. These factors and others prompted Obama to call on Ledbetter during his presidential campaign. (Ledbetter appeared in Virginia with Michelle Obama.) The candidate invoked her name during a nationally televised debate. After he was elected, Ledbetter joined the Obama family on the symbolic train trip they took to his swearing-in ceremony. She even danced with the new president at one of the inauguration balls.

The Lilly Ledbetter Fair Pay Act was the first law Barack Obama would sign as president of the United States. The law, approved by a Congress controlled by the president's party, closed the loophole Goodyear had slipped through to avoid the judgment of the jury in Anniston. However, it did not end the debate over fair pay. After the Ledbetter Act, politicians and academics would continue to argue over the size and nature of the wage gap between men and women, as well as its causes.

In the grossest measure, determined by comparing what women and men were paid overall, the difference was 20 percent or more. Skeptics would say that men and women worked in different fields and this explained the disparity. (They also cited the tendency for women to focus more on family life and on the possibility that men were simply better at demanding more money.) However, studies that compared men and women working in the same job also revealed gender gaps. Male chief executives enjoy a gender boost of $674 per week. In teaching, which has traditionally been a female occupation, men are paid $324 more weekly. No hard evidence could be found to prove men were better at asking for raises, and no social factor, including greater family responsibilities, could explain away the entire gap.

One new law, focused narrowly on the issue revealed by the

Ledbetter case, would not close the wage gap. However, it did put employers on notice of the risk they incurred if they used a two-tiered pay system. Throughout his presidency Obama pushed for the more sweeping reform contained in what was called the Paycheck Fairness Act, which would have added to the penalties ap-

Top 10 Occupations with the Worst Wage Gap
Median usual weekly earnings of full-time wage and salary workers, 2014 annual averages

	Women's earning as a percent of men's	Women's percent of occupation	Weekly earnings premium for men
Personal financial advisors	61.33%	40.00%	$633.00
Physicians and surgeons	62.24%	37.42%	$756.00
Securities, commodities, and financial services sales agents	65.12%	35.32%	$473.00
Financial managers	67.44%	53.49%	$544.00
First-line supervisors of housekeeping and janitorial workers	69.44%	41.83%	$220.00
First-line supervisors of production and operating workers	69.96%	17.49%	$283.00
Sales and related workers, all other	69.97%	49.73%	$285.00
Chief executives	69.99%	26.28%	$674.00
Retail salespersons	70.34%	39.20%	$207.00
Other teachers and instructors	70.44%	58.24%	$324.00

Source: Author's calculations of Bureau of Labor Statistics, "Labor Force Statistics from the Current Population Survey."
Available at http://www.bls.gov/cps/cpsaat39.htm (last accessed April 2015)

plied in cases of discrimination, barred retaliation against workers who complained, and required larger employers to report the rates of pay for men and women. The act was defeated in the Senate, more than once, and once the GOP took control of the Senate in 2014, its backers, including the president, would have no chance of making it into law.

Opponents of government action tended to frame the problem of the pay gap in a way that suggested it was so complex and nuanced that it defied solution. This was not true. Many countries report a much smaller wage gap than the United States. In countries as varied as Spain, Belgium, and New Zealand, it is below 10 percent. In Ireland it is less than 14 percent. Women fare better in these countries, and many others, because they offer lower-cost child care and paid leave for new parents. The policies countries have used to close the gender gap range from tax reforms to actual quotas for the hiring and promotion of women. German law requires that large corporations reserve 30 percent of board seats for women.

Economic engineering of the sort seen in parts of Europe would be all-but-impossible in the United States, especially with Obama blocked in Congress. However, in 2014 he did impose some of the rules contained in the Paycheck Fairness Act on federal contractors, requiring them to report their pay rates for men and women and barring them from retaliating when women lodged complaints. Two years later another executive order required all employers with more than one hundred workers to report what they were paying people by gender. If the next president leaves it in place, this rule

Gender Pay Gap Among Full-Time, Year-Round Workers

Percent

Source: Census Bureau, Table P-40.
Note that due to a change in income questions in the March Supplement in 2013, there is a trend break.

will provide the kind of information that might settle disputes of gender equality in tens of thousands of workplaces. The power of this kind of information was evident in the improvement that federal reports showed in the years since the Lilly Ledbetter Act was adopted. After getting worse during the Bush years, the gap actually closed slightly during the Obama presidency. Although it would be impossible to quantify, some evidence could be found to suggest that all the talk about fair pay for women could move employers to do the right thing on their own.

A case in point could be seen at the company Saleforce.com, where the chief executive officer believed he was already paying men and women equally. When two women employees told him they thought his assumptions were wrong, Marc Benioff asked his managers for a report on the matter. He discovered that the employees were right. He immediately spent $3 million to close the gap and committed managers to keeping the genders on par going forward.

Consistent in his support for Lilly Ledbetter, Barack Obama was a proponent of equal pay for women long before he was elected president, and he continued to champion the issue throughout his two terms in office. When he discussed the issue, he referenced his daughters and spoke with conviction.

In another major debate about equality—the fight for gay marriage rights—Obama's record was much less certain. David Axelrod, who worked for Obama in many campaigns, would recall that Obama long favored marriage equality. He had even indicated his support for it when filling out a questionnaire in 1996. But Obama began to hedge his position almost immediately because many of his African-Americans constituents opposed it on religious grounds. In 2004 he told the local Windy City Times, "I am a fierce supporter of domestic-partnership and civil-union laws." He added,

"I am not a supporter of gay marriage as it has been thrown about, primarily just as a strategic issue. I think that marriage, in the minds of a lot of voters, has a religious connotation."

The irony in this situation could not have been lost on Obama. After all, religion had been the basis of so-called antimiscegenation laws, which many states had used to ban interracial marriage until the late 1960s. The fight to overturn these laws had been an essential part of the civil rights struggle.

When it came to gay marriage, opponents cited religion and defined the effort to grant *more* people the right to marry as an assault on the institution itself. The Republican Party made opposition to marriage equality part of its official platform. In 1996 a large majority in Congress, among them many Democrats, supported a new law called the Defense of Marriage Act (DOMA), which codified the restriction of the government benefits granted to married people to heterosexual couples. Presented with the legislation during his campaign for reelection, President Clinton signed it, even though he called it "divisive and unnecessary."

Clinton won reelection in part due to his compromises on issues such as DOMA, which Republicans exploited to motivate voters who viewed politics through the lens of conservative Christianity. In 2004, religious and conservative activists got antiequality initiatives put onto ballots in eleven states and conducted aggressive campaigns to build support for these measures. The voters flocked to support these bans—every one was approved—and most also cast a vote to reelect President Bush. Bush had attached himself to the cause by declaring his support for a national, constitutional ban on gay and lesbian marriages. He said that such a sweeping measure was required because judges in Massachusetts had granted gay and lesbian couples equal rights and "their actions have created confusion on an issue that requires clarity."

As he campaigned for president in 2008, Obama and his team understood that gay marriage was a potent issue. He took the most neutral position available, in favor of "civil unions," which gave couples some of the rights of marriage but fell short of actual equality. Often uncomfortable when the question was asked, he would talk about how marriage put God "in the mix" and this made it hard for him to support marriages other than between a man and a woman. Axelrod would write, "Having prided himself on forthrightness, though, Obama never felt comfortable with his compromise, and, no doubt, compromised position." In fact, Axelrod would report that Obama was unhappy "bullshitting" and that "I just don't feel my marriage is somehow threatened by the gay couple next door."

Voters who wanted to know more about Obama's attitudes could consider his early commitment to the repeal of DOMA and to changing another Clinton policy that discriminated against gay men and women, called Don't Ask, Don't Tell. This rule prohibited any discussion of sexual orientation by people in the military, but it did not end the practice of dismissing from service people who were known to have same-sex relationships. By maintaining the rule against homosexuality, but then banning any discussing of orientation, Don't Ask, Don't Tell reinforced discriminatory attitudes. It also required that everyone in the service practice various kinds of deceptions to comply with regulations.

In his first State of the Union address, President Obama announced he would work with Congress "and our military" to repeal Don't Ask, Don't Tell. The military argument for discrimination against gay soldiers and officers had been based on the notion that somehow the presence of a gay person would affect the fighting abilities of a unit. However, the same argument had been made against the racial integration of the armed services, and when it finally occurred, no real disruption was seen. In the case of gay service members, General Colin Powell, former secretary of state, said he thought it was "a law that should be reviewed." However, as President Obama committed himself to the repeal of the law, more than a thousand former officers signed a petition supporting the policy, and Senator John McCain, whom Obama had defeated in the 2008 election, read it aloud at a Senate hearing. The letter said the law was essential "to protect good order, discipline, and morale."

As retired officers, those who had signed the letter represented a generation removed from the men and women in the rank and file in 2010. Over the years a wide gap had opened between the young and the old when it came to homosexuality. In 2010, the highly regarded National Opinion Research Center reported that only 26 percent of people under age thirty considered same-sex relationships "always wrong," but 63 percent of those over age seventy did hold this belief. (McCain was seventy-four at the time.) A similar difference was seen when researchers asked about marriage equality, with younger adults supporting equal rights by three to

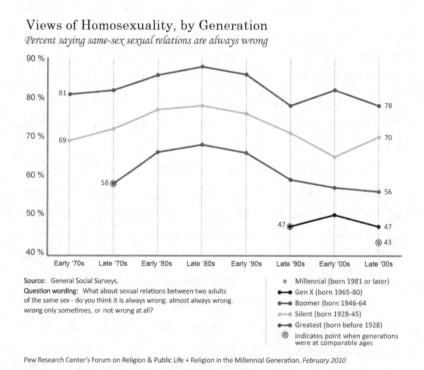

Views of Homosexuality, by Generation
Percent saying same-sex sexual relations are always wrong

Source: General Social Surveys.
Question wording: What about sexual relations between two adults of the same sex - do you think it is always wrong. almost always wrong. wrong only sometimes, or not wrong at all?

- Millennial (born 1981 or later)
- Gen X (born 1965-80)
- Boomer (born 1946-64
- Silent (born 1928-45)
- Greatest (born before 1928)
- Indicates point when generations were at comparable ages

Pew Research Center's Forum on Religion & Public Life + Religion in the Millennial Generation. *February 2010*

Courtesy Pew Research Center

one and a majority of older Americans opposed to it. In 2010, three of four major opinion surveys found a majority of all Americans supported openly gay people serving in the military.

With public opinion changing rapidly, Obama was in a position to make a concerted push for repeal. Stymied in Congress when McCain blocked a Senate vote, Obama waited for a Department of Defense study, which found that repeal would have minimal practical effect. The report included results from a survey of tens of thousands of service members and their wives and husbands. Less than a third of the respondents said the change would have a mainly negative effect. When the study was made public, Defense Secretary Robert Gates said that with the right effort by officers, ending the policy "would not be the wrenching, traumatic change that many have feared and predicted." Gates was supported by thirty military experts, including current and former military academy professors, who said the only rationale to support Don't Ask, Don't Tell "is prejudice."

Virtually every survey ever done on the subject showed that women were less prejudiced about sexual orientation than men, and a woman senator led the effort to overcome McCain on the issue of Don't Ask, Don't Tell. In December 2010, Republican Susan Collins of Maine noted that her party had won so many seats in the previous month's election that it would take control of the House in 2011. Then, any hope of repeal would likely be lost. Collins encouraged Democrats in the House to approve a repeal proposal and send it to the Senate. Once this was done, Collins and others rallied enough Republicans to overcome any effort to block repeal with a filibuster. One of those who voted in favor of repeal, Senator Joseph Lieberman of Connecticut, noted that fourteen thousand men and women had been forced out of the military because of the policy. "What a waste," he said.

President Obama signed the legislation repealing the policy within days of the Senate vote. At the ceremony where he put his

signature on the bill, he told a story about a soldier who had rescued a fellow private during World War II at the Battle of the Bulge.
Trapped in a snowy, forty-foot-deep ravine, Lloyd Corwin was
rescued by Andy Lee, who then waited more than forty years to tell
his friend that he was gay. "He had no idea," said Obama, of Corwin. "And he didn't much care. Lloyd knew what mattered. He
knew what had kept him alive; what made it possible for him to
come home and start a family and live the rest of his life. It was his
friend." Corwin's son was present at the White House as Obama
spoke and applauded the president's remarks.

Obama also quoted the Pentagon's study that supported changing the policy. He said, "One special operations war fighter said
during the Pentagon's review—this was one of my favorites—it
echoes the experience of Lloyd Corwin decades earlier: 'We have
a gay guy in the unit. He's big, he's mean, he kills lots of bad guys.'
No one cared that he was gay." As the people listening to the president laughed, he added, "And I think that sums up perfectly the
situation."

Follow-up studies on repeal did not reveal any of the negative
effects, let alone the "great damage" that Senator McCain had said
was being done. Military morale, recruitment, and readiness were
not changed, and even in the marines, where resistance to repeal
was greatest, General James Amos said, in 2013, "I'm very pleased
with how it has gone."

Repeal of Don't Ask, Don't Tell brought a measure of equal treatment to tens of thousands of men and women who had been forced
into second-class status within the military. Restrictions on gay
marriage affected millions of people, putting the force of the government behind bigotry rooted in custom and religion, which had
been the source of other forms of discrimination that had eventually fallen under the weight of history. As a distinguished graduate
of Harvard Law School who had been an instructor in constitu-

tional law at the University of Chicago from 1993 to 2004, Obama certainly understood the legal, as well as the moral, argument in favor of equality. In 2009 Obama had hosted the first-ever White House reception marking Gay Pride Month.

If Obama was unhappy with the campaign compromise he had made on gay marriage, as Axelrod reported, many of his supporters were, too. Having come to office by promising "change," the president faced high expectations among members of his party, especially when it came to civil rights. In August 2010, a writer for *The New Republic* published an essay calling Obama's inaction on gay marriage "a disgrace," adding, "Obama's stance seems to be a way of conveying to the country that he knows a lot of people still aren't completely comfortable admitting gays and lesbians as full participants in American life, and that this is OK because he isn't either." Soon Obama began saying that his position on the matter was "evolving," and in early 2011 he told the Justice Department to stop opposing lawsuits challenging the Defense of Marriage Act in federal court.

With the House of Representatives in GOP control, Obama could not hope to address gay marriage with federal legislation. Nevertheless, his supporters felt impatient with his leadership. In the summer of 2011 he went to New York for a fund-raiser sponsored by gay supporters and endured a bit of heckling. "Marriage, do you support it?" shouted some in the crowd. A month later, when California senator Diane Feinstein proposed legislation that would overturn DOMA, which had little chance of becoming law, the president announced he supported it. Then, in May 2012, Vice President Biden caused a stir when he said on TV, "The good news is that as more and more Americans come to understand what this is all about is a simple proposition: Who do you love? Who do you love, and will you be loyal to the person you love? And that's what people are finding out what all marriages at their root are about. Whether they are marriages of lesbians or gay men or heterosexuals."

While noting that the president set administration policy, Biden said he believed that all couple were "entitled to the same exact rights . . . all of the civil liberties."

Biden's statement prompted immediate coverage on news Web sites. Analysts saw it as such a firm departure from the president's position that they speculated it was an intentional trial balloon, uttered with the purpose of gauging public reaction. In truth, as writer Jo Becker reported in her book on the subject, *Forcing the Spring,* White House officials were caught by surprise, and some considered the statement disloyal to the president. (Biden was known for making off-the-cuff remarks and had occasionally run into trouble doing so.) According to Becker, Biden said that he "didn't go out volunteering a position, but when asked a question . . . I had to respond to it."

With an election less than six months away, and aides advising the president that support for marriage equality might cost him victories in key states, Biden's remark did put the president in a position where he would have to clear things up. Three days later, he sat for an interview with ABC news reporter Robin Roberts, who put the question to him directly. He talked about gay friends and colleagues and said, "I've just concluded that—for me personally, it is important for me to go ahead and affirm that—I think same-sex couples should be able to get married. Now—I have to tell you that part of my hesitation on this has also been I didn't want to nationalize the issue. There's a tendency when I weigh in to think suddenly it becomes political and it becomes polarized."

Opinion in the Obama family may have been polarized, too. The president told Roberts that his daughters had friends "whose parents are same-sex couples. And I—you know, there have been times where Michelle and I have been sitting around the dinner table. And we've been talking and—about their friends and their parents. And Malia and Sasha would—it wouldn't dawn on them that somehow their friends' parents would be treated differently. It doesn't make sense to them. And—and frankly—that's the kind of

thing that prompts—a change of perspective. You know, not want-
ing to somehow explain to your child why somebody should be
treated differently, when it comes to the eyes of the law."

After the president explained his position, Shep Smith of the
Right-leaning Fox News network praised him for taking a position that put him firmly "in the twenty-first century." Many
African-American leaders also announced that they would join the
president in support of gay marriage. John Lewis, longtime civil-
rights leader and a member of Congress from Georgia, said, "I fought
too long and too hard against discrimination based on race and color,
not to stand up and fight against discrimination based on sexual
orientation. . . . We must respect the dignity and the worth of every
human being whether they are gay or straight." The board of the
National Association for the Advancement of Colored People, the
oldest civil rights organization in the country, also announced its
support for an end to bans on same-sex marriage. The organization
announced, "We have and will oppose efforts to codify discrimination into law."

When voters went to the polls in the fall, Obama did lose two
states that he had carried in 2008: Indiana and North Carolina. In
the first instance his stand on marriage equality probably didn't have
much effect, since Indiana tended to be quite conservative and the
margin of defeat was greater than ten points. However, in North
Carolina the president lost by only two points, and it was possible
that the issue was important. Still, the president was the first since
Dwight Eisenhower to win more than 51 percent of the popular
vote two times in a row. Also, 2012 saw the country moving in his
direction on same-sex marriage as three states approved ballot measures to allow same-sex marriages and one defeated a proposal to
ban them. In no other election had advocates for equality won even
a single statewide referendum.

One month after the elections, the Supreme Court announced
it would hear two cases that challenged the constitutionality of laws

that denied same-sex couples the right to marry. In the more narrowly focused one, Edith Windsor of New York, who had married her longtime partner in a state that permitted same-sex unions, challenged the elements of the Defense of Marriage Act that prevented her from receiving marital benefits when her spouse died. In the other case, couples from California said that a recently approved voter initiative—Proposition 8—was unconstitutional because it denied a class of people, gay men and lesbian women, the rights enjoyed by heterosexuals. They said it was state-sanctioned discrimination. and the US Appeals Court in San Francisco agreed. The defendants appealed, which brought them to the US Supreme Court.

When he delivered his second inaugural address on the steps of the US Capitol, Obama made clear his support for gay rights and argued that this cause was a natural extension of the fight for gender and racial equality: "We, the people, declare today that the most evident of truths—that all of us are created equal—is the star that guides us still; just as it guided our forebears through Seneca Falls, and Selma, and Stonewall." (Stonewall was the name of a bar where, in 1969, a spontaneous and days-long protest erupted over police harassment of gays and lesbians.) In his speech the president added that the country's "journey" toward a more perfect union "is not complete until our gay brothers and sisters are treated like anyone else under the law—for if we are truly created equal, then surely the love we commit to one another must be equal as well."

The matter of equality in the Prop 8 case would be argued in the Supreme Court by private parties. On one side would stand the lawyers for the gay couples. On the other would stand attorneys representing organizations that wanted to protect Prop 8. However, the Obama administration also threw the weight of the federal government behind those seeking to abolish the law. According to many reports, the president was directly involved in setting out the argument that Solicitor General Donald Verrilli would make on behalf of the government. His amicus brief said the Supreme Court should uphold the Appeals Court decision, which governed nine Western states, and then extend the ruling to nine others that allowed gay marriage or civil unions. The idea here was that once a state granted certain marriage rights, it had to grant them all. The key passage in the document read, "Proposition 8, by depriving same-sex couples of the right to marry, denies them the 'dignity, respect, and stature' accorded similarly situated opposite-sex couples under state law and does not substantially further any important governmental interest."

With a similar brief, Verrilli also supported Edith Windsor. Few court cases attracted as much public interest as these two. When they were argued, thousands of gay rights supporters marched in the street in front of the court and waved banners and rainbow flags, which symbolized their commitment to a diverse country. Smaller, but no less vocal, contingents of people holding anti-equality views gathered to make themselves heard. Many of these people made religious arguments, including the crude sentiment on a sign that read GOD H8S FAGS. The religious zealotry leaked into the courtroom when the justices heard the Windsor case and a man shouted, "Homosexuality is an abomination!" and "You'll all burn in hell!" Verrilli was speaking and barely skipped a beat as the shouting man was escorted out of the courtroom by police. In response to a question from Justice Anthony Kennedy, Verrilli recalled how social attitudes toward gay people had changed. He said, "We understand now, in a way even that we did not fully understand in *Lawrence* [a previous case that ended legal prohibitions on same-sex relationships] that gay and lesbian people and gay and lesbian couples are full and equal members of the community. And what we once thought of as necessary and proper reasons for ostracizing and marginalizing gay people, we now understand do not justify that kind of impression."

When rulings were issued, the Appeals Court decision striking down Prop 8 was upheld, and Edith Windsor was affirmed in her effort to overcome the legal discrimination against her. A year later the court extended the right to marry to same-sex couples in all fifty states. These developments, which would have been hard to predict in 2008, completed a sweeping transformation of official policy. After brief periods of protest the country adapted to the new reality in a peaceful way.

The president welcomed the change and praised the Supreme Court's decisions at the annual White House celebration of Gay Pride Month, which had also become a rite for honoring bisexual and transgender Americans. He noted a number of accomplishments including new laws against hate crimes and to assure equal access to medical care. He also marveled at the change in social attitudes: "One thing is undeniable. There has been this incredible shift in attitudes across the country. . . . A decade ago people ran against LGBT rights. Today they are running toward them."

The proper context for the celebration—Obama was greeted by a boisterous crowd—would have to include the recollection of what Obama had said at the first White House gay pride event, which had coincided with the fortieth anniversary of the Stonewall uprising. At the time the president was under pressure from those who expected him to be a transformational leader. He spoke as if he understood the course he would follow. "I want you to know that I expect and hope to be judged not by words, not by promises I've made, but by the promises that my administration keeps. . . . We've been in office six months now. I suspect that by the time this administration is over, I think you guys will have pretty good feelings about the Obama administration."

Barack Obama did not make specific policy promises when it came to race, but during his first campaign he had often talked about unity. His most substantive comments about race came in March of 2008 when he faced withering criticism about the incendiary remarks made by the pastor of a church he'd attended in Chicago.

Obama condemned those statements and said, "They rightly of-
fended white and black alike." However, he also defended the
man, Jeremiah Wright, as someone who was not just fiery, but also
compassionate and inspiring. After reciting the history of race relations, Obama noted the country was in "a racial stalemate," which
he hoped that citizens would resolve together.

As he addressed the racial assumptions and expectations that
his candidacy evoked and conditions across the country, Obama was
both generous in his regard for Americans of all races and humble
about what he could accomplish. He recognized the frustrations and
anger of people who felt they had been denied an equal opportunity to thrive, and he insisted that the nation's race problems would
not be addressed in a full way by a single presidential candidacy,
"particularly a candidacy as imperfect as my own." However, no
matter what Obama said to dampen expectations, he was trapped
by the symbolism that came with being the first African-American
nominated by a major party and by his election and reelection. In
the minds of some, his mere existence was supposed to change
things for the better, or the worse.

Some of the most negative responses to America's first black
president came at the start of his presidency from so-called Tea Party
protesters, who shouted racist comments and waved signs decorated
with racist slogans. Racist jokes were offered by members of Congress and racist cartoons were distributed by GOP officials. But
the most insidiously negative assertions came from those who
insisted that with Obama's election race relations had immediately
soured. He was even blamed for fistfights between white and black
schoolkids.

The idea that race relations were worse because of Obama reflected age-old fears about the antiwhite backlash waiting to emerge
from black Americans. Broadcaster Glenn Beck declared, "This
guy is, I believe, a racist," and a Minnesota state senator named Mike
Parry said, "My opinion is that our president is arrogant and angry.

The fact is that he is a black man." Obama also faced the bizarre complaint, often voiced by whites, that he was somehow less than black. Former Illinois governor Rod Blagojevich said, "I'm blacker than Barack Obama. I shined shoes. I grew up in a five-room apartment. My father had a little Laundromat in a black community not far from where we lived. I saw it all growing up." All these comments were spoken in the *first year* of Obama's presidency. They would continue, and the feelings behind them would find expression in the persistent "birther" campaign that kept alive the notion that the Obama presidency was illegitimate because he wasn't an American citizen. Worse would come from pop figures of the political Right such as Ann Coulter, who referred to the president as a "monkey," and Ted Nugent, who used the Nazi-era slur "subhuman mongrel" to describe the president.

On the other side of the ledger of expectation, Obama encountered high hopes among those who thought that his election heralded a healing of the racial divide. To the frustration of many who hoped for more social progress, racial conflict persisted and at times received even greater press attention than in the past. In almost every instance, whether it was a police shooting of an unarmed black person or a lesser outrage, the president held no direct authority to intervene. However, the Obama Justice Department did pressure police departments to reform, and agencies charged with enforcing antidiscrimination laws and regulations stepped up their enforcement. The administration subjected more than twenty police departments to investigations of systemic misconduct in their dealings with minority communities. More important, where previously departments were permitted to resolve cases with memorandums, the Obama Justice Department sought more binding agreements that were overseen by federal judges.

Throughout his presidency, Obama repeated his commitment to serve all of the country, not just one group, and he approached issues with such analytical calm that he defied both those who would say he was an angry man and those who prayed he would show more emotion. The emotion came over time, especially as he mourned victims of both racial and seemingly random violence. The president was clearly and sorely pained by mass shootings, which occurred with alarming frequency and defied every effort anyone made to impose more regulations on the purchase of firearms.

Subject to powerful expectations and often hemmed in by the limits of his power, Obama nevertheless made a profound contribution to the cause of racial equality. His presidency, and the example he and his family set as the first family, changed forever the way the world imagines the United States. This achievement was accomplished with grace despite the insults hurled against him. It may also have set the stage for the presidents to follow to achieve more. This possibility was noted by the writer Michael Eric Dyson as Obama began his last year in office. Dyson wrote that were she to succeed him, Hillary Clinton had been prepared, by her own rough experience in politics and by what she saw while serving as Obama's secretary of state, to do even more for black America than the first black president could.

10

UNFINISHED BUSINESS (AND FAILURES)

"Hope" was the theme, the trademark, and the currency of Barack Obama's 2008 campaign for the presidency. The word appeared under his image on iconic campaign posters and in his speeches, and it invited mockery, which he acknowledged by imagining aloud how his critics spoke about him. "He's a hope-monger," said candidate Obama with a hint of a smile.

When required, Obama refined his message but never abandoned its poetry. "Hope is not blind optimism," he said. "Hope is not sitting on the sidelines or shirking from a fight. Hope is that thing inside of us that insists, despite all the evidence to the contrary, that there is something greater inside of us. . . . If you will work with me, like you've never worked before, then we will win. And we will win America. And then we will change the world."

Obama and his supporters delivered hope, won America, and, by many measures, changed the world. In the United States this truth is evident in the lives of people who now have jobs and health care and cleaner air and better schools and on and on. Abroad, Obama restored America's reputation, reduced the nuclear threat, began to address climate change, and on and on. Such is the power of rhetoric, imagery, emotion, and effort.

Hope did not solve all of America's problems or heal its divisions. No president could have produced the transformation that so many imagined would come with Obama's election. He was the first black president, the first born after the 1940s, and the first who carried a name that was not distinctly European. Widely judged to be the best presidential orator since Kennedy, Obama's charisma was balanced with a temperament that suggested he would be extremely effective. But no one could satisfy the promise that was Obama. Inevitably, he would disappoint many supporters and leave much for his successors to undertake. These are just a few examples of where Obama fell short of expectations and his own promises.

RACE RELATIONS

As Americans began to consider Obama's legacy, some of the loudest expressions of disappointment came from African-American leaders, whose hopes had soared in 2008. Commentator Tavis Smiley repeatedly pointed out that black Americans had lost ground, economically, in the Obama years. This fact, he said, proved Obama's failure to serve the African-American community. Columbia University professor Fredrick Harris said, "There is not enough focus or attention, particularly policywise, on addressing the legacies of racial inequality in this country." Others complained that in Obama's effort to demonstrate that he was president of all the country's people, he had failed to address, in an effective way, the racial problems symbolized by the many widely publicized instances of unarmed black men who were killed by police in places such as Houston, Ferguson, Missouri, and Staten Island, New York. In the meantime, public opinion polls showed that Americans, including black Americans, felt significantly more pessimistic about race relations.

In reality, Obama often faced a no-win situation in race relations. When he pointed to the often-lethal danger of merely being a young black man in America, he was criticized for failing to support law and order. When he called on black families and communities to raise their expectations for themselves, he was criticized for blaming those who are victims of bigotry.

Among whites it was easy to find those who complained about

Obama's leadership on race. In early 2016, Republican representative Mo Brooks of Alabama told a radio talk show host, "There probably has not been a more racially divisive, economic-divisive president in the White House since we had presidents who supported slavery." Senator Marco Rubio, R-FL, said of Obama, "We have not seen such a divisive figure in modern American history."

Other than for the weak evidence in opinion polls, it's difficult if not impossible to assess race relations in America. Certainly no metric could support the claims made by Rubio and Brooks. The well-publicized deaths of young black men who were either shot or restrained by police did spark a new protest movement and a more energized discussion of the unequal justice evident in that they were nine times more likely to die in this fashion than their white counterparts. But the discussion and the protests, not to mention the backlash against them, proved little when it came to whether blacks and whites got along.

Obama seemed to have no option other than to speak directly but carefully, lest he make matters worse. When unarmed black teenager Trayvon Martin was shot by a white neighbor who participated in civilian neighborhood watch patrols, Obama said that if he had a son, he would have looked like the victim. When rioters in Baltimore looted stores, Obama said, "They're not protesting, they're not making a statement, they're stealing." After the mass shooting perpetrated by a white supremacist at a black church in Charleston, South Carolina, called Emanuel AME, he said the state's flag, which incorporated elements of the flag of the Confederacy, was a "reminder of systemic oppression and racial subjugation." He was criticized for these remarks by the *National Review*'s Heather Mac Donald, who wrote of how Obama had used the tragedy "opportunistically."

Required to be the president for Heather Mac Donald, as well as for the congregation at Emanuel AME, America's first black president would walk a difficult path. Although he could, and did, direct the Justice Department to investigate racially charged cases, and he created a task force on policing, his main power in this area of American life was symbolic. As such, his mere presence in the Oval Office, and his family's presence in the living quarters of the White House, evoked intense pride but also animosity. Goodwill was balanced by cruel caricatures that circulated on the Internet and a vast number of death threats. In context, Obama's record of disappointing supporters and critics alike on the matter of race is no surprise. Much work would remain to be done when he left office, but he likely anticipated this outcome. He said as much in 2008 while he was campaigning for his first term:

> Contrary to the claims of some of my critics, black and white, I have never been so naïve as to believe that we can get beyond our racial divisions in a single election cycle, or with a single candidacy—particularly a candidacy as imperfect as my own. But I have asserted a firm conviction—a conviction rooted in my faith in God and my faith in the American people—that working together we can move beyond some of our old racial wounds, and that in fact we have no choice if we are to continue on the path of a more perfect union.

GUANTÁNAMO

When he campaigned for president, Barack Obama pledged to close the prison camp at Guantánamo Bay, Cuba, where hundreds of terror suspects have been incarcerated in what Amnesty International described as an American "gulag." The International Red Cross reported conditions at the US facility that amounted to "torture" of prisoners, and similar complaints were made by more than two hundred FBI agents who visited.

One of Obama's first acts as president was to order a shutdown of the Guantánamo camp by the end of 2009. However, the administration discovered, almost immediately, that camp records were in such disarray that they couldn't be certain about the backgrounds of many of those being held. A task force named to determine which prisoners might be tried, released, or transferred to other nations made slow progress. In the meantime, administration efforts to find facilities that would take detainees who would remain in US custody ran into opposition from state and local officials as well as members of Congress.

The story of the Guantánamo prison has always been clouded by misunderstanding. Widely assumed to be a secure facility for holding enemy combatants, it was actually filled mainly with people taken not in combat, but after their arrest in various foreign cities and towns. Of the nearly eight hundred people captured and sent to the prison, more than 85 percent were turned in to authorities by captors who were paid ransoms. As of early 2016, 683 had been released after serving long periods of detention without charge. Nine died in custody. Eight were prosecuted and convicted by military tribunals.

In the political struggle over the operation of the prison camp, the administration gradually lost the ability to act on the president's order. Congress barred closing the camp in the 2011 defense authorization bill, which Obama signed in order to fund the Pentagon. The law also prevented the president from bringing any of the prisoners to the US mainland for trial. This made the controversial military tribunals at the camp the only option for resolving many of the prisoners' fates.

The debate over Guantánamo was yet another example of the president's running up against political opponents who wanted to deny him the chance to fulfill one of his promises. However, those who worked to keep the prison open also argued that the men held there represented such a grave threat to the United States that they could not be managed elsewhere. They also understood, no doubt, that Americans generally opposed closing the prison.

In his effort to close the prison Obama was motivated not by politics, but by his belief that the camp was being used to detain

As you may know, since 2001, the United States has held people from other countries who are suspected of being terrorists in a prison at Guantanamo Bay in Cuba. Do you think the United States should – or should not – close this prison and move some of the prisoners to U.S. prisons?

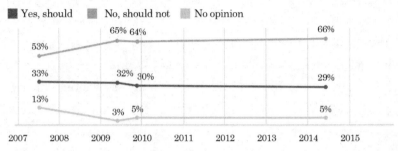

July 2007 wording: Do you think the United states should – or should not – close the prison at the Guantanamo Bay military base in Cuba?

American views on Guantanamo prison reported by Gallup   Courtesy Gallup

people without the usual rights of legal process, a betrayal by the United States of its own principles. As he said in his 2014 State of the Union address, "We counter terrorism not just through intelligence and military action, but by remaining true to our constitutional ideals, and setting an example for the rest of the world." In much of the world, Guantánamo represented the height of hypocrisy as practiced by a nation that held itself out to be a symbol of liberty and the rule of law. America's critics were quick to note cases such as that of Mohammed Ali Abdullah Bwazir of Yemen, who was imprisoned at Guantánamo in 2002 when he was twenty-two years old. Although he was originally accused of being a terrorist, he was never tried or convicted. However, he was, apparently, so broken by his treatment that when he was granted his freedom in early 2016, he refused to leave the camp.

As in so many other areas of conflict with Congress, the administration did act in ways to advance its agenda despite legislative obstacles. As of early 2016, the population at the prison had been reduced to ninety-one, and more than one-third of these had been approved for release. Just twenty-eight of the remainder were deemed so dangerous that they should be held for the foreseeable future.

THE WAR IN AFGHANISTAN

During the 2008 election campaign, Barack Obama did not bind himself tightly when it came to the wars in Iraq and Afghanistan. Nevertheless, he was determined to get US fighting forces out of Iraq as soon as he could. He held a different view about America's war in Afghanistan, where the Taliban government had actually supported the terrorist group that attacked America on 9/11. There he saw a worthy fight. However, he also recognized the cost and danger of a protracted conflict in a country where foreign armies had always found not victory, but defeat.

Getting out of a war is always more difficult than getting into one. This was the lesson of America's war in Vietnam, and it was offered again in Afghanistan. Although then secretary of defense Donald Rumsfeld had declared that major combat operations were over in 2003, and Western allies turned toward nation building, the Taliban were never fully defeated. Continued attacks kept US forces in Afghanistan to support a shaky, democratically elected government. In his campaign for the presidency Obama said he would deploy more troops in the hope that the local government forces could be trained to take over the defense of the country in 2014. This approach worked, but not completely. After seeking refuge in parts of Pakistan and dissolving into local communities, Taliban forces rejoined the fighting and gradually seized territory. America's withdrawal was slowed. The 2014 deadline came and went. In 2015 more than five thousand Afghan security officers were killed during a single Taliban offensive in Helmand Province. In September the Taliban took Kunduz, the fifth-largest city in Afghanistan. A month later the president announced he would not withdraw any more troops. About ten thousand would remain in Afghanistan, probably until after the end of the president's second and final term.

"I will not allow Afghanistan to be used as safe haven for terrorists to attack our nation again," said the president as he acknowledged he would not be able to end the war begun by his predecessor. He said the security situation in the country was "fragile" and that "Afghan forces are still not as strong as they need to be." The decision to keep a significant force would fulfill America's commitment to the Afghan government, he added, and demonstrate to the Taliban that "the only real way to achieve the full drawdown of US and foreign troops from Afghanistan is through a lasting political settlement."

Although polls showed the American public was eager to end the war, and the president had said he wanted to reach this goal, little criticism was heard after the decision was announced. Of the two wars begun after 9/11, Afghanistan was widely recognized as the one that was justified and necessary. Nevertheless, the announcement marked a disappointment for the administration.

THE WAR IN IRAQ

What was George W. Bush imagining as he donned a green *Top Gun* flight suit and got buckled into a navy jet for a short flight to an aircraft carrier positioned in the Pacific just off the California coast? Did he know that his swagger across the deck of the USS *Abraham Lincoln* would be regarded as both ridiculous and vain? Had he anticipated that his words—"Major combat operations in Iraq have ended"—would be followed by almost ten more years of fighting, four thousand more American deaths, and an insurgency that would morph into the ISIS terror network?

Bush never addressed all of the mistakes in judgment and perspective in his decision to declare victory in May 2003, when Saddam Hussein was still at large and fighting raged around the country. However, years later, as he conducted his last presidential press conference, the president did confess that decorating the ship with a huge banner that read MISSION ACCOMPLISHED had been an error. "It sent the wrong message," he said.

At the time it was begun, the administration predicted that the invasion of Iraq would be a quick operation conducted at a cost of roughly $80 billion. Twenty-one Senate Democrats and one Republican found the case for war unconvincing and voted against the bill authorizing the president's actions. In Chicago, then–state senator Obama made his opposition to the planned invasion clear in a speech in which he said, "I don't oppose all wars. What I am opposed to is a dumb war."

By the time Barack Obama reached the Senate, the justifications for the invasion—that Iraq had provided significant support for the 9/11 attacks and possessed so-called weapons of mass destruction—had been disproved and the war was becoming a quagmire. The number of civilians and combatants killed was well on its way to the five hundred thousand total, and the price of the American mission had exceeded $1 trillion, not counting the cost of caring for returning veterans. Before he got the chance to cast a vote on the war, Obama wrote about the issue in *Foreign Policy,* arguing it was a fight "that never should have been authorized and never should have been waged." He said he favored a policy that would get American combat brigades out of Iraq by 2008.

More than one hundred thousand American troops occupied Iraq on the day Obama was elected, but in that same month the United States and the government of Iraq agreed that the American armed forces should leave by the end of 2011. Both governments pushed to fulfill this agreement, and the United States withdrawal was completed in December 2011. But even as the president welcomed troops home, the United States continued to maintain the single largest embassy in the world on more than one hundred acres in the former Green Zone, which had served as the base of America's wartime operations. The embassy was staffed with thousands of civilian, military, and contractor employees.

The Americans left in Iraq witnessed the disintegration of the country under corrupt and inept central leaders and intensifying pressure from rebel and insurgent fighters of ISIS (Islamic State of Iraq and Syria). Led in part by military men of the Saddam Hussein regime (they were demobilized when Bush disbanded the Iraqi military), ISIS represented a worst-case outcome from the original American decision to invade. Even more fanatical than al-Qaeda, ISIS swept through parts of Iraq and Syria, defeating government forces in battle and seizing territory. With control over a self-declared state, the group was able to generate untold millions of dollars through crime and the sale of oil, and to support and inspire attacks in Western Europe and the United States.

ISIS's battlefield success and terror tactics, which included beheadings that were recorded and broadcast on the Internet, may have been enabled by Bush-era policies, but they were President Obama's problem. According to many analyses, the Obama administration had failed to recognize the severity of Iraqi prime minister Nouri al-Maliki's authoritarianism and did not heed the signs of the country's collapse. The rise of ISIS was marked by waves of kidnappings and murder, the displacement of more than 1.2 million Iraqis, and the group's spread to other countries in the Middle East and Africa. ISIS affiliates employed the same terror tactics—grisly execution, kidnappings, attacks on civilians—and produced the same fears and instability seen in Iraq.

America and its allies in Europe and the Middle East responded to ISIS with air strikes and by rushing Special Forces and military trainers to Iraq. Local forces, including Kurds, Shiite militias, and regular Iraqi military, began achieving victories against ISIS fighters and gradually retook territory in 2015 and early 2016. Air strikes killed thousands of fighters, and US forces seized some ISIS leaders.

By February the Iraqi government claimed it had retaken half the territory that had been lost. However, the government's optimism—officials predicted the fight would be completely won by the end of the year—was overshadowed by uncertainty. The Shiite militias fighting ISIS were being accused of war crimes, and the chaos in the country seemed without end.

The suffering caused by ISIS in Iraq and neighboring Syria was not solely the responsibility of President Obama. The violent internal power struggles that fueled the fighting are of ancient origins, and their current manifestations arose out of Bush's decision to dismantle the one strong institution in prewar Iraq, the military. Obama administration officials would say the Iraqis insisted on the withdrawal of US forces. However, the administration failed to resolve the problem that was Maliki, and its response to ISIS was too slow, too incremental, and incomplete. Thus the problem from hell that belonged to George Bush would not be resolved by Obama. Eight years would pass and he would hand it to his successor.

WAR AT HOME

The legacy of 9/11 included the creation of a huge new Homeland Security agency that became the third-largest bureaucracy in the US government, behind the Pentagon and Department of Veterans Affairs. The Federal Bureau of Investigation developed a domestic surveillance operation employing thousands of agents, and the collection of voice and data communications by the National Security Agency (NSA) and others constituted a sweeping and largely unchecked invasion of privacy.

Tasked with thwarting every plan to attack Americans, the enormous security bureaucracy operated in such secrecy that the public could access scant reliable data on its cost and effectiveness. (One estimate set the cost of counterterrorism at $16 billion annually. Another suggested that intelligence gathering cost many times as much.) What did Americans get for their money? This question was almost impossible to answer because claims about attacks that were prevented were subject to interpretation on many levels. Meanwhile disputes raged over the true threat from terrorism and how far the government should intrude on privacy to stop plotters.

The public's fear of terrorism was stoked by the horror that came with unexpected deadly attacks, such as the Boston Marathon bombing of 2013 and the mass shooting of 2015 in San Bernardino, California. Although many dangers—lightning, in-home accidents, car crashes—presented more substantial and immediate threats, Americans expressed consistent fear that they, or a family member, would become victims of an attack.

Worries About Becoming a Terrorism Victim Up in 2015

How worried are you that you or someone in your family will become a victim of terrorism – very worried, somewhat worried, not too worried, or not worried at all?

% Very/Somewhat worried

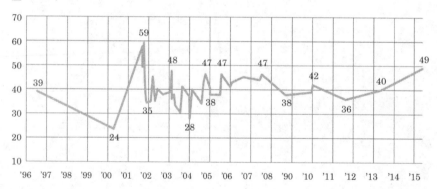

Americans' concerns about terrorism reported by Gallup   Courtesy Gallup

Although fear led some to say they were willing to cede privacy rights in exchange for security, Americans seemed generally concerned about the trade-off.

A broad and heated national conversation over privacy and the security state arose after an analyst named Edward Snowden copied tens of thousands of files, many of them classified, and gave them to journalists, who published accounts that revealed the breadth of the surveillance carried out. The reports revealed programs for spying on US citizens' telephone communications and e-mail, as well as for the collection of data from foreign leaders, corporations, and governments. Much of the spying was done by tapping into the flow of data passing through Internet and telephone companies.

In the uproar that accompanied Snowden's revelations, and his decision to seek asylum in Russia, Americans became more fully

More Continue To Be Concerned With Country's Protection Over Civil Liberties

Bigger concern about gov't anti-terrorism policies? (%)

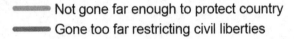
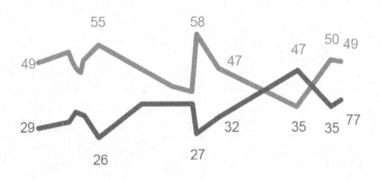

Survey conducted Jan. 7-11, 2015.
Volunteered responses of Both/Neither/Don't know not shown.

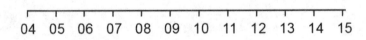

Courtesy Pew Research Center

aware of the shadowy system that permitted the government to monitor them. President Obama was shown to be as committed to this surveillance as his predecessor. Indeed, the scope and volume of data collected during his presidency was greater than ever before, and the administration disputed an independent review board's finding that the NSA's mass collection of data was illegal. The board cited "serious threats to privacy and civil liberties" and said the NSA should destroy what it had collected. A White House official said simply, "The administration believes that the program is lawful."

Civil libertarians and many other citizens took issue with the White House statement, but Obama's steadfast position and the limited opposition his policies faced in Congress meant that the issue soon receded from public consideration. Presidential candidates Ron Paul and Bernie Sanders mentioned civil liberties concerns during the 2016 campaign, but voters didn't seem moved by their arguments about surveillance of US citizens. No candidate appealed to the electorate over Obama's other civil liberty problems, including the administration's effort to stifle the rights of whistle-blowers and to intimidate the press with a Justice Department investigation of journalists. This effort included the secret seizure of phone records.

As a senator, Obama had called for security programs that would check terrorists while "protecting the privacy, and liberty, of innocent Americans." As a candidate, he said he would improve privacy protections for Americans and "hold government and business accountable for violations of personal privacy." As his presidency neared an end, Obama had not just fallen short of these goals, but he had made more compromises on civil liberties, in the pursuit of national security, than President Bush.

WALL STREET ACCOUNTABILITY

Although candidate Obama called for efforts to hold accountable the bankers whose frauds fed the Great Recession, his Justice Department convicted just one midlevel trader in connection with all the fraud that had been committed. The department secured no criminal convictions of top banking executives, even though banks paid nearly $200 billion in fines while admitting that criminal activity had taken place.

The Obama record on prosecuting financial fraud stands in contrast to the performance of the first President Bush. Back then, after the savings and loan crisis of the 1980s, more than one thousand men and women were convicted and served prison time. During the Obama years, prosecutors seemed to dither and delay until the five-year statute of limitations on criminal complaints ran out. When questioned about the lack of convictions, Justice Department officials said bankers had been especially clever about their misdeeds, which made it difficult to bring cases against them. "These are the kinds of cases that people come to the Justice Department to make," said Attorney General Eric Holder. "The inability to make them, at least to this point, has not been as a result of a lack of effort."

In the wake of the banking crisis that set in motion the Great Recession, investigators had collected documents from many firms and conducted interviews with insiders who revealed how investors had been duped and regulators had been evaded. However, the government lawyers did not use what they learned to support arrests. Instead they presented their findings to the targeted firms and offered executives the option of using corporate money, not their own, to settle cases. Bonuses continued to flow, and thanks to the agreements that settled cases, records were sealed. The public would never learn the true extent of the scandal even though, as former Federal Reserve Bank chairman Alan Greenspan said, "a lot of that stuff was just plain fraud."

Coming from a libertarian who enabled the bankers to run wild, Greenspan's characterization of the scandal supported those who favored prosecutions. Certainly those who participated in the Occupy Wall Street protest movement, and its many offshoots, felt that those most responsible for the suffering caused by the recession got away with their misdeeds. However, the protesters did not make a strong case for prosecutions. Instead they advocated for student loan forgiveness, less wealth inequality, more bank regulation, fewer mortgage foreclosures, and, most of all, a reduced role for corporations in the political system.

Long recognized as a problem by people on the Right and the Left, the political primacy of big money grew after the Supreme Court struck down limits on contributions in various cases, including the famous *Citizens United v. Federal Election Commission* case of 2010. As the court found that money was the same as speech and thus could not be restricted, cash poured into campaigns. In 2012 one wealthy businessman, Sheldon Adelson, spent $15 million on behalf of the failed primary campaign of presidential hopeful Newt Gingrich. In 2015, *The New York Times* reported that fewer than four hundred families had contributed almost half the money gathered by roughly twenty presidential contenders.

President Obama had done almost nothing to address campaign finance. The explanation, favored by his critics, matched the one they offered about the lack of fraud prosecutions: Obama and his party were beholden to moneyed interests. This claim seemed at least partly true. Obama's campaigns and those of many in his party had been funded with ample contributions from Wall Street. (Democratic senator Dick Durbin said of the banks and Washington, "Frankly, they own the place.") Also, many of those whom Obama had drafted to work in his administration had come from banking and investment firms and would return to them after their government services. One would not expect these people to push for criminal prosecutions or a major disruption of the status quo.

Barack Obama never explicitly promised to prosecute bankers, so his failure on this count is not proof of a broken promise. However, his inaction is one of his genuine failures. As time passed, Obama achieved many of the goals he set for himself, and in February 2016 he reiterated his commitment to what he called "the politics of hope." In that same month voters choosing candidates for the 2016 race gravitated toward those who spoke to their frustration with the status quo. Democrat Bernie Sanders and Republican Donald Trump both railed against Wall Street and won enthusiastic support among the middle class, and the poor, who were hurt the most by the transgressions of the bankers who got bonuses instead of prison terms. Their sense of grievance, which threw both the GOP and the Democratic Party into turmoil, had to be considered a part of Obama's legacy.

POSTSCRIPT: THE BENEFITS OF COOL

At the end of his presidency, Barack Obama won praise from two former Reagan administration officials who admired what he had accomplished in his second term, despite the fact that the GOP controlled Congress and were determined to obstruct him. Although presidents are usually slowed by political inertia, Obama had continued to achieve successes. "It may turn out that unlike virtually any other president, his second term is actually better than his first," said Reagan's arms negotiator Kenneth Adelman. The second-term achievements noted by Adelman and others ranged from the improved relations negotiated with Cuba and Iran to the successful defense of health care reform in the federal courts.

In many policy areas Obama reaped the benefits of his long-term approach to creating the kinds of change he had promised in his 2008 campaign. As late as 2016, he was still seeking to fulfill some of the commitments he had not met, including closure of the military prison at Guantánamo Bay, Cuba. He had also used his executive authority to improve background checks on gun buyers and address problems as wide ranging as cybersecurity and making government buildings less vulnerable to earthquakes. With these and other actions, Obama directed his administration to continue playing the game of governing into what he termed "the fourth quarter."

An avid basketball player, in politics Obama favored a flexible strategy that could work over the long course of the game. In the beginning of his presidency he sprinted to accomplish as much as possible as fast as possible—economic recovery, health care reform, financial reform—before his mandate from the voters faded and the Democratic Party lost its hold on Congress. In the two years before his reelection he moved carefully, in order to win a second term and get the time to complete more of his agenda. Once he gained a second term, he used the power that was available to him to fulfill many of his promises without the aid of Congress. He also began speaking more forthrightly about controversies such as gun violence and race.

When a racist young man killed nine black people who were studying the Bible at a church in South Carolina, the president pointedly called on the state to remove the Confederate battle flag from where it flew at the state capitol. He said the flag should be put in a museum and that doing so would "simply be an acknowledgment that the cause for which they [Confederate soldiers] fought, the cause of slavery, was wrong." At the funeral service for the church's pastor, Clementa Pinckney, the president observed that the killer's horrendous acts were leading to breakthrough conversations about how Americans got along with each other.

"Blinded by hatred," observed the president, "he failed to comprehend what Reverend Pinckney so well understood—the power of God's grace." Obama ended his eulogy and brought many to tears by singing the first lines of the hymn "Amazing Grace." The mourning people assembled in the church joined him in song.

Barack Obama was rarely more effective than when he comforted the nation in times of loss and crisis. One of the unwritten duties of the president of the United States is to act as a spiritual leader in such moments, and Obama generally handled the obligation in emotionally authentic ways. His instinct was to speak calmly and, when faith was called for, to express it in a generous and hopeful way. (His was a distinctly New Testament brand of belief.) However, he could also show flashes of anger, and he was especially affected by the mass shootings. For decades Congress had failed to address this problem in a meaningful way because of highly effective gun lobby groups, which are funded by firearms manufacturers. Over the years, calls for regulation followed horrific events, but nothing was done.

During the Obama presidency the United States suffered through more than twenty mass shootings. The worst, except for terrorist attacks, occurred at Sandy Hook Elementary School in Newtown, Connecticut, where a young man shot and killed twenty first-graders and six adults before he committed suicide. A particularly American problem—mass shootings are more frequent in the United States than in other developed countries—these incidents invariably prompted futile discussions about the easy availability of weapons designed solely to kill great numbers of people quickly. Although Americans own 42 percent of all the world's privately held guns, gun advocates say one solution to mass killings would be to get *more* guns into private hands.

With each tragedy the president seemed more grief-stricken and even shocked that lawmakers were not moved to action by the tide of innocent blood. After a mass shooting at a community college in Oregon, he despaired at the routine quality of the reporting on yet another tragedy and predicted an extreme reaction from the pro-gun lobby in Washington. "What is also routine," he said, "is that somebody, somewhere, will comment and say, 'Obama politicized this issue.' Well, this is something we should politicize. It is relevant to our common life together, to the body politic." In early 2016 the president took executive action to close loopholes that allowed people to evade the minimal background checks required of gun purchasers. Referring to individual citizens' rights to buy firearms and the death toll, he said, "We do not have to accept this carnage as the price of freedom."

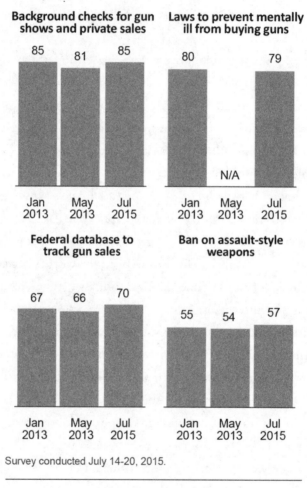

Little Change in Public Views of Gun Policy Proposals

% who favor...

Background checks for gun shows and private sales

85 81 85

Jan 2013 May 2013 Jul 2015

Laws to prevent mentally ill from buying guns

80 79

N/A

Jan 2013 May 2013 Jul 2015

Federal database to track gun sales

67 66 70

Jan 2013 May 2013 Jul 2015

Ban on assault-style weapons

55 54 57

Jan 2013 May 2013 Jul 2015

Survey conducted July 14-20, 2015.

Courtesy Pew Research Center

The president's appeal for the use of politics to balance competing concerns was grounded in the idea that citizens in a diverse and democratic society can respect their differences and reach meaningful compromises. Before taking office he had often expressed the hope that he could practice the constructive politics of compromise with Republicans in Congress, but he encountered in them not colleagues but obstructionists. Typical of the pattern was the wrangling over the 2011 federal budget when GOPers in Congress rejected deals that called for $3 in spending cuts for every $1 in new revenue.

Although some insisted that both parties had become more extreme and thus intransigent, the data showed this wasn't the case. About 90 percent of Democrats were political moderates, compared with only 10 percent of Republicans. Under these circumstances, the president had no one to talk to about compromises. This became more obvious after the 2011 budget talks when Republicans running for president were asked if they would accept a ten-to-one ratio of budget cuts to tax increases. Each one said no.

The partisan rancor was tinged by racial resentments. This problem was identified by political scientist Michael Tesler, whose studies found a marked return to what he termed "old-fashioned racism," or OFR, among GOP voters. Tesler noted that as recently as the 1950s a majority of Americans still considered whites to be racially superior to blacks. This crude expression of racism faded but fainter sentiments remained. They were revived, wrote Tesler, by Obama's election, which "had the ironic upshot of opening the door for old-fashioned racism to influence partisan preferences after OFR was long thought to be a spent force in American politics."

Tesler did not write that opposition to Obama's policies automatically signaled racism. Most of the debates over his initiatives were ideological, not race based. However, the intense feelings expressed by some of his opponents were influenced by prejudice. Consider how Congressman Doug Lamborn of Colorado explained why he couldn't work out policy differences with the president. "Even if some people say, 'Well, the Republicans should have done this or they should have done that,' they will hold the president responsible," said Lamborn. "Now, I don't even want to have to be associated with him. It's like touching a tar baby, and you get it, you're stuck, and you're a part of the problem now and you can't get away."

In addition to hurling the occasional slur, Obama's opponents worked hard to persuade the public that scandal plagued the president. Thirty-two congressional hearings were conducted to examine the 2012 attack on American facilities in Benghazi, Libya, in which four Americans were killed. (Congress held ten fewer hearings on the 9/11 attacks, which left nearly three thousand people dead.) In the end, Republican lawmakers found no wrongdoing in the Benghazi case and the hearings resulted in no disciplinary actions. The same outcome followed House investigations of alleged corruption at the Internal Revenue Service, the Department of Energy, and the Department of Homeland Security. In the latter case Representative Darrell Issa referenced the worst presidential scandal in history, Watergate, as he declared it "reeks of a Nixonian enemies list." No list was discovered, and in no case did House investigators identify a scandal involving the White House.

Instead of scandal, Obama had actually brought a level of rectitude not seen in the White House in decades. As of early 2016, not one high official in the Obama administration had been indicted on criminal charges, and just a handful had resigned under the pressure of investigations. In the previous presidency George Bush saw the perjury and obstruction of justice conviction of I. Lewis "Scooter" Libby, a top aide to Vice President Cheney, and guilty pleas or convictions of seven officials connected to lobbyist/felon Jack Abramoff. Many more resigned under clouds of controversy. Prior to Bush, President Bill Clinton's administration endured many investigations and even a failed impeachment trial of the president himself. During President Reagan's administration, thirty-two high officials were convicted (two verdicts were overturned on appeal) in various scandals including Iran-contra, in which the administration sold arms to Iran to circumvent a ban on direct aid to "contra" rebels in Nicaragua.

Although it might seem that he cleared a low bar—no impeachment, no convictions in eight years—Obama's record signaled an ethical high point for the modern presidency. His administration also demonstrated a remarkable level of competence. At several moments of crisis, political opponents and observers in the press insisted Obama's "Katrina" (for the Hurricane Katrina disaster) was at hand, but it never materialized. Events such as the massive oil spill in the Gulf of Mexico and the outbreak of Ebola virus in Africa prompted sustained efforts to cast the president in a negative light, but these problems and others were managed with effective calm. At times Obama's steadiness was also unacceptable. Maureen Down of *The New York Times* mocked "the Spock in him" and declared, "President Cool reached the limits of cool."

Obama's style was cool, especially when compared with George W. Bush's hot pursuit of war in Iraq and Bill Clinton's florid emotionalism. At times Obama's calm frustrated those who wanted to hear more of the soaring rhetoric he had offered when he addressed the Democratic National Convention in 2004 and at high points in his reelection campaigns. However, Obama did not rely too much on any one political tool. He was as calm as his public image suggested, and his authentic cool was what the nation needed in the chaos of the Great Recession. He was so cool that he was able to crack jokes at the White House Correspondents' Dinner after secretly ordering the military to capture or kill Osama bin Laden at the compound where he was hiding in Pakistan.

When the president did drop his reserve, it was often in unexpected encounters with those outside the realm of politics. Children brought out the best in him. He took delight in soothing a crying baby, playing on the Oval Office floor with a toddler, and donning a tiara with a group of Brownies. When Obama met students in Jamaica, he used local slang: "Greetings massive!" When a housefly landed on his hand during the recording of a TV interview, he paused, eyed it, and dispatched it with a swift slap. He then turned back to the interviewer and asked, "Now, where were we?"

In his willingness to show himself to be emotional and demonstrate odd personal abilities such as fly swatting, Obama demonstrated an even cooler level of cool. In the twenty-first century, real men who made themselves vulnerable revealed that they were, in fact, confident and brave. Similarly, Obama was so cool that he frequently dipped into pop culture venues that would have intimidated other politicians. In 2014 he sat for an "interview" with the comic Zack Galifianakis, who hosted a mock cable talk show called *Between Two Ferns,* to discuss health care. A year later Obama visited the garage/studio of comedian Marc Maron to record a podcast conversation. The president spoke as candidly as Maron's other interviewees and even ribbed his host for being "a little narcissistic" because he decorated the space with photos of himself.

As the president began to eye his legacy, he was typically determined in his effort to wring every last bit of progress out of his time in office. He urged his aides, and members of his cabinet, to keep trying to win policy successes because, despite the clock's ticking down, time was still left in the game. When the unexpected death of Supreme Court justice Antonin Scalia gave Obama an opportunity to nominate a replacement, he demonstrated a deft political touch by choosing Merrick Garland, chief of the federal Appeals Court in Washington, DC. The choice was well made for two reasons. First, Garland was a brilliant jurist who had reached the height of his profession, save the Supreme Court. Second, he had been amply praised by leading Senate Republicans, who supported his Appeals Court nomination in 1997. Many of these same GOP senators were refusing to consider any Obama nominee because, in their view, the last eleven months of a president's time in office didn't count when it came to Supreme Court nominations.

The choice of Garland presented the stonewallers of the Republican Party with several political problems. Many Americans would see their obstinacy, given their earlier support for Garland, as deeply hypocritical. Others, among them many moderate Republicans, would consider Garland, a moderate, far better than any nominee that might be made should a Democrat win the White House in the 2016 election. A court vacancy's going unfilled for a year or more was a another problem. With eight members, evenly divided in their politics, the court could be deadlocked on many important cases, and voters would surely blame GOP senators who refused to perform their function of considering and voting on the president's nominee.

The president seemed to take pleasure in acting, and speaking, as a leader who would never have to conduct another election campaign. This included candid reflections on his disappointments. In early 2016, Obama returned to the Illinois State Capitol, where his quest for the White House began, and reflected on the failure he felt most keenly: "One of my few regrets is my inability to reduce the polarization and meanness in our politics." He blamed the problem on himself, and on those in politics who promise so much more than they can accomplish "that their supporters will be perennially disappointed."

In his own case, Obama delivered on most of his promises, and where he fell short, he made a true effort. Yet much of what he achieved was accomplished quietly and would be seen only as complex pieces of legislation were translated into action and the interlocking strategy he'd employed became more evident. Seen from the perspective of 2016, it is apparent that Obama's economic policy dovetailed with his energy policy, which enabled his diplomacy and aided his environmental agenda. In an ever-more-connected world where problems such as climate change will yield only to an international effort, Obama's thoughtful and multifaceted approach may be the only thing that will work.

As to the looming symbolic challenge Obama faced as he became the nation's first black president, his calm, analytical way of approaching difficult issues must also be seen as the best possible option. His election, his reelection, and his successes say as much about the country as they do about him. They reveal America to be a better place than many of its critics assumed, and this image, of a country that is always reinventing itself, may be Obama's most significant and enduring legacy. This accomplishment makes him a consequential president whose service will only grow in significance with the passage and perspective of time.

In the meantime, the president would continue to endure harsh criticism from the Left, where writers such as Thomas Frank described the Obama years in terms of lost opportunities. In his 2016 book, *Listen, Liberal,* Frank expressed his disappointment in Obama because none of his reforms went far enough. Insurers remained embedded in the health care system. Wall Street retained its power in finances. Poverty was intractable, college students remained burdened by debt, and income inequality had worsened. *Listen, Liberal* was a stinging rebuke, but it was also unfair. Obama had been elected president, not monarch, and the American political system had been fashioned over generations to prevent the kind of sweeping change Frank would have preferred.

Instead of a revolution, Obama delivered progress on health care, which many previous presidents had failed to achieve, and the first real action on climate change in decades. A consequential president in style, as well as substance, Obama's intellectualism and perseverance, which annoyed so many of his critics, were actually welcomed by the public as a whole. As the 2016 GOP presidential candidates descended into ever-lower realms of rhetoric and behavior, Obama's poll numbers ticked steadily upward. In February 2016 the Gallup poll reported his favorability rating was 50 percent and climbing. In comparison, at the same point in their presidencies George W. Bush's favorability rating was 32 percent and Ronald Reagan's was 51.

In addition to his demeanor, Obama's popularity was likely the product of his success in foreign affairs, which is one policy area where a president can act most decisively. Under Obama the American people have seen a huge improvement in the nation's standing, as measured by public opinion, and historic openings to Iran and Cuba, where the president's record defied those who had dismissed him earlier in his presidency. In spring 2016 Obama highlighted his record with an official visit to Cuba, the first time a sitting US president had set foot in the country since 1928.

Obama's visit thrilled the Cuban people, who turned out in great numbers to see him. His main message was delivered at the Gran Teatro de La Habana, where he offered words of reconciliation and also provocation. Obama was applauded when he said, "I have come here to bury the last remnant of the Cold War in the Americas." He was applauded more loudly when he added, "I believe citizens should be free to speak their mind without fear, to organize, and to criticize their government, and to protest peacefully, and that the rule of law should not include arbitrary detentions of people who exercise those rights."

In referencing the rights that Cubans deserved, Obama vexed his host Raúl Castro, who later criticized the president in an article titled "Brother Obama." In the piece he insisted that Cubans did not need "gifts" from the United States and suggested that Obama was in no position to "develop theories about Cuban politics." Castro offered a litany of American interventions in the affairs of other nations and said that "syrupy words" were not enough to smooth over a history of conflict.

Castro's response was proof that Obama's visit had inspired hope in Cubans who yearned for more freedom. The tour was also a fitting bookend for a presidency that was foreshadowed, in 2008, by candidate Obama's address in Berlin, where two hundred thousand people cheered him at Tiergarten. In both appearances, Obama stood as a living symbol of hope. Hope for less conflict and more understanding; hope for an end to economic crisis; hope for equal rights; hope for the environment; hope for equal opportunity; hope for a more inclusive and respectful society.

More than most people understood, Obama had actually delivered the change that was the second part of his 2008 campaign message of "hope" and "change we can believe in." Partisan critics will forever sneer at this theme, insisting that the president fell short of his pledge. History, fairly told, will show he fulfilled his promise and in ways that will continue to be revealed, at home and abroad, for years to come.

Obama had history in mind as he gave the last of his eight addresses to the United Nations General Assembly in September 2016. As he spoke, the United States was poised to choose between Hillary Clinton and Donald Trump in an election that was less than sixty-days away. Trump was running as a close-the-borders xenophobe who would roll back trade agreements and constrict immigration in defiance of a century of experience that showed America prospered from free trade and the energies of new citizens from abroad.

Faced with the prospect of Trump, Obama chose to speak of optimism instead of anxiety, and yes, of hope rather than fear. In one of the most inspiring speeches of his entire public life, Obama held true to the themes of his 2008 campaign. "Each of us leaders, each nation, can choose to reject those who appeal to our worst impulses and embrace those who appeal to our best." This perspective was the message he offered the nation as he became president. It was the ideal that guided his time in office. And it is the foundation of the legacy.

ADDENDUM: ANTAGONISM AND FALSE ALARMS

Beginning with the vows taken by Republicans in Congress who sought to deprive him of policy achievements, Barack Obama faced an intensely organized and often irrational opposition from the first moment of his presidency. In an environment that independent analysts judged to be the most partisan in modern times, TV talkers, political opponents, and pundits offered predictions of doom and fantastic fabrications. For reasons rarely stated, except by fringe figures who considered Obama the Antichrist, this man who had devoted his life to public service and lifting others up, wanted to ruin the United States. Here is just a sampling of the false alarms, failed predictions, and antagonistic rhetoric of Obama's time:

- 11/18/08—"If General Motors, Ford and Chrysler get the bailout that their chief executives asked for yesterday, you can kiss the American automotive industry goodbye. It won't go overnight, but its demise will be virtually guaranteed." —Mitt Romney, *The New York Times*
- 1/16/09—"I don't need two hundred words. I just need four. 'I hope he fails.' The reason I said that is because I meant it. I hope he failed, because if Obama would fail, the country would survive, the country as founded." —Rush Limbaugh, RushLimbaugh.com
- 7/22/09—"None of [Obama's] bills are about what he says

they're about. The health care bill is reparations. It's the beginning of reparations. . . . The medical schools will get more federal dollars if they have proven that they are putting minorities ahead." —Glenn Beck, *The Glenn Beck Program*

- 8/7/09—"As more Americans delve into the disturbing details of the nationalized health care plan that the current administration is rushing through Congress, our collective jaw is dropping, and we're saying not just no, but hell no! And who will suffer the most when they ration care? The sick, the elderly, and the disabled, of course. The America I know and love is not one in which my parents or my baby with Down Syndrome will have to stand in front of Obama's 'death panel' so his bureaucrats can decide, based on a subjective judgment of their 'level of productivity in society,' whether they are worthy of health care. Such a system is downright evil." —Sarah Palin, *PolitiFact*

- 11/2/09—"When you look at the extreme czars, and you look at Barack Obama, and you look at the Barack Obama that portrayed himself one year ago as a very different candidate, you know, why—I feel like I have been vindicated. I was excoriated for saying he is far more radical than people know. You know, what do you see about him? Do you think he is far—do you think he's a socialist? Do you think he's—because I think this is—if we get nationalized health care, it's over. This is socialism, and that's a kind word." —Sean Hannity, *Hannity*

- 11/21/09—The health bill is "a triumph of the humanistic, atheistic philosophy. . . . It is a sham. Euthanasia is coming. You can call them death panels. That's exactly what they're going to be." —Cal Thomas, *America's News HQ*

- 1/13/10—"If they pass this thing, you are going to see insurrection. You're going to see an uprising. People are just not going to take this. I mean, your taxes are going to go through the roof. It's going to be a bloodbath when people find out how much this is going to cost, and for the first four years, they're not going to get anything." —Jim Quinn, *The War Room with Quinn & Rose*

- 3/19/10—"Obamacare will topple the stock market." —Jim Cramer, *The Kudlow Report*

- 4/7/10—"We're looking at a—the end of capitalism in America as we know it. . . . He will go down in American history as the worst president we have ever had. And I'm talking about national security, and I'm talking about economic issues." —Sean Hannity, *Conservative Victory*

- 8/1/10—"[President Obama and Secretary Duncan] are heading in the wrong direction. On their present course, they will end up demoralizing teachers, closing schools that are struggling to improve, dismantling the teaching profession, destabilizing communities, and harming public education." —Diane Ravitch, *The Huffington Post*

- 10/29/10—"Remember Hitler had the Brownshirts, and in the Night of the Long Knives, even Hitler got scared of the Brownshirts and killed thousands of them. So you say, 'Are there any signs that that's happened?'—and the truth is yes. If you read the health care legislation, which, by the way, nobody in Washington has read, but if you read the health care legislation, it's actually in the health care legislation. There are paragraphs in the health care legislation that talk about the commissioning of officers in time of a national crisis to work directly for the president. It's laying the groundwork for a constabulary force that will control the population in America." —Lieutenant General Jerry Boykin, MorningStarTV.com

- 2/25/12—"If you want ten-dollar-a-gallon gasoline, an anti-energy secretary, and in weakness requiring us to depend on foreigners for our energy, Barack Obama should be your candidate." —Newt Gingrich, NBC

- 8/24/12—Obama has shown "indifference to the impact of the debt on American citizens. . . . That's an awful burden to saddle our children and grandchildren [with]. It's also a burden that drags the economy down and redistributes wealth away from America to the rest of the world. Why? Because in the past much of our debt was owed to other Americans, but now a significant portion of our debt, about a third, is owed to foreigners. This is a transfer of hundreds of billions, in fact trillions of dollars, out of the United States and to other countries. My theory about Obama was that he wanted and wants global redistribution, and debt is a weapon of global redistribution." —Dinesh D'Souza, *2016: Obama's America*

- 9/9/12—"If this president's reelected you're going to see chronic high unemployment continue for another four years or longer. You're going to see low wage growth, if any growth at all. And of course there'll always be this fiscal calamity at our doorstep." —Mitt Romney, NBC

- 9/10/12—"We're headed toward an economic collapse, and we are the leader of the world. And when it happens to us, there are reverberations all over the world. It's not like some Podunk little European country collapsing that goes to another Podunk European country for a bailout. When we collapse, worldwide reverberation. How long is it going to take? I'm asking a serious question. Eighteen months? You throw Obamacare onto what we know what we are going to get from Obama, more debt, more spending, the expansion of the welfare state, how long can this go on?" —Rush Limbaugh, Fox News

- 9/12/12—"There's only one thing missing now. Leadership. It takes leadership that you don't get from reading a poll. You see, Mr. President—real leaders don't follow polls. Real leaders change polls." —New Jersey governor Chris Christie, *The Huffington Post*

- 7/3/13—"It is astonishing that President Obama is unilaterally imposing new regulations that will cost jobs and increase energy prices." —John Boehner, *CNN Money*
- 8/5/13—"If the exchanges are permitted to go into effect . . . there will be error, fraud, inefficiency, arbitrariness, and privacy violations aplenty. . . . Just as economic shortages were endemic to Soviet central planning, the coming Obamacare train wreck is endemic to big government liberalism. It's not a bug, it's a feature." —Bill Kristol, *The Weekly Standard*
- 1/16/14—"An 'all of the above' strategy is a compromise that future generations can't afford. It fails to prioritize clean energy. . . . It locks in the extraction of fossil fuels that will inevitably lead to a catastrophic climate future. It threatens our health, our homes, our most sensitive public lands, our oceans and our most precious wild places." —Letter to Obama from major US environmental organizations, *The Washington Post*
- 2/24/14—"On political grounds, the largest fiscal stimulus in history is close to being toxic. The Keynesian Humpty Dumpty was shattered the day Mr. Obama's stimulus was enacted. It is very hard to see how it will be put back together again. . . . Keynesianism has been supplanted by Austerianism." —Ed Luce, *Financial Times*
- 10/7/14—"Obama's been engaged in a civil war from the day he seized the presidency. He said he's going to transform America. What was that? What was that declaration? It's a declaration of war against the country's traditional values and freedoms." —Michael Savage, *World Net Daily*
- 10/10/14—"The fact of the matter is, with two years we're not gonna survive. We will not exist as a nation with firm

borders, with a single language, and with a cohesive culture. . . . He has been conducting a civil war on America's institutions from the day he seized power." —Michael Savage, *Steve Malzberg Show*

- 1/21/15—"A $320 billion tax hike to fuel more government spending is not going to promote a healthy economy or improve the standard of living for working Americans and their families. . . . Calling for expanding the death tax and raising the rates on capital gains . . . makes clear this White House is more about redistribution and populist class warfare than about actual bipartisan tax reform. In fact, if anything, these misguided proposals would only further clutter up the tax code and make it more confusing for taxpayers." —Senate Finance Committee chairman Orrin Hatch, *ThinkAdvisor*

- 1/28/15—"We're going to see unspeakable violence in this country. The Muslims are going to blow up schools, they're going to blow up malls. It's going to be done under the cover of a jihadist in the White House, a Marxist Muslim jihadist in the White House, planted there many years ago for this very day to bring down the nation. Mr. Obama's election was no accident, it was the culmination of a carefully planned, funded and executed strategy to bring down this country." —Rick Wiles, TruNews radio show, quoted on Right Wing Watch

- 10/13/15—"Are they members of ISIS? Is he bringing in an army to overthrow the people? What is he trying to do? At the same time he is bringing in one hundred thousand—no one knows how many—Syrian males of military age, he's moving to disarm the American population. You want to paint a scary picture? A crazy picture? A conspiratorial picture? Go ahead, I just did." —Michael Savage, radio show, quoted on Right Wing Watch

- 10/13/15—"I think Barack Obama's our number one national security problem or risk, whether by accident, by design. I don't know what else you'd call somebody who enables the Iranians to nuke up and then sees to it they end up with $150 billion to do with whatever they want, including buy new Boeing airliners and go out and sponsor terrorism in the Middle East." —Rush Limbaugh, *The Rush Limbaugh Show,* as reported on *Politico*

- 12/10/15—"We can't be politically correct stupid people. We have a president—I think he's a stupid person. . . . Our president is the greatest divider I've ever seen. Our country has never been more divided than what Barack Obama has done. Whether it's white on black, whether it's—our country has never been more divided." —Donald Trump, WHDH.com

- 1/7/16—"There's an assault on the Second Amendment. You know Obama's going to do an executive order and really knock the hell out of it. . . . I will veto. I will unsign that so fast." —Donald Trump, CNN

- 1/9/16—"The two most important issues for Americans are the economy and the terror threat posed by Islamic killers. Yet President Obama apparently believes global warming and increased gun checks are the most vital issues. It's kind of hard to fathom, but Mr. Obama's investing a huge amount of energy in climate and guns." —Bill O'Reilly, *The O'Reilly Factor*

ACKNOWLEDGMENTS

This book was imagined first by Thomas Dunne, whose instincts and talent show themselves with every scratch of his pen. I am grateful for the trust he placed in me. He and Peter Joseph, executive editor, steered this book project with steady hands and good humor.

I am grateful to colleagues who aided in research and editing and offered insights and encouragement. Among them are Steve Boldt, Mark Dagostino, Bart Jones, Lara Tillman, Jeff Katz, Dunstan Prial, Abby Lunney, and Amy Choi. I also received reliable feedback and guidance from Toni and Amy D'Antonio, whose insights into human nature increase my understanding of human motivations and the dynamics of change. This manuscript depended on political insights offered by John Manly and on social science shared by John Gerzema and William Johnson.

Among the subjects who gave their time and opened their doors to show me the effects of the Obama presidency on everyday life in America, I must offer special thanks to the staff and students of the Murkland School, cancer survivor Spike Dolomite, the workers of the GM plant in Spring Hill, Tennessee, and Mayor Rex Parris of Lancaster, California. These individuals, and communities across the country and around the world, testified freely to the achievements of a consequential president.

SELECTED CHAPTER NOTES

Chapter 1: Ending the Great Recession: It Was the Economy, Stupid

Susan Chandler, "The Baby Recession: Economic Woes Begin to Affect the Most Personal of Decisions: Whether or When to Have Children," *Chicago Tribune,* December 23, 2008, 1.

David R. Francis, "Recession Is a Given. Can We Avoid Depression?," *Christian Science Monitor,* March 24, 2008, 17.

Raghuram Rajan, "Has Financial Development Made the World Riskier?," http://www.nber.org/papers/w11728.pdf.

Justin Lahart, "Mr. Rajan Was Unpopular (but Prescient) at Greenspan Party," *Wall Street Journal,* January 2, 2009, http://www.wsj.com/articles/SB123086154114948151.

Paul Krugman, "How Did Economists Get It So Wrong?," *New York Times Magazine,* September 2, 2009, http://www.nytimes.com/2009/09/06/magazine/06Economic-t.html?_r=0.

"House of Cards," *60 Minutes,* January 24, 2008, http://www.cbsnews.com/news/house-of-cards-the-mortgage-mess/2/.

"The Job Impact of the American Recovery and Reinvestment Act of 2009," http://otrans.3cdn.net/ee40602f9a7d8172b8_ozm6bt5oi.pdf.

Laura Meckler and Jonathan Weisman, "Obama Warns of 'Lost Decade'—President Says Federal Government Is the Only Remaining Option to Jolt Economy," *Wall Street Journal,* February 10, 2009, A1.

Anne E. Kornblut and Michael A. Fletcher, "Obama Says Economic Crisis Comes First; President Tells Nation Stimulus Plan Must Pass, with or without GOP," *Washington Post,* February 10, 2009, A1.

"American Recovery and Reinvestment Act of 2009," breakdown of spending, https://en.wikipedia.org/wiki/American_Recovery_and_Reinvestment_Act_of_2009.

"South Carolina Economic Indicator Report," June 2010, South Carolina Department of Commerce.

Daniel Henninger, "Obama's 'Hair of the Dog' Stimulus," *Wall Street Journal,* February 19, 2009, A17.

Peter Nicholas, "Obama: Bill Is 'Beginning of the End' of Downturn; the President Lauds the Stimulus He Signs into Law, but an Aide Hints That Another Such Plan May Be Needed," *Los Angeles Times,* February 18, 2009, A9.

Sean Reilly, "Sen. Richard Shelby Now 'Confident' Obama Is Eligible by Birth for Presidency," AL.com, July 29, 2009.

Ben Smith, "Alabama Paper Stands by Shelby Story," *Politico.com,* February 22, 2009.

David Weigel, "And Now, Roy Blunt," *Washington Independent,* July 29, 2009.

Jonathan McDonald Ladds, "The Neglected Power of Elite Opinion Leadership to Produce Antipathy Toward the News Media: Evidence from a Survey Experiment," *Political Behavior* 32.1 (2010): 29–50, http://www.jstor.org/stable/40587306.

Paul Krugman, "Mission Not Accomplished," *New York Times,* October 2, 2009, A3.

Marco E. Terrones, Alasdair Scott, and Prakash Kannan, "Global

Recession to Be Long, Deep with Slow Recovery," IMF Research Department, April 16, 2009.

Allan Meltzer, "What Happened to the 'Depression'?," *Wall Street Journal,* September 1, 2009, A17.

Justin Lahart, "Currents: Gauging the Economy's Engine as It Sputters Along—Calling a Recession's End Is Tough amid Conflicting Data, but Here's a User's Manual to the Gears and Measures," *Wall Street Journal,* May 19, 2009, A12.

Dan Balz and Jon Cohen, "Confidence in Stimulus Plan Ebbs, Poll Finds; Obama's Approval Rating Remains High, but Shift in Public Outlook Has Political Implications," *Washington Post,* June 23, 2009, A4.

Stephanie Armour, "Foreclosure Rate Dips in May: But Pace Exceeds Year-Ago Level by 18% Despite Efforts," *USA Today,* June 11, 2009, B2

Don Lee and Jim Puzzanghera, "Unease Grows as Jobless Rate Rises to 10.2%; Obama's Options for Easing Unemployment Are Limited, Both Politically and Practically," *Los Angeles Times,* November 7, 2009, A1.

Peter Temin, "The Great Recession and the Great Depression," National Bureau of Economic Research Working Paper No. 15645, January 2010.

Chapter 2: Auto Industry Rescue: "The Doomsayers Were Wrong"

Ross Eisenbrey, "Management—Bad Management—Crippled the Auto Industry's Big Three, not the UAW," Economic Policy Institute, May 24, 2012, http://www.epi.org/blog/bad-management-crippled-auto-industry-big-three/.

Matthew Dolan, "Ford Benefits as GM, Chrysler Stumble—Union Givebacks, Rising Market Share Are Tied to Rivals' Bad News;

Why Some Shoppers Switch to Ford," *Wall Street Journal,* February 20, 2009, B1.

Nick Bunkley, "UAW Vows to Cede to Big 3: It Would Halt Its Jobs Bank and Weigh Contract Changes to Win Congress' Support of a Bailout," *Philadelphia Inquirer,* December 4, 2008, 1.

Kendra Marr, "Closer to Bailout, GM Prints Candid Apology," *Washington Post,* December 9, 2008, D1.

Greg Stoll and John Hitt, "Outside Pressure Grows for GM to Oust Wagoner," *Wall Street Journal,* December 8, 2008, A1.

Philip Elliott and Julie Hirschfeld Davis, "Senator Wants GM Chief to Resign," *Deseret News,* December 8, 2008, 2A.

Greg Hitt, Jeffrey McCrackern, and John D. Stoll, "Rescue Bid for Detroit Collapses in Senate," *Wall Street Journal,* December 12, 2008, A1.

Michael Kranish, "Bush Vows to Avert Auto Industry Failure in U-turn, Would Tap $700b Fund," *Boston Globe,* December 13, 2008, A1.

Peter Grier, "Big Three's Future Still in Balance," *Christian Science Monitor,* December 19, 2008, 1.

Michael O'Neal, "Big Expectations for Auto: Bailout Plan Calls for Radical Changes in Three Months," *Chicago Tribune,* December 20, 2008, 1.21.

"America's Most Dangerous Cities," Forbes.com, April 2009, http://www.forbes.com/2009/04/23/most-dangerous-cities -lifestyle-real-estate-dangerous-american-cities.html.

Sharon Silke, "Carty Poll Shows Lukewarm Support for Auto Rescue: Analyst Offers Grim Prospects for GM," *USA Today,* November 11, 2008, B3.

Bryan Bender, "Obama Cautions Auto Industry, Wants Change, Says CEOs Who Misuse Loans Should Go," *Boston Globe,* December 8, 2008, 1.

Kendra Marr, "Auto Sales Plummeted to 27-Year Low in Jan.; Industry Has 37 Percent Decline over Last Year," *Washington Post,* February 4, 2009, D1.

"The Miracle of Turin," *Economist,* April 24, 2008, www.economist .com/node/11089887.

Cheryl Jensen, "2008 J.D. Power Rankings Released," *New York Times,* June 4, 2008, http://wheels.blogs.nytimes.com/2008 /06/04/2008-jd-power-rankings-released/.

Andrew Ross Sorkin, "G.M.'s Bondholders Speak in the Voice of the Aggrieved," *New York Times,* March 31, 2009, B1.

Angela Tablac, "Chrysler Gets 'Death Papers'; Analyst Says Government's Expectations for Automaker Are Unrealistic," *St. Louis Post-Dispatch,* March 31, 2009, A8.

Maya Jackson Randall, "U.S. News: Treasury Has $134.5 Billion Left in TARP," *Wall Street Journal,* March 30, 2009, 3.

Michael J. de la Merded and Micheline Maynard, "Fiat Takes Over Chrysler After 42-Day Bankruptcy," *New York Times,* June 1, 2009.

"Chrysler's Turbulent History," http://www.nytimes.com/interactive /2015/05/24/business/chrysler-timeline.html.

Jay Alix, "How General Motors Was Really Saved: The Untold True Story of the Most Important Bankruptcy in U.S. History," *Forbes,* November 18, 2013.

Steven Rattner, *Overhaul: An Insider's Account of the Obama Administration's Emergency Rescue of the Auto Industry* (Boston: Houghton Mifflin Harcourt, 2010), 120–21.

David Hanna, "How GM Destroyed Its Saturn Success," *Forbes.com,* March 8, 2010, http://www.forbes.com/2010/03/08/saturn -gm-innovation-leadership-managing-failure.html.

"Detroitosaurus Wrecks: The Lessons for America and the Car Industry from the Biggest Industrial Collapse Ever," *Economist,* June 4, 2009.

"Government Motors No More," *Economist,* August 19, 2010.

"Examining the State of the Domestic Automobile Industry—Part

I," Committee on Banking, Housing, and Urban Affairs, US Senate, November 18, 2008.

"Examining the State of the Domestic Automobile Industry—Part II," Committee on Banking, Housing, and Urban Affairs, US Senate, December 4, 2008.

George Will, "Bailout Won't Fix the Dying Auto Industry," *South Florida Sun–Sentinel,* November 22, 2008, 19.

Daniel Dombey and Bernard Simon, "Bush Bails Out GM and Chrysler to Hand Detroit Crisis to Obama," *Financial Times* (London), December 20, 2008, 1.

Stephen Ohlemacher, "Divide Deepens over Auto Industry Bailout: Opponents Say Loans Would Just Put Off Demise of 'Dinosaur,'" *Chicago Tribune,* November 17, 2008, 29.

"The Bankruptcy of General Motors; a Giant Falls; the Collapse of General Motors into Bankruptcy Is Only the Latest Chapter in a Long Story of Mismanagement and Decline," *Economist,* June 4, 2009.

Jim Puzzanghera, "Desperate Auto Chiefs Plead Anew; Humbled Big 3 Leaders Say They'll Accept U.S. Oversight and Take the $34-Billion Bailout Installments," *Los Angeles Times,* December 5, 2008, 1.

Jim Rutenberg, Peter Baker, and Bill Vlasic, "Early Resolve: Obama Stand in Auto Crisis," *New York Times,* April 29, 2009.

Chapter 3: Health Care Reform: Saving Spike Dolomite

"Anti–Health Care Protest—Town Hall Health Care Reform Protesters—Tea Party Rally," https://www.youtube.com /watch?v=ZKBa9K_vAm8.

Louis Jacobson, "Julian Castro Says Seven Presidents before Barack Obama Sought Universal Health Care," Politifact.com, September 5, 2012, http://www.politifact.com/truth-o-meter/statements /2012/sep/05/julian-castro/julian-castro-says-seven-presidents -barack-obama-s/.

Kristina Davis, "Health Care Reform Meeting Draws Packed House," *San Diego Union Tribune,* August 30, 2009.

http://www.theguardian.com/commentisfree/cifamerica/2010 /oct/25/tea-party-koch-brothers mm.

Jane Mayer, "Covert Operations: The Billionaire Brothers Who Are Waging a War against Obama," *New Yorker,* August 30, 2010.

Ezra Klein, "Why Seniors, Who Have Government-Run Health Care, Oppose Reform," *Washington Post,* August 30, 2009.

Elizabeth Doctuer and Robert Berenson, "How Does the Quality of U.S. Health Care Compare Internationally?," Robert Wood Johnson Foundation, 2014.

http://www.theatlantic.com/health/archive/2014/06/us-health care-most-expensive-and-worst-performing/372828/.

Joseph J. Doyle Jr. "Health Insurance, Treatment and Outcomes: Using Auto Accidents as Health Shocks," *MIT Review of Economics and Statistics,* https://www3.nd.edu/~wevans1/class_papers /doyle_restat.pdf.

Elizabeth Ward et al., "Association of Insurance with Cancer Care Utilization and Outcomes," *Cancer Journal for Clinicians,* January–February 2008, 9.

Kristen Gerencher, "Coverage Plans Contrast Sharply," *St. Louis Post–Dispatch,* October 21, 2008, 1.

Paul Krugman, "Wrecking Health Care: McCain Would Privatize and Deregulate the Health Insurance System," *Pittsburgh Post–Gazette,* October 7, 2008, B5.

Robert G. Kaiser, "Election Shakes Up Notion of a Center-Right America," *Deseret News,* November 23, 2008, 3.

Scott Keeter, "Young Voters in the 2008 Election," Pew Research.

"Jimmy Carter: Wilson's Outburst Was Racist," http://www .nbcwashington.com/news/politics/NATL-Jimmy-Carter -Wilsons-Outburst-Was-Racist-59410277.html.

Sheryl Gay Stolberg, "Obama Nudging Views on Race, a Survey Finds," *New York Times,* April 28 2009, 1.

Philip Elliott, Associated Press, "Obama Mishandled Comments on Race, Opinion Poll Says," *Deseret News,* July 31, 2009, 1.

Norman Ornstein, "How Racists and Partisans Exploit the Age of Obama," *Atlantic,* December 11, 2014.

Rick Ungar, "Busted! Health Insurers Secretly Spent Huge to Defeat Health Care Reform While Pretending to Support Obamacare," *Forbes,* June 25, 2012.

"Health Care Coverage and Access in the Nation's Four Largest States: Results from the Commonwealth Fund Biennial Health Insurance Survey," 2014.

Derek Bok, "Political Leadership in the Great Health Care Debate of 1993–94," in *Public Discourse in America,* ed. Judith Rodin and Stephen P. Steinberg (Philadelphia: University of Pennsylvania Press, 2011).

Chapter 4: Energy: Sun, Wind, and Market Forces

"Lazard's Levelized Cost of Energy Analysis—Version 9.0," Key Finding (New York: Lazard, 2016).

Felicity Barringer, "With Help from Nature, a Town Aims to Be a Solar Capital," *New York Times,* April 8, 2013.

James Hamilton, "Causes and Consequences of the Oil Shock of 2007–2008," National Bureau of Economic Research, Cambridge, Mass., May 2009.

Andrew C. Revkin, "The Obama Energy Speech, Annotated," *New York Times,* August 5, 2008, http://dotearth.blogs.nytimes .com/2008/08/05/the-obama-energy-speech-annotated/.

Tom Troy, "Obama Plans Visit to Area Next Week; He'll Prep for Last Debate, but Site Unclear," *Blade,* October 9, 2008, A1.

Michael Grunwald, *The New New Deal,* 165.

David Jackson, "McCain, Obama Promote Nuclear Energy Plans," *USA Today,* August 6, 2008, 5.

Jon Gertner, "Capitalism to the Rescue," *New York Times Magazine,* October 5, 2008, 54–61.

Louis Jacobson, "Chris Matthews Says Cheney Got $34 Million Payday from Halliburton," Politifact.com, May 24, 2010.

Michael Abramowitz and Steven Mufson, "Papers Detail Industry's Role in Cheney's Energy Report," *Washington Post,* July 18, 2007, HR6.

Joby Warrick, "Federal Mine Agency Considers New Rules to Improve Safety," *Washington Post,* January 31, 2006.

Juliet Eilperin, "US Exempted BP's Gulf of Mexico Drilling from Environmental Impact Study," *Washington Post,* May 5, 2010.

Seth Borenstein, "Enforcement of Mine Safety Seen Slipping under Bush," *McClatchyDC,* January 6, 2006.

Bill Canis and Richard Lattanzio, "U.S. and EU Motor Vehicle Standards: Issues for Transatlantic Trade Negotiations," Congressional Research Service, February 2014.

"Trend in Energy Production from U.S. Energy Information Administration: Slower, Costlier, Dirtier, a Critique of the Bush Energy Plan," Natural Resources Defense Fund, http://www.nrdc.org/air/energy/scd/execsum.asp.

Justin Gerdes, "Obama Administration Marks 1 Million Homes Weatherized under Stimulus," Forbes.com, September 30, 2012.

Michael Grunwald, "Rise of the Smart Grid," *Time,* July 26, 2012.

Peter Singer, "Federally Supported Innovations: 22 Examples of Major Technology Advances That Stem from Federal Research Support," Information, Technology and Innovation Foundation, Washington, 2014.

"Further Actions Needed to Improve DOE's Ability to Evaluate and Implement the Loan Guarantee Program," GAO, July 2010.

Ronnie Greene, "Skipping Safeguards, Official Rushed Benefits to a Politically Connected Energy Company," Center for Public Integrity/ABC News, May 24, 2011.

Pete Kasperowicz, "Issa Warns Taxpayers' Loss on Solyndra Loan May Near $850 Million," *Hill,* October 22, 2012.

U.S. Department of Energy Office of Inspector General Special Report, "The Department of Energy's Loan Guarantee to Solyndra, Inc.," August 24, 2015.

"The Solyndra Mess," *New York Times,* November 25, 2011, 34.

"Issa Eyes Political Connections That Drove Loan Approvals Like Solyndra," Foxnews.com, October 9, 2011.

Darren Samuelsohn, "GOP Running out of Gas on Solyndra," Politico.com, March 27, 2012, http://www.politico.com/story /2012/03/gop-running-out-of-gas-on-solyndra-074564.

"President Announces National Fuel Efficiency Policy," White House, May 19, 2009.

Juliet Eilperin, "Obama to Tighten Fuel Efficiency Standards for Big Trucks," *Washington Post,* February 18, 2014.

"New Investigation Finds Decades of Government Funding Behind Shale Revolution," TheBreakthrough.org, December 20, 2011.

www.EPA.gov/hydraulicfracturing.

Eliza Griswold, "The Fracturing of Pennsylvania," *New York Times Magazine,* November 17, 2011.

Christina Nunez, "A Slew of Coal Plants Get New Lease on Life—with Gas," *National Geographic,* November 20, 2014.

James McBride, "Hydraulic Fracking Backgrounder," Council on Foreign Relations, June 10, 2015, http://www.cfr.org/energy -and-environment/hydraulic-fracturing-fracking/p31559.

"US Retail Sales Dipped in December; Low Gas Prices a Key Factor," Associated Press, January 15, 2016.

"Green Jobs Grow Four Times Faster Than Others," *Los Angeles Times,* March 19, 2013.

US Energy Information Administration Monthly Energy Review, 2015.

Chapter 5: Environment: Saving the Planet

Jonah Bromwich, "A Fitting End for the Hottest Year on Record," *New York Times,* December 23, 2015.

Damian Carrington, "2016 Set to Be Hottest Year on Record, Globally," *Guardian,* December 17, 2015.

Philip Shabecoff, "Global Warming Had Begun, Expert Tells Senate," *New York Times,* June 24, 1988.

David L. Chandler, "Climate Myths: CO_2 Isn't the Most Important Greenhouse Gas," *New Scientist,* May 16, 2007.

Catherine Brahic, "Climate Myths: Human CO_2 Emissions Are Too Tiny to Matter," *New Scientist,* May 16, 2007.

Naomi Oreskes and Erik Conway, *Merchants of Doubt* (New York: Bloomsbury Press, 2010).

https://www.documentcloud.org/documents/1676446-global -climate-science-communications-plan-1998.html.

Constance Lever-Tracey, *Routledge Handbook of Climate Change and Society* (New York: Routledge, 2010), 245–60.

"James Inhofe: There Is No Global Warming Because God," Fox News Radio, March 7, 2015.

"One in Four in U.S. Are Solidly Skeptical of Global Warming," Gallup, www.gallup.com.

William Yardley, "Whale Protection Bolstered as Palin Objects," *New York Times,* October 18, 2008, 11.

Riley E. Dunlap and Aaron M. McCright, "A Widening Gap: Republican and Democratic Views on Climate Change," *Environment,* September 2008.

Luntz Research Companies, "Straight Talk," https://www.mother jones.com/files/LuntzResearch_environment.pdf.

Amy Sherman, "Cap and Trade Legislation Was Originally 'a Republican Idea,' Wasserman Schultz Says," Politifact.com, May 23, 2014.

Richard Conniff, "The Political History of Cap and Trade," *Smithsonian,* August 2009.

"Inside Obama's Sweeping Victory," Pew Research Center, November 5, 2008.

Margot Roosevelt, "Obama Jumps In on Climate," *Los Angeles Times,* November 19, 2008.

"Bush Views Shift on Climate Change," NPR.org, February 1, 2007, ww.nrdc.org/bushrecord/airenergy_warming.asp.

Elizabeth Kolbert, "Midnight Hour," *New Yorker,* November 24, 2008.

Suzanne Goldenberg, "The Worst of Times: Bush's Environmental Legacy Examined," *Guardian,* January 16, 2009.

Al Gore, "Climate of Denial," *Rolling Stone,* June 22, 2001.

David Biello, "How Much Will Tar Sands Add to Global Warming?," *Scientific American,* January 23, 2013.

Brendan Sasso, "Does NSA Spying Leave the U.S. Without Moral High Ground in China Hack?," *National Journal,* June 14, 2015.

Howard Schneider, "U.S., China Agree on Climate Steps to Curb Emissions; Annual Strategic and Economic Talks Open with a call for China to Curb Cyber-Snooping on U.S. Firms," *Washington Post,* July 11, 2013.

"Obama Administration Running Out the Clock on Keystone XL," House Energy and Commerce Committee, http://energycommerce.house.gov/content/keystone-xl.

Linda Feldman, "Keystone XL Pipeline: Did Obama Just Drop a Big Hint About His Decision?," *Christian Science Monitor,* June 25, 2013, 11.

Lauren Carroll, "3 Keystone XL Questions Answered," Politifact.com, January 9, 2015.

"Remarks by the President on Climate Change," Georgetown University, Washington, D.C., June 25, 2013.

Jonathan Chait, "Obama Might Actually Be the Environmental President," *New York,* May 5, 2013.

http://www.presidency.ucsb.edu/data/orders.php.

"Statement by the President on the Keystone XL Pipeline," November 6, 2015.

Laudato Si, "On Care for Our Common Home," http://w2.vatican

.va/content/francesco/en/encyclicals/documents/papa-francesco_20150524_enciclica-laudato-si.html.

Samir Saran and Vivan Sharan, "Indian Leadership on Climate Change," Brookings, May 6, 2015.

Mitch McConnell, "Obama's Power Plan Grab," *Washington Post,* November 29, 2015, 25.

Jonathan Chait, "Why Are Republicans the Only Climate-Science-Denying Party in the World?," *New York,* September 27, 2015.

Chan Sewall, "Paris Accord Considers Climate Change as a Factor in Mass Migration," *New York Times,* December 12, 2015.

"Climate Negotiators Zero In on Key Issues as Planned End to Paris Talks Nears; New Draft of Agreement Has Unresolved Points," *Wall Street Journal,* December 9, 2015.

Coral Davenport, "Nations Approve Landmark Climate Accord in Paris," *New York Times,* December 12, 2015.

Chris Buckley, "China Is Burning Much More Coal Than It Claimed," *New York Times,* November 4, 2015, 1.

Edward Wong, "China Plans to Upgrade Coal Plants," *New York Times,* December 2, 2015.

"Understanding the IPCC Reports," www.wri.org/ipcc-infographics.

Chris Mooney, "Small Nations Noticed in Paris," *Washington Post,* December 12 2015, 1.

Joby Warrick, "Paris Climate Deal Nearly Unraveled Over 1 Word," *Washington Post,* December 14, 2015, 1.

"From Paris, a Good Moment for Our Earth; the Climate Agreement, by Nearly 200 Nations, May Have 'Saved the Chance of Saving the Planet,'" *Los Angeles Times,* December 14, 2015, 15.

Bill McKibben, "Falling Short on Climate in Paris," *New York Times,* December 13, 2015, http://www.nytimes.com/2015/12/14/opinion/falling-short-on-climate-in-paris.html?partner=bloomberg.

"Paris Climate of Conformity," *Wall Street Journal,* December 14, 2015, 16.

Chapter 6: Foreign Policy: Obama's World

Ramin Mostaghim and Sarah Parvini, " 'Freedom,' Iranians Chant as They Celebrate Nuclear Agreement," *Los Angeles Times,* July 14, 2015.

"Iran Nuclear Crisis, What Are the Sanctions," BBC, March 30, 2015.

Shreeya Sinha and Susan Campbell Beachy, "Timeline on Iran's Nuclear Program," *New York Times,* April 2, 2015, http://www .nytimes.com/interactive/2014/11/20/world/middleeast/Iran -nuclear-timeline.html?_r=0#/#time243_10809.

Michael R. Gordon and Jeff Zeleny, "Obama Envisions New Iran Approach," *New York Times,* November 2, 2007, http://www .nytimes.com/2007/11/02/us/politics/02obama.html.

"Obama to Restore Science to Its Rightful Place," *New Scientist Daily News,* January 20, 2009, https://www.newscientist.com /article/dn16452-obama-to-restore-science-to-its-rightful -place/#.VSTYRBDF8vE.

"President Barack Obama," *This Week* transcript, September 14, 2013, http://abcnews.go.com/ThisWeek/week-transcript -president-barack-obama/story?id=20253577.

David Andrew Weinberg, "What Netanyahu's Meddling in US Election Means for Obama, Romney, and Diplomacy," *Christian Science Monitor,* September 19. 2012.

United States Institute of Peace, "Iran Primer," www.usip.org.

IAEA, Iran timeline, https://www.iaea.org/newscenter/focus/iran /chronology-of-key-events.

"Iran's Nuclear Deal Becomes a Reality," *Economist,* January 14, 2016, http://www.economist.com/blogs/graphicdetail/2016/01 /graphics-iran-sanctions-and-nuclear-deal.

Saeed Kamali Dehghan, "Iran: Hassan Rouhani Wins Presidential Election," *Guardian,* June 15, 2013, http://www.theguardian.com

/world/2013/jun/15/iran-presidential-election-hassan-rouhani-wins.

Ken Ballen, "Iranians Favor Peace Deal with US," CNN.com, June 8, 2009.

Carl Hulse and David M. Herszenhorn, "A Coordinated Strategy Brings Victory to Obama on the Iran Nuclear Deal," *New York Times,* September 3, 2015, A1.

David E. Sanger and Michael R. Gordon, "Years of Trading and Compromise Sealed Iran Deal," *New York Times,* July 16, 2015, A1.

Terrance McCoy, "The Roots of Why Obama and Netanyahu Dislike Each Other So Much," *Washington Post,* February 26, 2015.

Amir Tibon and Tal Shalev, "Bibi and Barack, Scenes from a Failed Marriage," Huffingtonpost.com.

"AIPAC Official: PM's Congress Speech Hurt Iran Deal Opposition," *Times of Israel,* September 3, 2015, http://www.timesofisrael.com/aipac-official-pms-congress-speech-hurt-iran-deal-opposition/.

"Corker's Muddled Argument Against the Iranian Nuclear Deal, the Senate Foreign Relations Committee Chairman Isn't Clear on What Alternative He Would Offer," *Washington Post,* August 20, 2015.

"Opinions About the Iran Deal Are More About Obama Than Iran," Fivethirtyeight.com, July 14, 2015, http://fivethirtyeight.com/datalab/opinions-about-the-iran-deal-are-more-about-obama-than-iran/.

Stephen Walt, "The Secret to America's Foreign Policy Success and Failure," ForeignPolicy.com, July 27, 2015.

Matt Bradley and Nathan Hodge, "Iraq Signs Collaboration Deal with Russia, Iran, Syria, on ISIS Fight; Agreement Compounds U.S.'s Declining Influence in Middle East, *Wall Street Journal,* September 27, 2015.

Stephen Walt, "Delusion Point," Foreignpolicy.com, November 8, 2010.

Ron Suskind, "Faith, Certainty, and the Presidency of George Bush," *New York Times Magazine,* October 17, 2004.

"Reactions from Around the World," *New York Times,* November 5, 2008, http://thecaucus.blogs.nytimes.com/2008/11/05/reactions -from-around-the-world/.

Michael Oren, "How Obama Opened His Heart to the 'Muslim World,'" Foreignpolicy.com, June 19, 2015.

Garance Franke-Ruta, "Reaction: Obama Wins Nobel Peace Prize," *Washington Post,* October 9, 2009, http://voices.washingtonpost .com/44/2009/10/09/reaction_obama_wins_nobel_peac .html.

Council on Foreign Relations, Iraq War timeline, http://www.cfr .org/publication/18876/timeline.html?gclid=CjwKEAiArdG- 1BRCLvs_q-IObwxMSJACXbLtzonln_5bCt67dGzvufsVMoFro RsKXTsoCMdj7tk3IBxoCH1bw_wcB.

Council on Foreign Relations, Afghanistan War timeline, http:// www.cfr.org/afghanistan/us-war-afghanistan/p20018.

Matthew Rosenberg and Michael D. Shear, "In Reversal, Obama Says U.S. Soldiers Will Stay in Afghanistan to 2017," *New York Times,* October 15, 2015.

Gideon Rose, "What Obama Gets Right: Keep Calm and Carry the Liberal Order On," *Foreign Affairs,* September/October 2015.

Chapter 7: Education: Racing to the Top

Anthony Cody, "Rich Schools/Poor Schools: The Gap Grows," *Educationweek,* September 23, 2009.

"Federal Education Policy and the States, 1945–2009," New York States Archives, Albany, 2009.

"The Demographics of Wealth: How Age, Education and Race Separate Thrivers from Strugglers in Today's Economy," Fed-

eral Reserve Bank of St. Louis, https://www.stlouisfed.org
/~/media/Files/PDFs/HFS/essays/HFS-Essay-2-2015
-Education-and-Wealth.pdf.

Julie Bosman, "Obama Sharply Assails Absent Black Fathers," *New
York Times,* June 16, 2008.

"No Child Left Behind: What Worked, What Didn't," *Morning
Edition,* Public Radio, October 28, 2015.

Thomas Ahn, "The Impact of No Child Left Behind's Accountability Sanctions on School Performance: Regression Disconti-
nuity Evidence from North Carolina," University of Kentucky,
February 2013.

Jennifer Imakezi, "Is No Child Left Behind an Un (or Under)
Funded Federal Mandate? Evidence from Texas," *National
Tax Journal,* September 2004.

"Cut Loose: State and Local Layoffs of Public Employees in the
Current Recession," Center for Economic Policy and Research
issue brief, September 2009.

"Cutting to the Bone: How the Economic Crisis Affects Schools,"
Center for Public Education, October 7, 2010.

"Investing in Our Future: Returning Teachers to the Classroom," White House, August 2011.

Matthew Ronfeldt, Susanna Loeb, and James Wyckoff, "How
Teacher Turnover Harms Student Achievement," *American Educational Research Journal* 50, no. 1 (February 2013): 4–36.

"Repair for Success: An Analysis of the Need and Possibilities for a
Federal Investment in PK-12 School Maintenance and Repair,"
prepared by the 21st Century School Fund, November 16,
2009.

"Official Says Maine High School Falling Apart," *Boston Globe,* October 15, 2009.

Allison Manning, "Termites Drive Actors Buggy," *Quincy Patriot
Ledger,* March 20, 2009.

"CMD Publishes Full List of 2,500 Closed Charter Schools,"

September 22, 2015, http://www.prwatch.org/news/2015/09
/12936/cmd-publishes-full-list-2500-closed-charter-schools.

"Massachusetts: Race to the Top Report," http://www.doe.mass
.edu/rttt/2014-01yr3report.pdf.

"Best State in America: Massachusetts for Its Educational Success,"
Washington Post, July 11, 2014.

"Race to the Top: What Have We Learned from the States So Far?
A State-by-State Evaluation of Race to the Top Performance,"
Center for American Progress, March 26, 2012.

"The New Rules, Testing Our Schools," *Frontline,* PBS, March 2002.

Stephanie Simon, "PISA Results: 'Educational Stagnation,'" Polit-
ico.com, December 3, 2013.

Rebecca Meade, "Obama's Change of Heart on Testing," *New
Yorker,* October 28, 2013.

David L. Kirp, "Why the New Education Law Is Good for Children
Left Behind," *New York Times,* December 10, 2015.

Emmarie Huetteman, "Senate Approves Overhaul of No Child Left
Behind Law," *New York Times,* December 9, 2015.

Thomas Doe and Brian Jacob, "The Impact of No Child Left
Behind on Student Achievement," National Bureau of Economic Research, November 2009.

Allie Grassgreen, "Obama Pushes For-Profit Colleges to the Brink,"
Politico.com, July 1, 2015.

Chapter 8: Financial Reform: Boring Is Better

Obama speech on regulatory reform, Dayton, Ohio, October 9,
2008.

Edmund L. Andrews, "Greenspan Concedes Error on Regulation,"
New York Times, October 23, 2008.

Gingrich statement from ABC TV, November 8, 2011.

McCain statement on deregulation from CBS News, September 21,
2008.

Data on polling, issues, and preferences from Frank Newport et al., *Winning the White House 2008* (New York: Checkmark Books, 2009).

"Conclusions of the Financial Crisis Inquiry Commission," http://FcicStatic.Law.Stanford.Edu/Cdn_Media/FcicReports/Fcic_Final_Report_Conclusions.Pdf.

"Financial Crisis Cost Tops $22 Trillion, GAO Says," *Huffington Post,* February 14, 2013.

"Financial Regulatory Reform: Financial Crisis Losses and Potential Impacts of the Dodd-Frank Act," GAO-13-180, February 14, 2013.

"Remarks by the President on Financial Reform," January 21, 2010, https://www.whitehouse.gov/the-press-office/remarks-president-financial-reform.

" 'The Only Thing Useful Banks Have Invented in 20 Years Is the ATM,' " *New York Post,* December 13, 2009.

"Volcker Praises the ATM, Blasts Finance Execs, Experts," Marketbeat, *Wall Street Journal,* December 8, 2009.

Michael Hirsh, *Capital Offense* (Hoboken, N.J.: Wiley, 2010), 294–300.

Timothy F. Geithner, *Stress Test* (New York: Broadway Books, 2014), 424–25.

Tamara Keith, "New Consumer Protection Agency Faces Opposition," NPR, July 21, 2011.

Adam J. Levitin, "The Consumer Financial Protection Bureau: An Introduction," Boston University.

Jake Sherman, "Goldman Fills Political War Chests," Politico.com, April 21, 2010.

Elison Elliott, "Greenspan Backs Obama Consumer Protection Plan," Foreign Policy Association, September 28, 2009, http://foreignpolicyblogs.com/2009/09/28/greenspan-backs-obama-consumer-protection-plan/.

Louis Uchitelle, "Elders of Wall St. Favor More Regulation," *New York Times,* February 16, 2010.

"Big Majority Wants Wall Street Regulation," Reuters, March 11, 2010.

Louis Uchitelle, "S.E.C. Accuses Goldman of Fraud in Housing Deal," *New York Times,* April 16, 2010.

John Harwood, "The Caucus; Two Senators Cross the Aisle for a Brief, but Failed, Pass at Bipartisanship," *New York Times,* March 15, 2010.

Frank Rich, "Fight On, Goldman Sachs!," *New York Times,* April 26, 2010.

For Scott Brown's demands see Geithner, *Stress Test,* 423.

Helene Cooper, "Obama Signs Overhaul of Financial System," *New York Times,* July 21, 2010.

Gretchen Morgenson, "Beware of Exploding Mortgages," *New York Times,* June 10, 2007.

Elizabeth Warren, "Unsafe at Any Rate," *Democracy,* Summer 2007, http://democracyjournal.org/magazine/5/unsafe-at-any-rate/.

Elizabeth Warren appeared on *The Daily Show,* April 15, 2009.

William D. Cohan, "The Elizabeth Warren Fallacy," *New York Times,* September 30, 2010.

"Many Successes in Just a Few Years: The Consumer Financial Protection Bureau Turns 5," Center for American Progress, July 21, 2015, https://www.americanprogress.org/issues/housing/news/2015/07/21/117803/many-successes-in-just-a-few-years-the-consumer-financial-protection-bureau-turns-5/.

Noah Bierman, "US Chamber Calls Elizabeth Warren Threat to Free Enterprise," *Boston Globe,* August 15, 2012.

Suzanna Andrews, "The Woman Who Knew Too Much," *Vanity Fair,* November 2011.

Andrew Sorigel, "A Stabilizing Force," *US News and World Report,* July 21, 2015.

Michael Grunwald, "The College Loan Bombshell Hidden in the Federal Budget," *Politico.com*, February 5, 2015.

Chapter 9: Equality: Expectations, Limits, Progress

Nina Totenberg, "Fair Pay Law Strikes a Blow for Equal Pay," NPR, January 29, 2009.

Howard J. Wall, "The Gender Wage Gap and Wage Discrimination: Illusion or Reality?," https://www.whitehouse.gov/sites /default/files/page/files/20160128_cea_gender_pay_gap _issue_brief.pdf.

Lilly Ledbetter interview, www.makers.com/moments/sexual -harrassment-boss.

For decision and dissent in *Ledbetter v. Goodyear,* www.supremecourt .gov/opinions/06pdf/05-1074.pdf.

"In Debate, McCain Had Joe the Plumber, Obama Had Lilly Ledbetter," *US News and World Report,* October 16, 2008.

Francine Blau and Lawrence Kahn, "The Gender Pay Gap, Have Women Gone as Far as They Can?," *Academy of Management Perspectives* 21, no. 1 (February 2007):7.

Gender pay gap Europe, http://ec.europa.eu/justice/gender-equality /files/gender_pay_gap/140319_gpg_en.pdf.

"President Obama on the Gender Pay Gap. How Does Your Country Compare to the US?," World Economic Forum, February 2, 2016, http://www.weforum.org/agenda/2016/02/president -obama-on-the-gender-pay-gap-how-does-your-country -compare-to-the-us.

"The Global Gender Gap Index 2014: Business and Policy Implications," World Economic Forum.

James Puzangherra, "Obama Moves to Close Gender Wage Gap," *Los Angeles Times,* January 29, 2016.

James Dao, "Same Sex Marriage Issue Key to Some GOP Races," *New York Times,* November 4, 2004.

"Gay Marriage: A Campaign Wedge Issue," Foxnews.com, October 5, 2004.

Transcript of Bush statement on gay marriage, February 24, 2004, http://www.cnn.com/2004/ALLPOLITICS/02/24/elec04 .prez.bush.transcript/index.html.

Walter Shapiro, "Presidential Election May Have Hinged on One Issue," *USAToday,* November 4, 2004.

David Axelrod, *Believer* (New York: Penguin Press, 2015), 447.

Peggy Pascoe, "Why the Ugly Rhetoric Against Gay Marriage Is Familiar to This Historian of Miscegenation," History News Network, www.historynewsnetwork.or/article/4708.

"Remarks by the President in State of the Union Address," 2010, https://www.whitehouse.gov/the-press-office/remarks-president-state-union-address.

Bernard D. Rostker, Susan D. Hosek, and Mary E. Vaiana, "Gays in the Military Eventually, New Facts Conquer Old Taboos," *RAND Review* (Rand Corporation), Spring 2011.

Ed O'Keefe and Greg Jaffe, "Sources: Pentagon Group Finds There Is Minimal Risk to Lifting Gay Ban During War," *Washington Post,* November 11, 2010.

Cathy Renna, "Military and Civilian Professors Say That 'Don't Ask, Don't Tell' Debate Is Over," Palm Center, November 30, 2010.

Elizabeth Bumiller, "Pentagon Sees Little Risk in Allowing Gay Men and Women to Serve," *New York Times,* November 30, 2010.

Carl Hulse, "Senate Repeals Ban Against Openly Gay Military Personnel," *New York Times,* December 18, 2010.

"The President Signs Repeal of 'Don't Ask Don't Tell': 'Out of Many, We Are One,'" TheWhiteHouse.gov, December 22, 2010.

"Two Years After 'Don't Ask, Don't Tell' Repeal, Threats of Gay 'Chaos' Still Groundless," Human Rights Campaign, September 19, 2013.

Charlie Savage and Sheryl Gay Stolberg, "In Shift, U.S. Says Marriage Act Blocks Gay Rights," *New York Times,* February 23, 2011.

Richard Just, "Obama's Gay Marriage Position Called a Disgrace," CBS News, August 23, 2010.

Michael A. Memoli and Kathleen Hennessey, "Obama Declares Support for Same-Sex Marriage," *Los Angeles Times,* May 9, 2012.

David Nakamura, "Obama Backs Bill to Repeal Defense of Marriage Act," *Washington Post,* July 19, 2011.

Biden comments on gay marriage were made on *Meet the Press,* May 6, 2012.

Edward-Isaac Dovere, "Book: W.H. Scrambled After Biden Gay Marriage Comments," Politico.com, April 16, 2014.

"Obama: 'I Think Same-Sex Couples Should Be Able to Get Married,'" ABC News, May 9, 2012.

Igor Volsky, "The Obama Effect: Growing Number of African Americans Come Out for Marriage Equality," Thinkprogress .com, May 17, 2012.

Laren Markoe, "Election 2012 Shows a Social Sea Change on Gay Marriage," *Huffington Post,* November 8, 2012.

"Inaugural Address by President Barack Obama," January 21, 2013, https://www.whitehouse.gov/the-press-office/2013/01/21 /inaugural-address-president-barack-obama.

Barack Obama speech "A More Perfect Union," March 18, 2008.

"10 Horrifying Racist Attacks on Obama," Alternet.com, September 20, 2009.

Sarah Netter, "Racism in Obama's America One Year Later," ABC News, January 27, 2010.

Norm Ornstein, "How Racists and Partisans Exploit the Age of Obama," theAtlantic.com, December 11, 2014.

Michael Eric Dyson, "President Obama's Racial Renaissance," *New York Times,* August 1, 2015.

Michael Eric Dyson, "Yes She Can," *New Republic,* November 29, 2015.

Chapter 10: Unfinished Business (and Failures)

Michael Powell, "Embracing His Moment, Obama Preaches Hope in New Hampshire," *New York Times,* January 5, 2008.

E. J. Dionne, "Obama's Poetry Beating Clinton's Prose," *Washington Post,* January 8, 2008.

"Hope Is Not Optimism," May 17, 2008, speech.

Jennifer Senior, "The Paradox of the First Black President," *New York,* October 5, 2015.

George E. Condon Jr. and Jim O'Sullivan, "Has President Obama Done Enough for Black Americans?," *Atlantic,* April 5, 2013.

Janell Ross, "Are Race Relations Really Worse Under President Obama?," *Washington Post,* August 4, 2015.

"Alabama Congressman Calls Obama 'the Most Racially-Divisive President' Since Slavery," theGrio.com, January 17, 2016.

Jon Swaine et al., "Young Black Men Killed by U.S. Police at Highest Rate in Year of 1,134 Deaths," theGuardian.com, December 31, 2015.

Heather MacDonald, "The Shameful Liberal Exploitation of the Charleston Massacre," *National Review,* July 1, 2015, http://www .nationalreview.com/article/420565/charleston-shooting -obama-race-crime.

"A More Perfect Union," March 18, 2008, speech, http://www .politico.com/story/2008/03/transcript-of-obama-speech -009100.

"Amnesty International Report 2005," May 25, 2005.

Neil A. Lewis, "Red Cross Finds Detainee Abuse in Guantánamo," *New York Times,* November 30, 2004.

Mark Denbeaux, "Report on Guantánamo Detainees: A Profile of

517 Detainees Through Analysis of Department of Defense Data," Seton Hall University School of Law.

Karen DeYoung and Peter Finn, "Guantánamo Case Files in Disarray," *Washington Post,* January 25, 2009.

Peter Finn, "Most Guantánamo Detainees Low-Level Fighters, Task Force Report Says," *Washington Post,* May 29, 2010.

Laura Bult, "Suspected Taliban Operative Refuses to Leave Guantánamo After Release, Lawyer Compares Him to 'Shawshank Redemption' Character," *New York Daily News,* January 22, 2016.

"Guantánamo by the Numbers," American Civil Liberties Union, https://www.aclu.org/infographic/guantanamo-numbers.

Timeline of war in Afghanistan, Foreignpolicy.com, http://www.cfr.org/afghanistan/us-war-afghanistan/p20018.

Matthew Rosenberg and Michael D. Shear, "In Reversal, Obama Says U.S. Soldiers Will Stay in Afghanistan to 2017," *New York Times,* October 15, 2015.

Sheryle Gay Stolberg, "Mistakes, I've Made a Few, Bush Tells Reporters," *New York Times,* January 12, 2009.

Michael B. Kelley, "The Staggering Cost of the Last Decade's US War in Iraq, in Numbers," *Business Insider,* June 20, 2014.

"Barack Obama and What He Said on the Iraq War," *Telegraph,* December 14, 2011.

Dexter Filkins, "What We Left Behind," *New Yorker,* April 28, 2014.

Peter Beinart, "Obama's Disastrous Iraq Policy: An Autopsy," *Atlantic,* June 23, 2014.

Aaron David Miller, "Does Obama Have Any Regrets About His Middle East Policy?," *Foreign Policy,* September 29, 2015.

Zack Beauchamp, "The US Uses Iraq's Shia Militias to Fight ISIS. They Just Got Accused of Ethnic Cleansing," Vox.com, February 5, 2016.

Ali Khedery, "Why We Stuck with Maliki—and Lost Iraq," *Washington Post,* July 3, 2014.

Dana Priest and William M Arkin, *Top Secret America: The Rise of the New American Security State* (New York: Little, Brown, 2011).

James Bamford, "The NSA Is Building the Country's Biggest Spy Center (Watch What You Say)," *Wired,* March 15, 2012.

Risa Brooks, "Homegrown Terrorism Is Not on the Rise," *Boston Globe,* April 27, 2013.

Adam Goldman, Jia Lynn Yang, and John Muyskens, "The Islamic State's Suspected Inroads into America," *Washington Post,* January 29, 2016.

Drew Desilver, "US Spends over $16 billion Annually on Counter-Terrorism," Pew Research, September 11, 2013.

"White House Rejects Review Board Finding That NSA Data Sweep Is Illegal," Foxnews.com, January 23, 2014.

"Associated Press Says US Government Seized Journalists' Phone Records," Associated Press, May 13, 2013.

Caroline Houck, "Barack Obama on Surveillance, Then and Now," Politifact.com, June 13, 2013.

Darrell Delamaide, "Obama Legacy Includes Banker Impunity," *USA Today,* August 19, 2015.

William D. Cohan, "How Wall Street's Bankers Stayed out of Jail," *Atlantic,* September 2015.

Andrew Clark, "Goldman Sachs Breaks Record with $16.7bn Bonus Pot," *Guardian,* October 15, 2009.

Nicholas Confessore, Sarah Cohen, and Karen Yourish, "Buying Power: Here Are 120 million Monopoly Pieces, Roughly One for Every Household in the United States," *New York Times,* October 10, 2015.

Eric Lichtblau and Nicholas Confessore, "From Fracking to Finance, a Torrent of Campaign Cash," *New York Times,* October 10, 2015.

Ryan Grim, "Dick Durbin: Banks 'Frankly Own the Place,'" *Huffington Post,* May 30, 2009.

Postscript: The Benefits of Cool

Samuel Warde, "2 Reaganites Praise Obama for Unprecedented 'Successful' Second Term," *Liberals Unite,* July 20, 2015.

Gregory Korte, "Obama Signs Two Executive Orders on Cybersecurity," *USA Today,* February 9, 2016.

Associated Press, "Obama Orders More Earthquake Resilience for Gov't Buildings," *Seattle Times,* February 2, 2016.

Stephen Collinson, "Obama on Oregon Shooting: 'Somehow This Has Become Routine,'" CNN.com, October 2, 2015.

David Frum, "Mass Shootings Are Preventable," *Atlantic,* June 23, 2015.

"Fact Sheet: New Executive Actions to Reduce Gun Violence and Make Our Communities Safer," White House, January 4, 2016.

Victor Luckerson, "Read Barack Obama's Speech on New Gun Control Measures," *Time,* January 5, 2016.

Ryan Grim, "John Boehner Rejects Obama's Grand Bargain on Debt Ceiling," *Huffington Post,* July 9, 2011.

Steve Benen, "Ten-to-One Isn't Good Enough for the GOP," *Washington Monthly,* August 12, 2011.

Charles Ingraham, "This Astonishing Chart Shows How Moderate Republicans Are an Endangered Species," *Washington Post,* June 2, 2015.

Michael Tesler, "The Return of Old-Fashioned Racism to White Americans' Partisan Preferences in the Early Obama Era," *Journal of Politics* 75, no. 1 (December 2012): 110–23, http://www.jstor.org/stable/10.1017/S0022381612000904.

Patrick Jonnson, "What Were Two Republicans Thinking, Calling Obama 'Tar Baby' and 'Boy'?," *Christian Science Monitor,* August 3, 2011.

Max J. Skidmore, *Presidential Performance: A Comprehensive Review* (Jefferson, N.C.: McFarland, 2004), 350.

David Weigel, "Nine Times That the Media Has Declared a 'Katrina Moment' for Barack Obama," Slate.com, July 7, 2014.

Maureen Dowd, "Captain Obvious Learns the Limits of Cool," *New York Times,* January 9, 2010.

"Remarks by the President in Address to the Illinois General Assembly," White House, February 10, 2016.

BIBLIOGRAPHY

Axelrod, David. *Believer*. New York: Penguin Press, 2015.

Barofsky, Neil. *Bailout*. New York: Free Press, 2012.

Brill, Steven. *America's Bitter Pill*. New York: Random House, 2015.

Doyles, Larry. *In Bed with Wall Street*. New York: Palgrave Macmillan, 2014.

Draper, Robert. *Dead Certain*. New York: Free Press, 2007.

Frank, Thomas. *Listen, Liberal*. New York: Metropolitan Books, 2016.

Gates, Robert M. *Duty: A Memoir of a Secretary at War*. New York: Knopf Doubleday, 2015.

Geithner, Timothy. *Stress Test*. New York: Broadway Books, 2014.

Grunwald, Michael. *The New New Deal*. New York: Simon and Schuster, 2012.

Harvey, David. *The Enigma of Capital*. New York: Oxford University Press, 2010.

Kabaservice, Geoffrey. *Rule and Ruin*. New York: Oxford University Press, 2012.

Klein, Edward. *The Amateur*. Washington, D.C.: Regnery Publishing, 2012.

Klein, Joel. *Lessons of Hope: How to Fix Our Schools*. New York: HarperCollins, 2014.

McLean, Bethany, and Joe Nocera. *All the Devils Are Here*. New York: Portfolio/Penguin, 2010.

Newport, Frank. *Winning the White House.* New York: Infobase Publishing, 2009.

Obama, Barack. *The Audacity of Hope.* New York: Three Rivers Press, 2006.

———. *Change We Can Believe In.* New York: Three Rivers Press, 2008.

Panetta, Leon. *Worthy Fights: A Memoir of Leadership in War and Peace.* New York: Penguin Press, 2014.

Paulson, Henry M., Jr. *On the brink.* New York: Business Plus, 2010.

Plouffe, David. *The Audacity to Win.* New York: Penguin Books, 2009.

Rajan, Raghuram G. *Fault Lines.* Princeton, N.J.: Princeton University Press, 2010.

Rattner, Steven. *Overhaul.* New York: First Mariner Books, 2010.

Remnick, David. *The Bridge.* New York: Alfred A. Knopf, 2010.

Richardson, Heather Cox. *To Make Men Free.* New York: Basic Books, 2014.

Rogak, Lisa. *Barack Obama in His Own Words.* New York: Public Affairs, 2007.

Schultz, Jeffrey D. *Presidential Scandal.* Washington, D.C.: CQ Press, 2000.

Smiley, Tavis. *Accountable.* New York: Atria Books, 2009.

Taibbi, Matt. *Griftopia.* New York: Spiegel and Grau, 2011.

Todd, Chuck. *The Stranger.* New York: Little, Brown, 2014.

Woodward, Bob. *Obama's Wars.* New York: Simon and Schuster, 2010.

INDEX